THE COMPLETE GUIDE TO
REMODELING YOUR HOME

THE COMPLETE GUIDE TO
REMODELING YOUR HOME

A Step-by-Step Manual for Homeowners and Investors

Kent Lester & Una Lamie

Betterway Publications, Inc.
White Hall, Virginia

Published by Betterway Publications, Inc.
Box 73
White Hall, VA 22987

Every precaution has been taken in preparing *The
Complete Guide to Remodeling* to make your home remodeling as safe and successful as possible. Neither
Betterway Publications, Inc. nor the authors, however,
assume any responsibility for any damages incurred in
conjunction with the use of this manual.

Library of Congress Cataloging-in-Publication Data

Lester, Kent
    Complete guide to remodeling your home.

    Includes index.
    1. Dwellings--Remodeling. I. Lamie, Una
II. Title.
TH4816.L45 1987   643'.7   87-6593
ISBN 0-932620-73-6 (pbk.)

Printed in the United States of America
0 9 8 7 6 5 4 3 2

Dedicated to

THE REMODELER

who wishes either to build the house of his dreams or to accumulate wealth by finding, remodeling and selling homes and rental property.

ACKNOWLEDGMENTS

*Many illustrations in this edition appear
courtesy of the United States Department of
Housing and Urban Development and
the United States Department of Agriculture.*

CONTENTS

INTRODUCTION...11

SECTION I: PLANNING

1. Remodeling as an Investment 17
2. The Tax Laws and Remodeling...............................21
3. Legal and Financial Issues 25
4. Finding the Right Property 31
5. Evaluating Remodeling Potential...........................35
6. Evaluating the Structure..43
7. Stretching the Remodeling Dollar...........................61
8. Estimating the Remodeling 67
9. When to Use the Experts 97
10. Working with Subcontractors.................................99
11. Working with Material Suppliers............................103

SECTION II: IMPLEMENTATION

12. Starting the Renovation 109
13. Kitchen 117
14. Baths...127
15. Adding Space 135
16. Foundation 149
17. Floor System..153
18. Siding..159
19. Roof System 167
20. Openings..173
21. Doors...177
22. Insulation and Moisture Control 185
23. Interior Items 193
24. Special Items 207
25. Porch...211
26. Painting 215

GLOSSARY...211

APPENDIX 235

INDEX 267

INTRODUCTION

The purpose of this book is simple - to help you make and save money through remodeling. Whether you are remodeling your own home or an investment property, this book will arm you with the essential information necessary to make maximum use of your remodeling dollar. Most people underestimate the knowledge and commitment in time necessary to achieve remodeling results of which you can be proud. This book will instruct you on all the techniques necessary to become a master remodeler, for fun or for profit.

HOW TO FIND GOOD REMODELING POTENTIAL

This book will tell you how to find the kind of remodeling projects worth tackling. You'll learn how to ferret out good potential projects from sources overlooked by others.

HOW TO EVALUATE PROPERTY

Not all remodeling challenges were meant to be conquered! Evaluating the potential of a remodeling project requires the skills of a keen detective. Many construction flaws are hidden and require close examination to detect. You will learn how to spot the danger signals.

HOW TO ESTABLISH FINANCIAL INDEPENDENCE BY REMODELING

Remodeling is one of the few high-yield investments that can be done part time. This book will show you how to maximize the return on your investment either on your personal home or your investment property.

STEP-BY-STEP INSTRUCTIONS

Once you have determined the work to be done, this book will provide the detailed instructions needed to accomplish the task. If you have the work done by professionals, these instructions will provide you with the knowledge to evaluate the work of others.

Benefits of Remodeling Over New Construction

Increases in the cost of new home construction has renewed interest in the renovating of existing homes and investment properties. The financial return from remodeling can be much greater than that of new construction because with remodeling you can provide much of the labor and/or management which is built into the cost of new construction. In addition, recent tax laws have made remodeling even more attractive to the investor by limiting the tax writeoffs allowed on new investment property. Remodeling, on the other hand, adds equity and therefore capital gains that can be deferred until the property is sold.

If you are remodeling for yourself, you may not be concerned about the investment potential as much as your desire for a homey and comfortable abode. You should weigh carefully, the advantages and disadvantages of remodeling over building a new home. This decision is a highly personal one and depends quite often on your tastes in housing. Remodeling an older home may require you to give up some of the modern conveniences and design flexibility associated with new construction; however, an older house can provide the warmth and charm not easily attained in new construction.

In addition, rehabilitation of your own home has other advantages:

- Upgrading your present home eliminates the need to relocate to a new neighborhood. You can stay in familiar surroundings while the work is being done. If the house is a recent purchase, the property can usually be occupied immediately, even while the remodeling is taking place.

■ Remodeling can save moving expenses. Moving to a new house has several hidden costs, since you are likely to spend money to redecorate the new house to fit your tastes; such as, adding new carpeting, draperies, etc.

■ Remodeling can save the legal, real estate and closing cost expenses involved in purchasing a new home.

■ Some older houses provide more amenities than are available in new homes of comparable price.

■ Rehabilitation can usually be done as finances become available, reducing your immediate financial burden.

■ Low interest rate mortgages can sometimes be assumed on older homes. Owner financing is often available on older homes because sellers are eager to sell their older homes. Owner financing is extremely valuable because it does not require the stringent qualifications of government-regulated loans. For investors with several properties, this can sometimes be the only way to obtain new properties.

■ There is a high potential for finding good bargains.

■ Tax laws provide numerous incentives for remodeling, especially in areas designated as historical districts.

■ Money can be saved by doing much of the work yourself.

■ Older neighborhoods are generally located closer to metropolitan areas.

■ Remodeling offers a higher return on investment. The value you add to the house through remodeling will be much greater than the retail value of the work, especially if you do much of the work yourself. As equity: increases, you can obtain nontaxable equity loans on the additional value.

Figure 1–The period styles of many older buildings are not always available in new construction.

CAUTIONS

Remodeling is not easy. Make sure you are aware of the work involved before forging ahead. Prepare yourself mentally for the potential frustrations which may be encountered. Rest assured; problems **will** occur. Be ready for them:

■ Many subcontractors ("subs") are hesitant to do remodeling because of the hassles involved. Good remodeling contractors are hard to find; many require payment by the hour.

■ The true cost of remodeling may be hard to determine before starting the project because of hidden factors (rotten wood, air infiltration, foundation flaws, poor wiring, poor plumbing, etc.).

■ The improvements on the house may upgrade it to a value above the surrounding neighborhood, holding down the resale value of your home and making it difficult to realize a return on your investment. Consider though, that these same factors can work in your favor if you buy the least expensive home in the area.

■ Appraisers have a hard time determining the final remodeled value of a home before the work is complete.

■ Utility costs in older homes are usually higher due to less or poorer quality insulation. Sometimes this factor can be difficult or impossible to overcome.

LET'S GET STARTED!

If you are ready, remodeling can be a profitable and rewarding endeavor. It is hard to beat the satisfaction gained by restoring a piece of history to its former grandeur! Homes hold a powerful grasp over a person's feeling of well being and accomplishment. There is an excitement in watching an older home flourish through your personal efforts. This book will take you through all the steps necessary to find, evaluate, and renovate your next home. Let's get started!

SECTION I:
PLANNING

1. REMODELING AS AN INVESTMENT

Remodeling Your Own Home

If you are a novice remodeler, your first project will usually be your own home. This is good because it allows you to get a feel for the effort and complications involved, while still giving you ample time to make mistakes, correct them and learn from them. Don't fool yourself; you will make mistakes! You, however, will make a more forgiving subject than a new tenant in an investment property.

BUILD EQUITY RAPIDLY BY REMODELING

Remodeling is probably one of the country's most popular cottage industries. It allows you to rehabilitate your home, while still holding down a full-time job. You will realize a tremendous increase in equity over a very short period of time because you can provide most of the labor, saving the costs of remodeling contractors and skilled laborers. These markups can add up to 75% to the cost of the remodeling project.

The remodeling you provide will add to the value of your home, but at the retail price of the remodeling contractor, not at your cost. You will be paying yourself as the remodeler in tax free dollars that are added to the equity of the house. These dollars are essentially tax free until the house is sold. If the additional profit is applied toward your next house purchase, it may never be taxed! This is because the IRS allows you to defer profits on principal residences as long as the purchase price of your new home meets or exceeds the sales price of the house sold.

USE "SWEAT EQUITY" AS A SOURCE OF FUNDS

The equity you build in your home can be a source of additional tax-free investment funds.

As your property appreciates, second mortgages based on the increase in equity will provide you with a source of money that is not taxable. Loans are not considered taxable income, but the interest on home loans is deductible. By deferring the sale of your home, but using its equity in the form of a loan, you can use your personal home as a substantial tax shelter and source of income because new tax changes have reduced the source of other tax shelters, *making your home investment even more valuable.*

Buying and Remodeling Investment Properties

Soon after realizing the monetary gains of your first personal remodeling project, you will be tempted to use your new found talent to rapidly build investment equity. The main reason for investing is to increase your net worth and to eventually provide a constant source of income. With that goal in mind, let's look at the reasons why remodeling will accelerate this process, providing you with net worth at an astounding rate.

THE ULTIMATE IN CREATIVE FINANCING

Hundreds of books have been written about creative "No Money Down" financing of investment property. The secret of this strategy is to find "Don't Wanters", sellers who are so eager to sell that they are willing to provide personal financing on their homes. Owner-financed homes do not require the investor to meet the stringent credit qualification that government-backed loans require. In addition, most banks severely limit the amount of debt that an aggressive investor can accumulate. Astute investors can bargain quite competitive terms on owner-financed loans, building ownership in properties at an astounding rate. See the "Legal and Financial Section" for creative financing details.

Typically, "Don't Wanter" homes are older homes in bad need of repair. The success of your investment strategy, therefore, will oftentimes hinge on your ability to renovate these homes effectively. You must be able to evaluate the structural and aesthetic condition of these properties before buying and be able to accurately estimate the cost to renovate. Because older homes seldom continue to appreciate steadily due to their age, the return on investment will be directly related to the amount of additional value that can be added to the home through carefully planned and controlled renovation.

In terms of immediate cash flow, remember that improvements to rental property usually increase the amount of rent that can be charged. A little improvement can go a long way toward increasing rental levels.

Before purchasing a run-down investment property, estimate carefully the complete cost of renovation. Add this cost to the price of the home before completing an investment analysis. Make sure to include any additional rent that can be charged as a result of the renovation.

BUILD EQUITY TO BUILD PROFITS

Normally, increases in a property's net worth comes from two sources:

1. Appreciation of the property through natural inflationary pressures.
2. Reduction of the principal (mortgage loan amount) through rent payments.

In a noninflationary economy, this process can be very slow. Property values (especially on older properties) may increase very slowly or not at all. Older properties are generally poorly maintained by the tenants. Don't expect them to have a sense of pride in your property if you don't! The reduction of the principal through mortgage payments is also extremely slow. In

five years of payments on a 30-year mortgage, the principal will only be reduced 3-1/2 percent.

Remodeling can change this slow process into a rapid one. There are five main reasons to renovate rental property:

1. To further increase the value or equity of the property

2. To reduce maintenance expenses

3. To increase the monthly rent

4. To raise the level and quality of the tenant

5. To reduce the time spent in managing the property

THE INVESTOR'S NEMESIS

Negative cash flow can sap an investor's strength. This occurs when the debt service and expenses on the property exceed the rent collected each month, requiring you to "subsidize" the property with your own cash. It doesn't take many "Alligators" (properties that eat away your cash) to create a "cash poor investor". With the number of intangibles involved in remodeling, you must make absolutely sure that you have a cash reserve available to take care of unpredictable problems. Take a lesson from Murphy's Law - "If anything can go wrong, it will, *at the most inopportune time.*". The last thing you need is a portfolio of properties begging for cash each month.

REDUCE MAINTENANCE COSTS

Older properties are notorious for hidden maintenance problems which add significantly to your monthly expenses. This is one of the main reasons to renovate. Eliminate those irritating and recurring problems that are caused by the age of the property. You will find that the tenants will cooperate once the property is properly maintained. It is a well known fact that tenants will take greater care of a property if it is maintained well by the landlord.

Many "Don't wanter" investment properties are sold by frustrated investors who are fed up with the incessant demands on their time that an older property requires. This type of property is your "mother lode" of opportunity. Turn those "time wasters" into "gold mines".

INCREASE RENTS

The improved quality of the unit can also add to cash flow through increased rent. Don't be afraid to ask for increased rent after a major renovation project. This is one of the primary ways to justify the expense of remodeling. You may be tempted to "give the tenant a break" for any inconveniences caused by the renovation. If you do, make it clear to the tenant that you are giving a temporary discount of the higher rental fee in exchange for their inconvenience. Don't allow the "grace period" to extend more than 3 months, or the tenants will resist the increase when it occurs.

AVOID VACATING THE PROPERTY

In many cases, major renovations will require that the property be vacated. This will impact negative cash flow and prompt you to finish the renovation project as soon as possible. Because of the drastic effect on rental cash flow, try to avoid renovations of this magnitude if at all possible. You may be able to time the renovations in phases so that tenants may continue to occupy the property. This will require a patient and cooperative tenant.

If the property is vacated, make sure to increase the rent before the new tenants move in! It may take a year of increased rents to make up for two months of rentless property.

2. THE TAX LAWS AND REMODELING

Real Estate - The Ultimate Tax Shelter

Real estate investments have long been known as excellent tax shelters, reducing the amount of taxes paid on income. Income tax law has long given real estate investments preferential treatment. Investors have been able to write off noncash expenses; such as, depreciation (if applicable), as well as cash expenses (such as repairs and interest expense). Since noncash expenses are deductible, these excess deductions can "shelter" income from other sources. These preferential laws have helped bolster the national real estate rental market and have acted as a "subsidy" to hold rent at artificially low levels.

The New Tax Law

The 1986 Tax Reform Act has changed all this. The tax bill has closed many of the popular tax shelters completely and has significantly reduced the effects of real estate tax shelters. This tax bill represents the most sweeping tax law change in recent American history and will change the way people invest, rent and purchase houses. If this change sounds grim, take heart! This new law will accomplish two things of great importance to the serious investor:

1. Change real estate investment from an industry motivated by *avoiding taxes* to an industry motivated by *producing profits*.

2. Increase the tax related benefits of owning a home and *remodeling* your existing home!

Let's summarize the changes that will most directly affect you as a homeowner, investor and remodeler:

THE INDIVIDUAL TAX RATE HAS BEEN REDUCED

The first and most obvious benefit of the new tax law is a reduction in the real tax rate. The old tax tables have been scrapped and have been replaced with a two-tier system. These reduced tax rates will reduce the investor's incentive to *shelter* income by reducing taxes since the savings will be much lower. Future investor incentives will be the creation of wealth, not the sheltering of income.

MOST INTEREST DEDUCTIONS ARE ELIMINATED

The new tax law eliminates deductions of interest on *consumer* purchases, including car loans, credit card accounts and other consumer loans. This should greatly reduce consumers' incentives to buy new products or cars simply to increase their tax writeoffs.

PERSONAL MORTGAGE INTEREST CAN STILL BE DEDUCTED

An "exception" to the interest rule is the personal mortgage. Interest on personal mortgage loans are still fully deductible *as long as* the loan mortgage covers your **principal residence** or a **second home** such as a beach cottage. No deductions for mortgage interest are allowed on more than two personal dwellings.

So how can you afford that new luxury sedan or your children's college tuition? Finance these expenditures with a home equity loan. The IRS doesn't care what you use the home loan to purchase - the mortgage interest will still be deductible. The lesson to learn here is : *Build equity in your home as rapidly as possible and use this equity to finance other purchases and investments.*

The Tax Law has anticipated this use of home equity and has imposed some restrictions. The law has a ceiling on the amount of mortgage interest which can be deducted. The mortgage interest can only be deducted as long as the total of all loans do not exceed the original purchase price of the home, plus the cost of any improvements. This means that, if the majority of your excess equity comes from appreciation rather than loan reduction, then you may not be able to deduct all the interest. This is seldom as bad as it looks since banks seldom will make loans on 100% of the value of the home. As the value of the home increases, this additional amount can be borrowed against and will still be deductible.

Let's look at an example. Suppose you bought a home five years ago for $100,000 at 10% interest. The bank required a 10% down payment and issued a $90,000 mortgage. Today, your home is worth $130,000 and you would like to take a second mortgage to purchase a new sailboat. You have paid down your original mortgage to $87,000. Most banks will only approve 2nd mortgages up to 80% of the appraised value of the home; so, your bank will approve a second mortgage for $17,000 (80% of $130,000 minus the balance of the original loan.) Since the original purchase price of the home was 100,000, you may deduct interest on $13,000 of the loan ($100,000 original cost minus the $87,000 remaining principal). Note that the first mortgage is valued at its *remaining balance* not the original loan value.

When calculating home value, make sure to include all costs of purchasing the home; such as, closing costs, legal fees, insurance costs and realtor fees. When you remodel, keep accurate and thorough records of everything you spend on the remodeling project. Routine maintenance and repairs cannot be included in these figures; account for only those items which actually increase the value of the home. The lesson here is, if possible, postpone needed repairs until your remodeling project. For example, if you foresee a large expense for plumbing repairs or for painting, you should consider scheduling your remodeling at the same time. If you remodel a bathroom, replacing the old fixtures and updating the color scheme, you can add these total costs to your basis. If you just repair a plumbing leak without including it in a remodeling project, it will be considered routine maintenance and cannot be added to your home value.

What happens if the total loan amounts exceed your home's value plus improvements? The excess interest is not tax deductible, *with two notable exceptions:* educational and medical costs. As long as you use the excess for these two endeavors, your interest is *still* deductible. In this sense, you can look at your remodeling project as the educational nest egg for your children.

Even with its limitations, the home mortgage deduction is a powerful tax-reduction tool. By remodeling your home, you can provide yourself with the only tax-deductible, loanable equity allowed under the new tax law.

REDUCED REAL ESTATE DEDUCTIONS

The new tax law distinguishes between active and passive income derived from investments. Real estate losses (passive investment) cannot be offset against active income from employment or stocks. If your real estate writeoffs exceed rental income, the excess losses can be carried forward to cover subsequent years' earnings. These losses can be carried forward indefinitely until the property is sold, at which time the losses can offset earnings from the sale. There is an exception to this rule that seems to be designed specifically for the small investor. If your income is under $100,000 per year and you are actively involved in the daily business of your investment properties, you can carry over $25,000 of your losses to use against other income. If your income is greater than $100,000, the amount you can carry over diminishes as your income increases, and finally vanishes at an income of $150,000.

In essence, what this law does is prevent larger investors from taking advantage of excess losses on their investments to cover other earnings. Your real estate investments will become self-supporting. You don't lose the writeoffs; you just have to restrict them to real estate income only. So, these writeoffs **will** still help to shelter the profit you may make on your other real estate investments. This is very important because the purpose of investing is to increase the property's value and therefore your equity. This, in turn, will increase your profits when you sell. Your deductions, therefore, will be needed to shelter these profits.

REDUCED DEPRECIATION

The new tax law has reversed the trend of increasing depreciation rates and has lengthened the depreciation period to 27-1/2 years. The depreciation must be calculated on a straight line basis; no longer are the accelerated methods allowed.

NO MORE CAPITAL GAINS

The long term capital gains treatment for property held for more than one year has also been abolished. The old maximum rate was 20% for capital gains; the new maximum tax is 28%.

CREDIT FOR REHABILITATIONS STILL EXIST

The new tax law still retains credits for rehabilitating older structures. The buildings must be located in registered historic districts or must have been built before 1936. These districts contain some of the best potential rehabilitation projects.

Predictions

■ More people will want to buy homes, driving up the prices and increasing equity buildup. Buyers will be eager to move up to higher priced housing to maximize their tax writeoff.

■ As the shortage of new homes becomes more acute, homeowners will look for properties to renovate that are located closer to the center of town. This will drive prices higher.

■ As homeowners move up to larger and ever more expensive houses, renters avoiding higher rents will move into these entry level homes.

■ The equity in your home and in investment properties will become the single most important source of sheltered profits available for further investments or other expenses.

Strategies

With all these changes, is it still possible to build wealth in real estate? The answer is a resounding YES! If anything, these changes will increase the value of renovating old structures, while providing the average investor with an honest tax break.

CONCENTRATE ON EQUITY BUILDUP

Most of your profits will come from appreciation and increased equity on your properties. Look for loans that will reduce your principal rapidly. On your rehabs, try to get the maximum increase in property value for every dollar you spend. As equity builds, you can refinance to obtain money for other investments or renovations. Your deductible losses will accrue over the life of your investment. When you sell, these losses will help to offset profits made on the property.

UTILIZE A SHORT SALES CYCLE

Since most equity build up will come from renovation, sell the properties soon after the renovations are done. The property's sales price will be at its peak before the renovations have had a chance to degrade from normal wear and tear. This strategy, of course, requires common sense judgment on your part. If the neighborhood is in the beginning stages of renovation, you may want to hold the property until at least 50% of the neighborhood is renovated. This will help to pull up the value of your property. Remember this primary investor's rule: "*Never be the highest price property in the neighborhood*".

DON'T SELL EVERYTHING AT ONE TIME

Most of your real estate tax writeoffs can be used to shelter other real estate income. Time the sale of property so that your accrued "paper losses" from depreciation, etc. on other properties can be used to offset profits from the sale. If timed properly, this technique can shelter all of your real estate profits, allowing them to be reinvested into new and larger properties.

LOOK FOR RENTAL HOME CONVERSIONS

Many disgruntled investors burdened with an excess of "tax shelters" will be unloading unprofitable rental properties in the next few years. Look for rental houses at bargain prices that can be rehabilitated and sold as renovated homes. These investors are familiar with creative financing deals and will be willing to structure innovative financing bargains.

3. LEGAL AND FINANCIAL ISSUES

Financing

Obtaining financing for your home will be one of the most critical and demanding phases of your remodeling project. Unless you are one of the few who remodel with cash, the home improvement loan or second mortgage is a necessity. You must be bookkeeper, financier and salesman. The lender will want evidence that you know what you are doing and that you can finish your project within budget.

THE HOME IMPROVEMENT LOAN

The home improvement loan is an unsecured loan, meaning that its security is not attached to the property. Most banks limit the amount of home improvement loans to under $10,000, with a maximum five-year term. It is typical for interest on a home improvement loan to be several few points higher than permanent financing. This gives you further incentive to finish the project as quickly as possible to cut your finance costs. Remember, changes and upgrades can be expensive and should not be considered once the project is in progress unless you are willing to pay for them out of pocket.

THE SECOND MORTGAGE

Like the first mortgage on a property, the second mortgage is a secured loan attached to the value of the property itself. This is the most common loan for major renovation projects and can be obtained from banks or savings and loan companies. The interest on second mortgages are usually 2 points above the market rate for first mortgages. Most lenders restrict the total principal amounts of the first and subsequent mortgages to 70%-90% of the total appraised value of the property. You may be required to obtain a certified appraisal if the property has appreciated significantly since the first mortgage.

THE HOME EQUITY LOAN

A recent development in the home loan business, the home equity loan provides the homeowner with a line of credit that is secured by the home or other property. In this way, the home equity loan is like a second mortgage, except that the borrower has a line of credit; he can borrow the funds at-will, up to the limit of the loan. This is a very flexible loan that can be used for any number of reasons. Since the money can be borrowed and paid back at any time, the interest expenses can be reduced somewhat by borrowing the money at the last minute and paying it back as soon as possible. Don't worry, you can borrow against the line of credit again at any time.

APPLYING FOR YOUR LOAN

Make sure that your financial package is complete before visiting the lender. The package should be neat, informative, well organized and should comply with all of the lender's requirements. Your lender will want to be sure that you can keep good records. Your financial package should include the following:

- Personal financial statement.
- Resume or personal biography.
- Total cost estimate of the project.
- Description of materials.
- Set of blueprints or drawing of project

The Personal Financial Statement should include all your assets and liabilities. Make sure to include everything of value you own including personal property. Many people tend to underestimate the value of items like furniture and clothing. Your liabilities should include any loans, charge accounts and credit balances. Ask your lender for one of their own standard forms.

The Resume is designed to sell yourself to the lender. Start with a standard job resume, but be sure to emphasize any construction interests or experience.

The Cost Estimate will be very important because your remodeling loan will be based on it. Make sure to include a 7 to 10% cost overrun factor in your estimates as a cushion for unexpected expenses. Many lenders can provide you with a standard cost sheet form. If not, use the one included in this book.

The Description of Materials form will aid the lender's appraiser in estimating the appraised value of your property. Many lenders use the standard FHA form for this purpose, but check to see if your lender uses a different format.

A Set of Blueprints, complete with all intended changes, should be submitted.

Creative Financing Techniques

The ultimate success of your remodeling ventures will hinge on your ability to use *other people's money* to finance your projects. Anytime you purchase *anything* on credit - a car, boat or home; you are using someone else's money. This is called "leverage" and is the foundation of all successful investing. With a little of your money and a great deal of someone elses' money, you can "multiply" or "leverage" the effect of your funds to accomplish more than would be possible with cash. If you have $10,000 cash, you may be able to renovate one house with that cash; but, with an additional $30,000 from the bank, you could now remodel *four* houses. This multiplies the profits you can make.

Unfortunately, obtaining the money from investors or lenders is not so simple. If you are about to start a large remodeling project, you may need financing. For instance, you have just purchased an older house for $60,000 with a down payment of 10% or $6,000. You want to do $20,000 worth of renovations that will make the property worth $100,000; so, you go to the local bank for a second mortgage loan. The lender will only loan up to 80% of the value of the home, but it already has a first mortgage *equal to 90%* of its current value. He will send you on your way, because he has no guarantee that your $20,000 expenditure will increase the home's value to the claimed $100,000. In essence, the bank will not lend you the money *until you don't need it* - after the project is complete.

Don't despair. Creative individuals and investors have found many innovative solutions to this "cart before the horse" problem. You are only limited by your imagination in finding financing options; that's why its called *creative financing*. Let's look at a few ways to generate financing.

Solution #1: The most obvious solution is to ask for an *unsecured* home improvement loan. If you have good credit, most banks will lend you a healthy sum ($2,000-6,000) on your credit standing alone. If you can obtain financing from several banks, you can accumulate quite a bit of unsecured funds. Most banks are very strict about disclosure of all other loans you possess; so, make sure to list all pre-approved loans. It is not necessary to list loans for which you have applied, but have not received approval.

Solution #2: Credit cards are a great source of quick cash. Because of their high interest rates, banks are eager to provide you with sizable credit limits. Most card services have cash withdrawal options; if not, simply live off the card while using your regular cash for remodeling. If you submit applications for 5 or 6 cards at a time, you may be approved for at least half. Even though the interest rates are high, credit cards function like a line of credit; you may pay them back at any time. Simply finance the renovation with the credit card and then apply for a second mortgage after the renovation is complete. The house will now be valued at its appreciated rate of $100,000, allowing a second mortgage of $24,000. The $56,000 original mortgage + $24,000 = $80,000; exactly 80% of the $100,000 value. Use this money to pay off the credit cards and you can start all over again.

Solution #3: Another source of credit is the regular unsecured line of credit. This source of money will be the result of carefully thought-out strategy on your part. You should immediately start to cultivate credit relationships with as many banks as possible. Open checking accounts with several banks and ask for small loans at first and build up to larger ones. Make sure to pay back each loan *slightly* ahead of time. As time goes by, you will be surprised how much unsecured credit you can accumulate.

Solution #4: Use a combination of all the above.

Solution #5: Owner financing is by far the best source of money. The seller is eager for you to purchase his property and is often willing to extend credit with much more lenient requirements than banks. This is especially true when the seller is a "don't wanter". This owner financing will be used to reduce or eliminate the down payment on the property. By avoiding a large down payment, you can save your cash reserve for the renovation. Let's look at several no-money-down strategies.

PURCHASE MONEY MORTGAGE

The purchase money mortgage entails obtaining financing from the seller to cover the down payment. It is usually in the form of a second mortgage on the property. This no-money-down technique is commonly used by creative investors as the primary way to purchase numerous properties with little or no cash. This requires an eager seller that is willing to accept a note instead of a cash down payment. This can be difficult if the investor wants a long term note. If you plan to remodel promptly, you can offer to pay back the note to the seller in 1 or 2 years, giving yourself plenty of time to finish the renovation. The short pay back period makes the mortgage much more appealing to the seller. Once the renovation is complete, you can apply for a second mortgage on the new appraised value or refinance the property.

EQUITY LOANS

If you are buying several properties, take advantage of the domino effect that occurs with successive purchases and renovations. As you build equity in existing properties, free up this equity by financing it with second or third mortgages. This cash can then be used for future down payments. This technique is used frequently by creative investors; however, it works even better for remodelers, since equity on remodeled property grows so much faster.

LEASE WITH OPTION TO BUY

This technique was made for remodelers! Let's look at an example.

You have found a quaint one-story, two-bedroom house with one bathroom in an up-and-coming neighborhood. Upon examination, you realize that the roof pitch is steep enough to allow the attic to be finished off as living space. Three cute dormers on the front will turn this small cottage into a 3-bedroom, 2-bath 1-1/2 story home. The seller wants $65,000 cash and is not willing to finance the down payment.

The current loan is not assumable; so, you will have to obtain new financing. You estimate that the improvements will add $25,000 to the value of the house, but the renovations will cost you approximately the $12,000 which you now have in cash.

If you get a new loan and put 10% down ($6,500), you will not have enough cash to complete the renovation. The bank cannot give you a mortgage for the new value of the house until the renovation is complete. You are trapped in the "cart before the horse" dilemma. What do you do?

Ask the seller to *lease* the property to you for a monthly rent equal to his mortgage payment. The lease will include an option for you to buy the property within the first year. Explain that you are a professional remodeler and plan to renovate the property. If you do not choose to buy the property, the seller will inherit the improvements you have made at no cost. If you choose to buy, you will pay the full asking price minus your monthly payments.

The seller is happy because he will be receiving tax writeoffs on his new "rental property" that can be used to offset the profits made when the property is sold. When you have finished the renovation, you exercise your option to buy and apply for a new mortgage for $81,000 (90% of the home's new appraised value of $90,000).

The result?: You just paid $12,000 for the renovation and $65,000 to the seller; a total of $77,000. But note that these payments are fully paid by the new $81,000 mortgage! You walk away with $4,000 cash and a new house worth $90,000. This type of deal works so well that you can afford to bargain aggressively with the seller if he resists this type of arrangement.

CONCLUSIONS

The point of these examples? There is no limit to the type of financial bargains you can devise. All it takes is a willing seller and *creativity*.

Once you know the needs and circumstances of the seller, you are ready to use your creativity to put together an innovative deal where both parties will benefit!

Legal Considerations

Depending upon the size of your project, you may need legal counsel. To avoid unpleasant surprises, consult the appropriate professionals -- attorneys, insurance agents, and financial lenders -- whenever faced with key legal issues; such as:

Easements
Covenants
Zoning
Variances
Liens
Subcontractor contracts
Builder's risk insurance
Building permits
Workmen's compensation

Easements

Easements can affect where and what additions you may make to the house. Easements give rights of traverse to local governments (sidewalk easements), utility companies (sewer or power line easements) or to individuals for various reasons. Consult your survey or conduct a title search to reveal any easements presently affecting your property. Make sure any additions you make to the structure do not violate existing easements.

Covenants

Covenants are building restrictions; such as, minimum square footage or the type and style of construction materials. These restrictions are usually placed on houses in the subdivision by the developer in order to protect the value of the homes in the subdivision. Ask your lawyer to check for any building restrictions in the public record before purchasing the property. The renovation project you planned may not be allowed by covenant restrictions!

Zoning Restrictions

Zoning restrictions, like covenants, control the use of, and the type of structures which can be built on, the property. These restrictions are placed by the local government planning board in order to protect land values in the area. Check with your local planning office; they can tell you the zoning or provide you with a zoning map of the county for a nominal fee.

Zoning laws also define the actual area which the structure can occupy upon the lot; i.e., the "minimum setback", which is the minimum distance the home must be from neighboring homes. There may also be restrictions on the minimum size of your backyard and sideyard. Make sure that any planned additions to the house do not encroach on these sideyard and backyard setback limits. In many planned subdivisions, these boundaries are strictly enforced in order to make the homes appear consistent, orderly and planned. In order to avoid hefty fines and possible reconstruction, it is imperative to acquaint yourself with the baselines and zoning restrictions prior to commencing your remodeling project.

VARIANCES

Variances, when granted, allow you to "deviate" within prescribed approved limits from standard state and local zoning ordinances. For example, if you want to extend your home to within 30 feet of the front curb, but the local zoning ordinance requires a 40-foot setback, you must apply for a 10-foot setback variance. Unless your request adversely affects neighborhood appearance or safety, your variance will usually be approved.

To obtain a variance, you must apply at the zoning office, paying an application fee. Then, a hearing will be set at which you will appear to describe or illustrate your intentions and the reasons for them. Usually a notice of your variance request will be posted on your lot so that the public is aware of your intention to request a variance and of the date on which the hearing will be held. Anyone has the right to appear at the variance hearing to either support or oppose your request.

LIENS

Liens, because of their potential effect on the remodeling project, are extremely important to a remodeler. A lien is a claim to a portion of the property. For example, if the plumbing contractor does not feel that he was fully paid for his work, he may file a lien against the property. When filed, the lien becomes a matter of public record. It will prevent the sale or mortgaging of the property until it is released by resolution of the conditions which led to its being filed. It is important to note that many states do not require the owner be notified of the lien; so, be sure your title search is done carefully in order to avoid nasty surprises!

If you are contracting the remodeling, you can protect yourself from liens by requiring your suppliers and subcontractors to sign a subcontractor's affidavit. This agreement states that all bills have been paid and that the subcontractor has no legal claim against your property. This will prevent him from filing any liens on the property. So, for your protection have all subcontractors with whom you deal sign a subcontractor's affidavit!

SUBCONTRACTOR CONTRACTS

Subcontractor contracts, like affidavits, protect you from surprises. All arrangements must be in writing, no matter how good your or his memory, reputation or integrity. "Subs" often develop "contract amnesia" if a problem arises. Your contract should include job specifications, time frame for completion and a schedule of payment. To avoid having to pay for rushed, below standard work, it is wise to include a statement such as "Final payment will be made when work is satisfactorily completed".

BUILDER'S RISK INSURANCE

Builder's risk insurance is another "ounce of prevention" necessary before starting your project. This insurance will protect you should someone be injured on the building site.

BUILDING PERMITS

Building Permits must be obtained from your City or County Building Inspector's office before construction can begin. They usually cost a certain amount per $1000 of construction value or per square foot. Obviously, construction value is somewhat intangible; so, you may be forced to accept the authority's estimate of construction value. The permit is usually required even if the remodeling project is only on the interior of the building Once a permit is issued, the building inspector will schedule the required inspections before, during and after the remodeling project. This permit must be

displayed in a prominent location at the site.

WORKMEN'S COMPENSATION

Workmen's Compensation is required in every state to provide workers with hospitalization insurance for job-related injuries. This accident insurance must be taken out by any person or company who has employees. Each building trade is assessed an insurance rate depending on the relative risk involved in the work. For instance, roofers will be charged a higher rate than trim carpenters. If your remodeling sub-contractors do not carry the proper insurance, you may be liable for injuries occurring on your property. So, make sure your subcontractors are properly insured. If a subcontractor carries a policy for his own workers, obtain the policy number and expiration date and call the carrier to verify coverage. Contact your local insurance agent for more information about workmen's compensation in your state.

Don't underestimate the importance of this policy. You are liable for any work-related injuries that occur on your property. Without this policy, a negligence lawsuit could deplete your life savings. Look for any situations around the project which could nullify Work-men's Compensation coverage. For example, in some states, drywall subcontractors who use drywall stilts are not covered.

4. FINDING THE RIGHT PROPERTY

If you have decided to renovate, you must begin a thorough search for potential properties. This chapter will help you to find bargains that others may overlook. The best bargains are, by definition, going to be the hardest to find. The universal law of economics states that "If it's easy to find, it's no bargain." To find the *real* bargains you must go where others seldom tread. The more difficult the search, the greater the opportunity. Begin your search with the most obvious sources first in order to develop a list of sample properties. Then, dig deeper into less obvious areas.

REAL ESTATE AGENTS

Most house purchases in the United States are made through real estate agents. This has become especially true in the larger cities, where the number of houses to choose from is overwhelming. Real estate agents can save you considerable time in looking for properties. Find a reputable agent and have him scour your primary areas for bargains. Real estate agents have access to Multi-Listing services that can cut a comprehensive search down from weeks to days. This activity costs you nothing and can yield valuable information and many bargains. Many times the aid of a competent agent will save you more than the cost of the real estate commission. The quality of real estate agents varies tremendously; so, shop carefully. Look for an agent with building or remodeling experience.

WANT ADS

The favorite pastime of a serious bargain hunter should include searching the want ads each Sunday. This is the first place to look for "FSBO's" (For Sale By Owner). Purchase a map of your town and outline the areas of greatest interest. As you read the want ads, look up the street address to locate the property on your "opportunity map". Drive by the

properties to see if the ad description matches your "real world" perception.

The biggest source of bargains will come from the "Don't Wanter". The "Don't Wanter" is a seller so eager to sell that he will look seriously at almost any deal. The want ads are full of "Don't Wanter's", pleading with the public to make them an offer. A typical "Don't Wanter" ad is easy to spot. Phrases like "desperate to sell", "$10,000 below market value", "Retiring, need to sell", "Price - $50,000 or any reasonable offer" indicate a willingness to sell. People become "Don't Wanters" for many reasons. One of the main reasons can be physical problems with the house. Many older home-owners have reached an age where working on their home is not attractive or possible. Quite often, their houses have reached the age that requires constant attention. This type of structure is your primary remodeling possibility.

Take extreme caution here! There is a fine line between the house begging for attention and the lemon with too many problems to overcome. Remember, the buyer knows the house and its idiosyncrasies much better than you. A seller hesitant to show you around the house may be hiding something.

Consider putting an ad in the paper asking for properties to buy. Potential sellers of houses will be reading the ads either looking for their own ad or other ads to copy. Try something like this:

> "I buy older houses. I am looking for houses with remodeling potential and atmosphere. Don't call unless you are serious about selling and will accept flexible terms. Call 555-1234."

You may be surprised at how many responses you get. This low-effort technique can help you to get the jump on other bargain hunters before the property is even advertised. There is another advantage. If you are the first to make an offer, the seller may be eager to avoid the hassles of selling and may take a lower offer then he intended. If you have checked out the property and it appears to be a good bargain, make an offer as quickly as possible and indicate that you will not wait around for him to make up his mind. Without other offers to compare to yours, the seller may well accept a low bid.

FHA AND HUD FORECLOSURES

These governmental agencies publish periodic listings of repossessed homes which quite often can be purchased for a fraction of their original value. The big advantage here is that the agency will provide preferred financing on each property. Contact your local real estate board and FHA office and ask to be put on their mailing lists.

AUCTIONS

Auctions of homes and properties have become an increasingly popular means of selling in the past years. Houses may be put up for auction for any number of reasons. Families may turn to auctions to sell off the personal property of deceased relatives. Developers and banks may unload excess property this way or owners may auction property to avoid foreclosure. Check the local newspapers for announcements of auctions or check the yellow pages for names of auction companies. Call them and request that you be put on their mailing lists.

COUNTY COURTHOUSE

The local courthouse can be a gold mine of information. Talk to the local authorities about the up and coming areas of town and the areas affected by zoning changes. All properties are listed in the public record deeds and plats. If you have seen several interesting properties,

look them up on the plat maps to determine the owners and their length of ownership.

Look for any notices of foreclosure or delinquent taxes. In most counties, these events must be on public notice for a certain length of time before any action can be taken. Most counties also require that the information be published in the local newspaper. Many a home has been auctioned on the courthouse steps for next to nothing. If the notice concerns delinquent payments, contact the owner. Chances are, he will be eager to avoid foreclosure and will be ready to deal.

DRIVE BY'S

Drive By's are the number one tool of the serious real estate buyer. Although time consuming, driving through an area is the only way to fully assess the neighborhood and available houses. Keep an eye out for **FOR SALE BY OWNER** signs. When you see one, stop and talk to the owner about the property, even if you are not particularly interested. Find out the asking price. Take notes on the property -- your likes and dislikes, as well as attractive features. Ask the seller if he knows of any other neighbors about to sell. Your best source of knowledge about remodeling will come from these personal experiences -- *and it's free*!

This is also your chance to get a feel for the neighborhood. Look for areas where several existing houses have been recently renovated. If you see a house that interests you, go to the courthouse and look up the owner in the plat records. Write a letter that states your interest in the house. This can get many owners interested in selling.

Don't make the mistake of many eager homeowners and buy the first decent deal around. It won't be the only great deal you find. Be patient. Make sure you have a good feel for all opportunities and the effort involved before making the plunge. You don't want your first remodeling project to be your last. The more you look, the more assured you will be of finding your **Dream Home!**

5. EVALUATING REMODELING POTENTIAL

If your house hunting has been successful, you should have found several prospective homes from which to choose. The time and effort you spend in evaluating your choices will determine the success or failure of your remodeling project; so, study your choices carefully. The items that make a home desirable are a combination of several factors and considerations, all of which add up to the total value or sales price of the home. These are:

- Land value
- Location of home (proximity to schools, shopping centers and work)
- Status and trend of the neighborhood
- Condition of the site
- Condition of the home
- The "flavor"'or "romance" of the structure
- The functionality of the structure

Many would-be remodelers get caught up in the "dream" of remodeling and the potential of the structure and fail to pay enough attention to the other "livability" factors. Before you even begin to analyze the structure itself, look at the following factors. Only after they all meet the acceptability test are you ready to judge the structure itself.

The Lot

Study the lot carefully. Make sure to check with the local county zoning office to determine the lot "setbacks" and future zoning plans for the neighborhood. Does the yard have sufficient room for possible expansion of the house? Is there room for the addition of a carport or garage to the side or back of the house? Will you be able to socialize in the back yard in relative privacy?

Many old houses have mature trees and bushes that contribute to that "lived in" look. This shrubbery can be very valuable as a buffer zone between your house and the next. Check the condition of these plants to determine if they are in good health. Many older plants encroach on neighboring yards or hang precariously close to the house and may have to be removed or trimmed back. Many older shrubs have reached the age that pruning the plant back to a proper size will risk killing it. If the plants are in healthy condition, they can add significantly to the atmosphere, energy efficiency and desirability of the lot.

The drainage of the lot is also very important. Look for washed out areas around the foundation or driveway. These can be never ending problems that are difficult to repair. Bad drainage can also restrict the location of new construction or cause difficulties during construction. Drainage trenches or washed out areas running across your lot are sure signs of runoff from neighboring yards or, worse, runoff from your yard to neighboring properties. If you find evidence of these, talk with neighbors to get a history of the neighborhood and their reactions to the drainage. You may find that one of the homeowner's reasons for selling is to avoid litigation from neighbors!

If the area has no public sewer, make sure to investigate the condition of the septic tank. Older septic systems are notorious for problems. Ask the seller and neighbors if any drainage problems exist. If some problems are indicated and you are serious about purchasing, consider having a percolation test run on the soil. This test determines the capacity of the soil to drain properly and can be administered by local surveyors or city sewage engineers.

Location of the Property

Real Estate agents like to say that the three most important factors in choosing a home are "location, location and location". In our increasingly mobile society, the location of your home has become even more important as a buying factor. This can work to your advantage, since older homes tend to be located nearer to metropolitan developments. The factors considered most important are the home's proximity to shopping, schools and work. Take a city map and draw a circle around the house you are evaluating at intervals of 1, 5 and 10 miles. If all three activities are located within the one-mile circle, consider the location to be excellent. If all three activities are located within 5 miles, the location is still quite good. Activities farther than 10 miles away may spell trouble. Of course, these figures should be adjusted if your home is located in a large city with a minimum of close-in housing.

The condition and makeup of the neighborhood is another vitally important issue. The best location in the city can be ruined if your house is in a rundown or crime ridden area. Drive around the neighborhood at all times of the day and night. Take notes on the condition of the neighbors' houses. Are they run down or ill kept? Ideally, the neighborhood should be on its way up. Many older neighborhoods follow a definite aging cycle. During the first few years of development, the neighborhood is at its peak. Age begins to take its toll by the tenth year, and the neighborhood starts downhill as the homes age and become "out of style". At some point, however, these homes will begin to rise in value for several reasons. First, when homes reach their lowest level, they have nowhere to go but up. Second, the homes reach an age where they are considered "antiques"; their out-of-date qualities become quaint reminders of a fargone age. At this stage, usually 30-50 years after development, these houses become assets to the community because of their central location. Of course, not all areas will experience a rebirth. Some neighborhoods will continue the spiral downward until commercial development or condemnation reclaims the land. Judging the direction of the neighborhood takes a keen eye for social trends and attitudes. Good signs of an area on the rise are:

1. The granting of historical district status to the area or surrounding areas.

2. Other remodeled houses or renovation projects in the vicinity.

3. A renewed "sense of pride" in the area, characterized by clean up projects or other public service projects.

4. New shopping developments or school renovations in the surrounding area.

5. Resistance of the area to encroachment by commercial or multi-family projects.

6. New home or condominium construction on reclaimed property in the area.

Look for these signs in your drive-by survey and by research at the local building inspector's or zoning office. These officials know the trends in the local community and are usually more than happy to share their knowledge.

Danger signals for an area include:

1. Commercial or industrial development nearby.

2. The closing of local schools.

3. The migration of local retail stores to other areas.

4. The proliferation of low income or multi-family developments in and around the area.

5. Excessive parking on the street. Drive by the area at night and on weekends to see if overflow parking occurs from local bars or stadiums.

6. An abnormally large number of for-sale signs in the area -- evidence that something is scaring away the residents. Many "Don't Wanter" sales occur because the seller is aware of something that will reduce the value of his property. He will do anything to sell the property. **Make absolutely sure before purchasing that you know the future of the neighborhood!**

If a neighborhood has just started its upward trend, you should consider purchasing only if you plan to retain the property long enough for the local property values to escalate. This increase in value will happen slowly. Your safest investment is a rundown property in a neighborhood that is well on its way to recovery. Don't try to be the "pioneer" who is going to "turn the neighborhood around." Remember, pioneers are the ones with the arrows in their backs!

Interior Layout

The pleasure of living in your new home will be greatly affected by its interior layout and appearance. Examine carefully, the relationship and convenience of areas to each other, traffic circulation, privacy and room size. Many houses will not lend themselves to an ideal arrangement without excessive cost and restructuring. The restrictions imposed by loadbearing walls may make it impossible to achieve suitable living conditions without some sacrifice in arrangement.

TRAFFIC PATTERNS

Observe the circulation and traffic patterns of each room. A floor plan with good circulation should keep traffic flow to one side of the room rather than through its center. Some circulation problems can be improved simply by moving doors to the corners of rooms or by placing furniture in a manner that will direct traffic where it will be the least objectionable.

LAYOUT

Ideally, your house should have rooms arranged in three areas - the private or bedroom area, the work area consisting of kitchen and utility rooms and the relaxation area consisting of dining and living rooms. A family room, a den or a recreation room may exist in or between these general areas. The den should be out of the general circulation areas and, if it is part of the bedroom area, may double as a guest room.

Kitchen Area
The location of the kitchen in relation to other areas of the house is critical. It should have direct access to the dining area and should be accessible to the garage or driveway for ease in unloading groceries. Being near the utility room is also convenient if you plan to have work in progress in the kitchen and utility room at the same time. Traffic should not pass through the kitchen work area.

The size of the kitchen is important. There was a time when small kitchens were thought to be convenient, but with the advent of so many modern appliances, not to mention the growth in popularity of the "breakfast nook", kitchens now require much more space. So, if the kitchen is too small, a major addition or alteration may be necessary.

Private Areas
To ensure privacy, the bedroom and bathroom area should be separated both visually and acoustically as much as possible from the living and work areas of the house.

Check to see that every bedroom is accessible to a bathroom without going through any other room and that at least one bathroom is accessible to the work and relaxation areas. One of the basic rules of privacy is to avoid traffic through one bedroom to another. Check the size of the bedrooms. They should have a floor area of at least 125 square feet for a double bed and 150 square feet for twin beds.

Living Areas

The living areas include the dining room, living room and den. In most older homes, these areas are broken into individual rooms. The den area is usually located at the front of the house, but rooms at the side or rear may be desirable, particularly if this provides a view into a landscaped yard. If the house has a separate parlor or living room and dining room separated by an arch, check to see if the interior partitions can be removed to give a more spacious feeling. The main entrance is usually at or near the living room. Check for a coat closet near this entrance and a passage into the work area without passing though the living room.

The effect of loadbearing walls

When evaluating the floor plan layout, pay careful attention to the location of loadbearing walls. These walls are usually located near the center of the structure and support loadbearing floor or ceiling joists. These walls are difficult and expensive to move, restricting floor plan changes.

APPEARANCE

Taste is so subjective that only basic guidelines can be given. The quaint feel of older houses may be obscured by years of painting and redesigning. Simplicity and unity of design are the major things for which to look. Homes of historic significance are in a special category, and professional advice should be obtained for their appraisal.

Simplicity is one of the first principles. Observe the main lines of the house. The house should have simple, classic lines or have a definite historical style. Some variety adds interest, but numerous roof lines at a variety of slopes present a busy, confused appearance. Strong horizontal lines are usually desirable in a conventional residence to give the appearance of being "tied to the ground." Strong vertical lines tend to make a house look tall and unstable.

Unity is as important as simplicity. The house should appear as a unit, not as a cluster of unrelated components. Windows and trim should be in keeping with the style of the house. Shutters should be one-half the width of the window so that, if closed, they would cover the window. Porches and garages should blend with the house rather than appear as haphazard, last minute "add ons".

If the dwelling appears unattractive, consider how paint and landscaping may affect it. Even an attractive house will not look good without being properly painted or landscaped.

Appraisal

In order to decide on the wisdom of buying a particular house, you must confirm that the appraised value of the property matches the selling price. Houses in older neighborhoods are notoriously hard to price because of the many variables created by their age. What is a fair price? Often, the fair price is one that satisfies to a reasonable degree both the needs of the buyer and the needs of the seller. You, as the buyer or the seller, will want to bring to the bargaining table as much cost information as possible. Although subjective, a reasonable and fair price can be determined by one of many methods.

COST METHOD

This method adds up all the costs of the individual components of the house -- land, construction costs, materials, legal and other fees, etc. -- and then subtracts depreciation to arrive at the final figure. To calculate the construction costs, you must first decide whether you will use the reproduction cost or the replacement cost.

The replacement cost would be the cost to replace the structure with a building of like kind. This is quite difficult since any replacement would be a new structure when compared with the old one. There is no way to artificially age the property to approximate the old one. For this reason, replacement cost has little use except when figuring insurance settlements.

The reproduction cost would be the cost of producing an exact replica of the original structure, using today's methods at today's cost. This method would be used when appraising an older home with great historical significance. Many areas designated as historical districts require that the structure be returned to its original form. Obviously, appraising a house at reproduction cost may value the property at a price no one will be willing to pay unless the home is that of a famous person. For this reason, the cost approach is seldom used as a serious means of appraising most older structures.

INCOME METHOD

The income method is only used for rental property and compares the rent a property can produce against its property value. Properties with equal rental income should have roughly the same property value. First, determine the average rent for properties in the same area and with the same features as the property you are investigating. Take the monthly rate and multiply it by 110. This is the gross rent multiplier and varies somewhat from location to location. Check with local real estate agents for the appropriate multiplier for your area. The resulting figure represents the average property value for the income producing properties in the area. If the average rent is $750 per month and the GRM (Gross Rent Multiplier) in your area is 110, then the value of the house would be $82,500. This figure is only approximate since other factors will also affect the rent.

MARKET COMPARISON METHOD

By far the most widely used appraisal technique is the market comparison method, or competitive market analysis as it is sometimes called. This is a method of appraising based on comparing the subject property to similar properties that have sold recently. Most Real Estate agents and professional appraisers use this technique. There are three basic steps to performing a market analysis:

1. Locate the comparable properties

2. Adjust the comparables for differences in the subject property

3. Apply the comparisons to the subject property

Finding comparable properties

Ideally, the properties should be as similar to the subject property as possible. The best "comps" will come from the same neighborhood as the subject property. These comps should have been sold within the last year to avoid price differences resulting from inflation or deflation. The properties should be of approximately the same size, style and state of repair. For example, if you are appraising a two-story victorian house, look for other victorian houses in the same locale. The more similar they are to the subject property, the fewer adjustments you will have to make.

How do you find sales records? The most comprehensive source is your county's public deeds and records office. All real estate transactions are filed and available for public scrutiny. Ask for assistance to find properties which have sold recently in the subject area. The deeds will not reveal the sales price; however, most counties charge a deed transfer fee based on the cost of the house. This fee amount is recorded on the deed and can be used to determine the sales price. If this data is insufficient, contact a local real estate agent. Most multi-listing services carry records on previous sales for use by agents in preparing their comparables. Do not use the listing prices or advertised selling prices for comparisons. These figures seldom match the actual selling price.

Adjusting for differences

Once you have found three to five appropriate properties, adjustments to their statistics must be made. Adjust for all differences which fall into the following four categories:

■ Differences in financing
■ Date sold
■ Location
■ Size and features

financing differences will affect the selling price of the house. If the seller offers a low-interest, no-money-down, assumable loan, he will be able to command a much higher price than a seller with a conventional loan at a higher interest rate. The selling price, therefore, must be adjusted up or down depending on the attractiveness of the financing.

The selling date of the comparables will affect their comparison prices. Adjust the sales price of the comparables by the rate of inflation or deflation in house prices since the property was sold. If prices have been rising, adjust the price upward. *If the prices are falling*, take another look at the feasibility of the property!

The location must be taken into account if the comparable properties are located in neighborhoods or lots that differ in desirability from the subject property. If the comparable property is located in a less desirable area, then adjust the price up, and vice versa.

The features of the comparable properties seldom match the subject house exactly. For instance, the subject house may have more bedrooms, bathrooms, etc. If the subject house has one less bathroom than the comparable, as an example, you would expect it to be less valuable. You want to adjust the comparable's price up or down to *adjust out* the difference in features. How do you determine the relative value of an extra bedroom or bath in an older home? This can be tricky. The best way is to first compare several sold properties to spot any selling price differences that may be attributed to differences in features.

Here is an example: Comparable property A has two bathrooms while comparable property B has only one. Both properties sold at approximately the same time and are located in the same neighborhood. The difference in price between A and B is $1500. If you judge that the two properties are equally attractive, it is safe to assume that the difference in price can be attributed to the extra bathroom. Therefore, the value of the extra bath can be assumed to be around $1500 for that type house.

If one of the comparables has one more bath than the subject property, you should adjust the price of the comparable *down* $1500, since the extra bath would cause the comparable to be worth more than the subject property. Remember, the goal is to make the comparable properties as *similar to the subject property as possible*. Then you can use the average price of the comparables to determine the *inferred* price of the subject property.

Obviously, appraising is an art as much as a science. You must use your common sense and judgment to even out prices between the comparables and the subject property. Even then, there is no guarantee that the owner will sell the property at your appraised value. Even with these limitations, the appraisal process can be extremely valuable in spotting good values or potential lemons. As you research these other properties, your ability to distinguish real value potential in remodeling projects will develop.

THE PROFESSIONAL APPRAISAL

Determining the appraisal value of older properties can be tedious and difficult. Professional appraisers do this for a living and have access to comparable pricing information which makes their work potentially more accurate than that of an amateur. Professional appraisals can cost anywhere from $100 to $500, but they can prove invaluable when you are seriously negotiating with a seller. If possible, ask the seller to pay for the appraisal by making the sales contract contingent on a stated value from an appraiser. If you are confident that the appraisal will show a lower value than the asking price, consider bringing the appraisal to the bargaining table as a negotiating tool. Most sellers of older homes will find it hard to argue with a professional appraisal. Make sure to hire an appraiser who is a member of one of the professional appraisal societies; such as, The American Institute of Real Estate Appraisers or The Society of Real Estate Appraisers. The highest level of designation is the MAI appraiser (Member of the Appraisal Institute).

LOCATION EVALUATION CHECKLIST

Lot Address _____ Owner _____

ACCESSIBILITY:

_____ Distance to nearest school

_____ Distance to nearest shopping

_____ Distance to metro area or office complex

STRENGTHS:

_____ Lot on sewer line. Sewer is in good repair.

_____ Landscaping is in good repair. Trees and shrubs are healthy and not too close to home or adjoining lots. Pruning of trees or shrubs possible without permanent damage.

_____ Safe, quiet atmosphere.

_____ Clean well kept neighboring houses.

_____ Higher priced and recently renovated houses nearby.

_____ Good drainage from lot and around house.

_____ Situated in improving/growth area

_____ Area is zoned exclusively for single family

_____ Underground utilities. Phone, electrical, cable TV

_____ Recreational areas nearby

_____ Sufficient lot clearance for room additions or garage

_____ Adjoining neighbors are friendly

WEAKNESSES:

_____ Sandy or unstable soil base with washouts or signs of erosion. Evidence of recent flooding. Signs of drainage across neighbor's lots from your lot.

_____ Property in flood plain. (Check with local authorities for verification.)

_____ Area on septic tank. (Ask seller and neighbors if any septic tank problems exist.)

_____ On or near major thoroughfare. Future road development nearby.

_____ Near airport, railroad tracks, landfill, exposed electric power facilities, industrial areas, or swampy areas (mosquitoes).

_____ Steeply sloped lot. Lot slopes toward house. Difficult to mow. Difficult access by car if iced over.

_____ Located in or near declining neighborhood

_____ Isolated from services/amenities such as shopping, schools, parks, etc.

_____ Apartment, commercial, or industrial development prevalent in area.

_____ Unfriendly or untidy neighbors

_____ Narrow or crowded street. Parking on street.

_____ Zoning or deed restrictions prevent improvements to the property.

6. EVALUATING THE STRUCTURE

The Unseen Dangers

No home is a good bargain if it harbors undetected problems that will surface after the sale. A well-built house that is properly maintained should last for over 100 years. Tests conducted by the Forest Products Laboratory show that, when abnormal environmental factors are not present, wood does not deteriorate in strength or stiffness for periods of 100 years or more.

In spite of the permanence of the wood frame house, many older houses are slowly being destroyed by decay, insects, rodents and the elements. Many of these houses have deteriorated to a point where rehabilitation would be impractical. You want to make sure not to fall in love with a house in this condition! This section will assist you in spotting the danger signals that should spell *caution*!

You should plan to examine the property carefully to look for structural problems. These problems can often be hidden from view and will require an astute detective to flush them out. Arrange for a detailed walk-through of the house with the seller present. Whenever you notice anything suspicious, ask the owner specific questions about any problems with the house. Even when the seller attempts to hide problems from you, careful observations of his reactions will often signal a potential problem.

Plan your own walk-through before hand, so that you know exactly for what to look. Use a checklist to insure that you do not overlook any details. You will only have a short time to evaluate the house, so make every minute count.

With careful evaluation, you can make sure that your dream house can be restored to a sound condition and can be updated to modern standards of convenience and comfort.

MASONRY AND CONCRETE

Foundations
The most important structural component of a house is the foundation. Structural problems here will be difficult and expensive to repair. Look for general deterioration; this may indicate that moisture or water has entered the basement. It is costly to repair this damage and, more importantly, to prevent a recurring problem with seepage. Check for uneven settlement, which can distort or even pull apart the house frame. Uneven settling may have caused your windows and door frames to be pulled out of square, or it may have loosened the interior finish and siding, creating cracks that can cause drafts and heat loss.

A minor settling problem can be corrected by releveling beams or floor joists. Widespread uneven settlement, however, may require a new foundation or, more critically, may make the house unsuitable for renovation. Be sure to check the joint between the foundation and the wood frame construction. If you find gaps of an inch or more, this may be an indication of significant settling -- a danger signal that more severe problems exist. Further structural investigation is needed to determine the extent of remodeling which may be necessary.

Masonry Walls and Piers
If the house has a stone or brick foundation supported on masonry piers, check the masonry for cracks and crumbling mortar. This common defect can usually be repaired, depending on its extent. Extensive deterioration, however, may indicate the need for major repair or replacement.

If the house has a crawl space, it probably has a foundation wall or piers supporting the floor joists. Check these supports for cracks and settlement, just as you have checked the perimeter foundation.

YES!

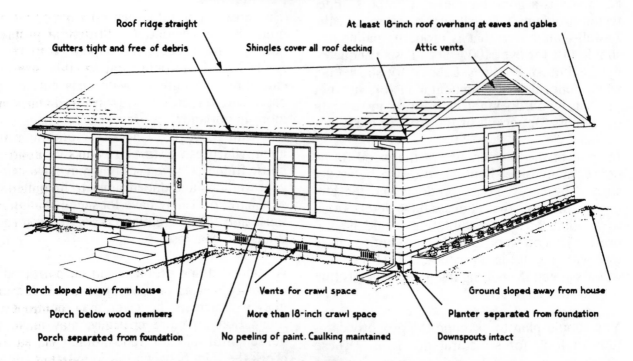

Roof ridge straight

At least 18-inch roof overhang at eaves and gables

Gutters tight and free of debris

Shingles cover all roof decking

Attic vents

Porch sloped away from house

Vents for crawl space

Ground sloped away from house

Porch below wood members

More than 18-inch crawl space

Planter separated from foundation

Porch separated from foundation

No peeling of paint. Caulking maintained

Downspouts intact

NO!

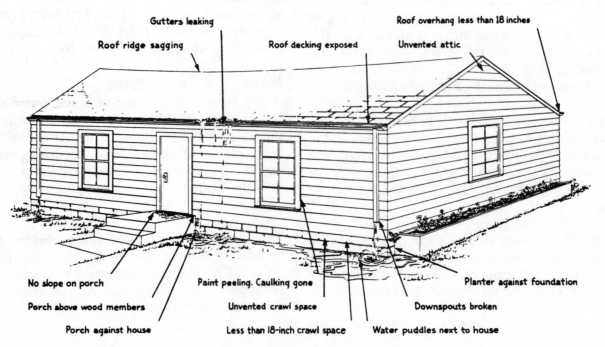

Gutters leaking

Roof overhang less than 18 inches

Roof ridge sagging

Roof decking exposed

Unvented attic

No slope on porch

Paint peeling. Caulking gone

Planter against foundation

Porch above wood members

Unvented crawl space

Downspouts broken

Porch against house

Less than 18-inch crawl space

Water puddles next to house

Basements

Damp or leaky basement walls may require major repair, especially if you wish to convert the basement space into a living space. Dampness and water encroachment can ruin a renovation project, creating costly delays, constant repairs and even making the new living space unlivable.

Possible causes of dampness are clogged drain tiles, clogged or broken downspouts, cracks in walls, incorrect sloping of the finished grade away from the house foundation or a high water table. Be sure to determine the cause of your problem before proceeding. Some causes may be easily remedied; others may be too costly or too extensive to undertake.

Check for dampness by examining the basement a few hours after a heavy rain. Look for cracks in the foundation or signs of leakage in the basement that seem to emanate from one location. Examine the walls for signs of dampness. Deposits of white flaky material on the surface of the wall indicate minerals leeching out of the concrete or block itself. This less localized seepage requires extensive waterproofing measures. Well-localized leaks, however, can sometimes be patched with waterproofing compound.

The most common source of dampness is surface water; such as, that from downspouts discharging directly at the foundation wall or that from surface drainage flowing directly against the foundation wall. The cardinal rule is to keep water away from the foundation; this is best accomplished by proper grading.

A high water table is a more serious problem. There is little possibility of achieving a dry basement if the water table is high, even if only periodically. Heavy foundation waterproofing or footing drains may help; but, since the source cannot be controlled, it is unlikely these

measures will do more than minimize the problem.

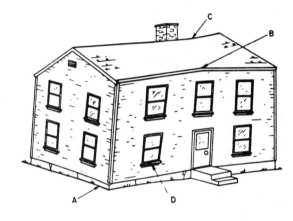

Figure 2—Uneven foundation settlement, A, may result in a house badly out of square. Evidence may include B, eaveline distortion; C, sagging roof ridge; or D, loosefitting frames or even binding windows and doors

Masonry veneers

Uneven settling of the foundation will cause cracks in brick or stone veneer. Cracks can be grouted and joints repointed, but large or numerous cracks will be unsightly even after they are patched,. The mortar also may be weak and crumbling, with joints which are incompletely filled or poorly finished. If these faults are limited to a small area, regrouting or repointing may be feasible. For improved appearance, the veneer can be cleaned with water or chemicals.

It is important to prevent water from entering the masonry wall or from flowing over the face of the wall. Examine flashing or caulking at all projecting trim, copings, sills and intersections of roof and walls. Plan to repair any places where flashing or caulking is not provided or where need of repair is apparent. Clear water repellent should be used with caution on brick or stone because it can trap moisture within the material.

Chimneys and Fireplaces

Look for cracks in the masonry or loose mortar in your chimney. Such cracks are usually the result of settling of the foundation or of the attachment of television antennas which put undue stress on the chimney. Cracks are a particular hazard if the flue does not have a fireproof lining.

If the chimney is masonry, it should be supported on its own footing. (Pre-fabricated fireplaces do not require footings, because of their light weight.) Look in the attic to see that ceiling and roof framing are no closer than 2 inches to the chimney -- either of these defects is a fire hazard and should be corrected immediately.

Does the fireplace have a damper? If not, add one to prevent heat loss up the flue when the fireplace is not in use. A fireplace that looks like it has been used a lot probably draws well; however, make sure by lighting a few sheets of newspaper in the fireplace and observing the flow of smoke. A good fireplace will draw immediately; a usable one will draw after about a minute.

WOOD FRAME CONSTRUCTION

Examine the building frame carefully to see if it is distorted as a result of foundation failure or improper/inadequate framing.

Floor Supports

If your house has a basement, its interior support is probably provided by wood or steel girders supported on wood or steel posts. Wood posts should be supported on pedestals and should not be embedded in the concrete floor,

where they may collect moisture and decay. Steel posts are normally supported on metal plates. Always examine the base of wood posts for decay even if they are set above the floor slab. Check wood girders for sag and for decay around the perimeter of the wall. Some sag is common in permanently loaded wood beams and is not a problem unless parts of the house have obviously distorted. Some deflection -- about 3/8-inch deflection in a 10-foot span girder -- is acceptable in design. Excessive sagging can usually be corrected with permanent floor jacks that will raise the floor back to its original level.

Floor Framing

The sill plates, or joists and headers if sill plates are not used, rest on top of the foundation. So, they are exposed to moisture and therefore vulnerable to decay or insect attack. Carefully examine these members, as well as the entire floor framing system, for decay and insect damage, particularly if the basement or crawl space is very damp.

Joists, like girders, should be examined for sag. Here, too, some sag can be expected and is not necessarily a sign of structural damage. Sag is not usually a serious problem unless the foundation system has settled unevenly, causing excessive deflection in parts of the floor system. Look for local deflection due to inadequate support of a heavy partition load that runs parallel to the joists. It might be considered excessive if it is readily apparent from a visual appraisal of the levelness of a floor.

If your floor seems to be excessively springy when walking across it, remedy this by adding extra joists or girders to increase stiffness.

Some builders estimate that 50 percent of the houses built have inadequate framing around stairs. So, also check the framing of the floor joists around all stair openings. Check the floors around these openings for levelness. Where floors are sagging, the framing will have to be carefully leveled and reinforced.

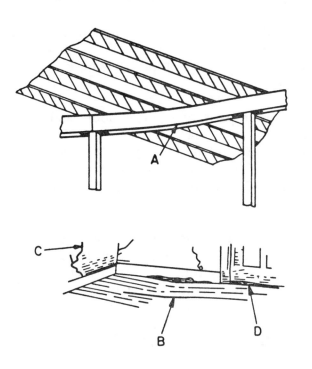

Figure 3--Sagging horizontal member, A, has resulted in: B, uneven floor; C, cracked plaster; and D, poorly fitting door.

Wall Framing
The common stud wall has much more than adequate strength. It may, however, still be distorted and require adjustment for some of the reasons covered in preceding sections. Open and close all doors and windows, observing their fit. Minor adjustments are easily accomplished, but large distortions will require new framing. Also check for sagging of the headers over wide window openings or in the wide openings between rooms. Where sag noticeable, new headers will be required.

Roof Framing
Examine the roof for sagging of the ridge, rafters and sheathing. Simple visual observation is all that is needed. The ridge will sag due to improper support, inadequate ties at the plate level or from sagging of the rafters. If the ridge

line is not straight or the roof does not appear to be in a uniform plane, some repair may be necessary. Rafters will sag due to inadequate stiffness or because they were not well seasoned when installed. Sheathing sag may indicate too wide a spacing between rafters or strip sheathing; it may indicate the plywood is too thin or it has delaminated.

EXTERIOR

Exterior wood on a house will last many years if it is kept free of moisture and is given reasonable care.

Siding and Trim
The main problems encountered with siding and trim occur as a result of excessive moisture, which can enter from either inside or outside your home. One of the main contributors to the problem is the lack of a proper amount of roof overhang, allowing rain to run down the face of the wall. Another source of excessive moisture may come from inside the house because of the lack of a vapor barrier, causing condensation within the wall.

Look for excessive space between horizontal siding boards by standing very close to the wall and sighting it. Minor cracks can be caulked, but extensive cracks and gaps will require new siding. If the boards are not badly warped, simple renailing may solve the problem. Always remember to check siding for decay. Examine the areas where two boards are butted end to end, all corners and around window and door frames.

Your shingle siding, if in good repair, should appear as a perfect mosaic; whereas, worn shingles have a ragged appearance and close examination will show individual shingles to be broken, warped and upturned. New siding will be required if the shingles are badly weathered or worn.

Windows

Windows usually present one of the more prevalent and difficult-to-repair problems of old wood frame houses. If they are loose fitting and not weatherstripped, they will be a major source of both uncomfortable drafts and considerable heat loss. Examine the sash and sill for decay. Also check the operation of the window. Casement windows should be checked for warp at top and bottom; the fit should be tight.

When replacement of windows is planned, check the window dimensions. If the window is not a standard size or if a different size is desired, the opening will have to be reframed or a new sash may have to be made, both of which are expensive.

In cold climates your windows should be double glazed or you should install storm windows. Both will reduce heat loss and avoid condensation. To determine if your windows have double panes, open the window and press your fingers against both sides of the window. A gap between your fingers of more than a quarter of an inch indicates double glazing; however, don't expect to find double glazing on houses of more than 10 years old which still have the original windows. Heat retention can be improved with storm windows or interior acrylic glazing products. Be advised, though, that storm windows are expensive for windows which are not a standard size.

Doors

Exterior doors should fit well without sticking. Weather stripping will help to avoid air infiltration. If you have difficulties in latching a door this can usually be attributed to warping. A simple adjustment of the latch keeper will solve most of these problems, but badly warped doors should be replaced.

Storm doors are necessary in cold climates not only for heat saving and comfort, but also to avoid moisture condensation on or in the door and to protect the door from severe weather.

If the door frame is out of square due to foundation settlement or other racking of the house frame, the opening will probably have to be reframed.

The lower parts of exterior doors and storm doors are particularly susceptible to decay and should be carefully checked. Also observe the condition of the threshold, which may be worn, weathered or decayed, requiring replacement.

Porches

One of the components of a house most vulnerable to decay and insect attack is the porch. Since it is open to the weather, windblown rain or snow can easily raise the moisture content of wood members. This leads to conditions which promote the growth of wood destroying organisms. Also, steps to the porch are often placed in contact with soil; this is always a poor practice with untreated wood.

Check all wood members for decay and insect damage. Give particular attention to the base of posts or any place where two members join and where water might get into the joint. Decay often occurs where posts are not raised above the porch floor to allow air to dry out the base of the post. It may be worthwhile to replace only a few members; however, the porch that is in an overall deteriorated condition should be completely rebuilt or removed.

Finishes

Exterior finish failures result most commonly from excessive moisture in the wood. This may result either from direct rain or from moisture vapor condensing in the walls. Finish failures may also be caused by poor paints, improper application of good paints, poor surface preparation or incompatible successive coatings. Many types of paint are incompatible and will cause peeling when future owners paint over old paint without knowledge of the makeup of the previous finishes. You, too, can cause this problem when repainting a surface you originally painted. So, be sure to note the composition of all paints you use. You will need this information when deciding what paints to use when, a few years from now, you decide to repaint.

Excessive peeling may require complete removal of the paint. Since this can be very expensive and time consuming, residing may be a better solution.

Roof

If the roof is actually leaking, it should be obvious from water damage inside the house. Look for water stains on the ceiling around the perimeter of the house and at wall junctions in each room. Extensive water damage will cause the ceiling tile or drywall to sag.

A look in the attic may also reveal water stains on the rafters, indicating small leaks that will eventually cause damage. Damage inside the house is not always attributable to roofing leaks, but it could also be caused by faulty flashing or condensation problems.

Asphalt Shingles

Asphalt shingles are the most common roof covering and are made in a wide range of weights and thicknesses. The most obvious deterioration of asphalt shingles is loss of the surface granules. The shingles may also become quite brittle. More important, however, is the wear that occurs in the narrow grooves between the tabs or sections of the shingle, or between two consecutive shingles in a row. This wear may extend completely through to the roof boards without being apparent from a casual visual inspection. A good asphalt shingle should last 18 to 20 years.

Wood Shingles

Wood shingles also find considerable use for covering of pitched roofs and are most commonly of durable woods such as cedar in No. 1 or No. 2 grades. A good wood shingle roof should have a uniform appearance; whereas, a roof with worn shingles will show splitting and a ragged appearance. Individual shingles on the worn roof will be broken, warped and upturned. The roof with this worn appearance should be completely replaced even though there is no evidence of leaking. Excessive shade may cause fungus growth and early shingle deterioration. A good wood shingle roof will last up to 30 years under favorable conditions.

In recent years, several types of fake (composite) wood shingles have reached the market. These shingles preserve the appearance of wood shingles, but are much more durable.

Built-Up Roofing

Built up roofing -- popular in the fifties on flat or low sloped roofs -- should be examined by going onto the roof and looking for bare spots in the surfacing and for separation and breaks in the felt. Bubbles, blisters or soft spots also indicate that the roof needs major repairs; however, an alligator texture alone may not be a failure of the roof. The life of a built-up roof varies from 15 to 30 years, depending on the number of layers of felt and quality of application.

Flashing

Flashing should be evident where the roof intersects walls, chimneys or vents and where two roofs intersect to form a valley. Check for corroded flashing and replace it to prevent future problems. Likewise, check for corroded gutters and downspouts. Some can be restored; however, if severely corroded, replacement will be needed.

Overhang
If the house was built with no roof overhang, the addition of an overhang should be considered in the remodeling plan. It will greatly reduce your maintenance on siding and window trim, not to mention how it will improve the appearance of your house.

INTERIOR

Interior surfaces deteriorate due to wear, distortion of the structure and the presence of moisture. Sometimes the problem is further complicated by the use of cheap or improper materials, improper application of wall coatings or floor surfaces or excessive layers of wallpaper.

Flooring

Wood Floors
In checking wood floors look for buckling or cupping of boards that can result from high moisture content of the boards or wetting of the floor. Also notice if the boards are separated due to shrinkage. This shrinkage is more probable if the flooring boards are wide. If the floor is generally smooth and without excessive separation between boards, refinishing may put it in good condition; however, be sure there is enough thickness left in the flooring to permit sanding. Most flooring cannot be sanded more than two or three times. If it is softwood flooring without a subfloor, even one sanding might weaken the floor too much. Similarly, sanding of plywood block floors should also be quite limited. If your floors have wide cracks or are too thin to sand, some type of new flooring will have to be added.

Resilient Tile
Floors with resilient tile should be examined for loose tile, cracks between tile, broken corners and chipped edges. Look to see if any ridges or unevenness in the underlayment are showing through. Replacement of any tile in a room may necessitate replacing the flooring in the whole room because tiles change color with age and the new tile will not match the old.

Walls and Ceiling

Interior Covering
The interior wall covering in old houses is usually plaster, but it may be gypsum board in more recently built or remodeled homes. Wood paneling may also be found, but it is usually limited to one room, a single wall or an accent area.

Plaster almost always has some hairline cracks, even when it is in good condition. Minor cracks and holes can be patched, but a new wall covering should be applied if large cracks and holes are numerous, and if the plaster is loose in spots. The same general rule applies to ceilings.

If walls have been wallpapered, check the thickness of the paper. If more than two or three layers of paper are present, they should be removed before applying new paper. All wallpaper should be removed before painting.

Painted Surfaces
The paint on painted surfaces may have been built up to excessive thickness. It may be chipped due to mechanical damage, incompatibility between successive layers or improper surface preparation prior to repainting.

Trim, Cabinets and Doors
Trim should have tight joints and fit closely to walls. If the finish is worn but the surface is smooth, refinishing may be feasible. If the finish is badly chipped or checked, removing it will be laborious regardless of whether the new finish is to be a clear sealer or paint. Trim or cabinetry of plain design will be less difficult to prepare

for refinishing than that having ornately carved designs.

If any trim is damaged or if it is necessary to move doors or windows, all trim in the room may have to be replaced as it may be difficult to match the existing trim. Small sections of special trim might be custom made, but the cost should be compared with complete replacement. Check with your building supply dealer to see if the particular trim is still being made. Also check some of the older cabinet shops to see if they have shaper knives of this trim design.

The problems with interior doors are much the same as those explained for exterior doors, except there are no decay or threshold problems.

RECOGNIZING DAMAGE BY DECAY AND INSECTS

Decay

Look for decay in any part of the house that is subject to prolonged moisture. Decay thrives in a mild temperature and in wood with a high moisture content.

One indication of decay in wood is abnormal color and loss of sheen. Abnormal coloring in its early stages may be a shade which is deeper than normal; in its advanced stages, cracking and collapse occur. Abnormal coloring may also be a lightening which eventually progresses to a bleached appearance. Fine black lines within the bleached appearance may also be present.

Fungal growths, appearing as strandlike or cottony masses on the surface of wood, indicate excessive exposure to water and consequently the presence of decay.

Just seeing the evidence of decay does not necessarily reveal the extent of it. The two

strength properties severely reduced by decay are hardness and toughness. To test hardness, prod the wood with a sharp tool and observe its resistance to marring. Compare this resistance with that of a sound piece of wood. To determine loss of toughness, use a pointed tool to jab the wood and pry out a sliver. If toughness has been greatly reduced by decay, the wood breaks squarely across the grain with little splintering and lifts out with little resistance. Sound wood tends to lift out as one or two relatively long slivers, and breaks are splintery.

Decay may exist in any part of the house, but some areas are particularly vulnerable. Special attention should be given to these areas:

Foundations and Floors

Decay often starts in framing members near the foundation. It may be detected by paperlike, fanlike growths that are initially white with a yellow tinge and turn brown or black with age. Look for these growths between subfloor and finish floor and between joists and subfloor. They may become exposed by shrinkage of flooring during dry weather. These growths may also exist under carpets, in cupboards or in other protected areas that tend to stay damp.

Siding and Exterior Trim

Where siding is close to the ground, look for discoloration, checking or softening. Also check for signs of decay where siding ends butt against each other or against trim.

Roof System

Observe wood shingles for cracking, softening and breaking of the exposed ends. Asphalt shingles have deteriorated if they can be easily pulled apart. Edges of roofs are particularly vulnerable if not properly flashed. If the roofing is deteriorating, check the underside of the roof sheathing for evidence of condensation or decay.

Porches

Give particular attention to step treads or deck surfaces that are so cracked or worn that they trap water. Also check joints in railings or posts. Enclosed porches may have condensation occurring on the underside of the deck and framing. Check the crawl space for signs of dampness and examine carefully areas where these signs occur to determine their origin.

Windows and Doors

Look for brown or black discoloration near joints or failure of nearby paint. Both are signs of possible decay. Also check the inside for water stains on the sash and sill resulting from condensation running down the glass. Wherever these stains exist, check for softening and molding.

Insect Problems

The three major kinds of wood-attacking insects that cause problems in wood frame houses are termites, powder post beetles and carpenter ants. Where there is any indication of one of these insects, probe the wood with a sharp tool to determine the extent of damage.

Termites

There are two main classifications of termites:

1. **Subterranean Termites** - which require access to the ground or other water source, and
2. **Nonsubterranean Termites** - which do not require direct access to water.

Examine all areas close to the ground for subterranean termites. One of the most obvious signs is earthen tubes built over the surface of foundation walls to provide runways from the soil to the wood above. Termites may also enter through cracks or voids in the foundation or concrete floors. They do not require runways to the soil where there is a source of water such as a plumbing leak or condensation.

Another sign of the presence of termites is the swarming of winged adults early in the spring or fall. Termites resemble ants, but the termites have much longer wings and do not have the thin waist of an ant. Where there is an indication of termites, look for hollow tubes in the wood that follow the grain; usually leaving a shell of sound wood.

Nonsubterranean termites live in damp or dry wood without outside moisture or contact with the ground. One of the early signs of these termites is sandlike excretory pellets that are discarded outside the wood. They cut freely across the grain of the wood rather than following the grain as the subterranean termites do.

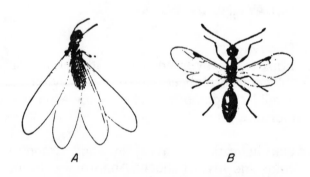

Figure 4–Differences between winged termite, A; and winged ant, B.

To combat termites, contract a certified professional exterminator. This is one job you don't want to leave to chance.

Powder Post Beetles

Powder post beetles are most easily recognized by their borings, which are about the consistency of flour. Many borings remain inside the wood. The adults leave the wood through a hole about the diameter of a pencil lead, leaving the wood with the appearance of having been hit by birdshot. Such holes may be just the result of a previous infestation; so, check for fresh, clean sawdust as a sign of current activity. Activity may also be recognized by the rasping sound the beetles make while tunneling.

Figure 5–Relative hazard of termite attack in the United States.

Look for powder post beetles in humid locations such as near the ground. Sometimes the homeowner may destroy them with an approved insecticide , but in severe cases, fumigation by a professional exterminator is required.

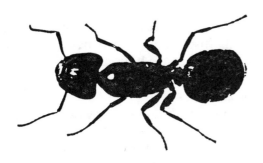

Figure 6–Black Carpenter Ant

Carpenter Ants

The presence of carpenter ants is often discovered by their chewed wood, which resembles coarse sawdust and is placed in piles outside the wood. They do not eat the wood, but only nest in it. Working ants may be as much as half an inch long. They make a rustling noise in walls, floors, or woodwork. Look for signs of carpenter ants in softwood in high humidity locations.

INSULATION AND CONTROL OF MOISTURE

Good insulation cuts heating costs and adds to comfort by making the temperature in the house more uniform. Humidifying the air increases comfort and saves fuel by reducing the temperature level required for comfort. While both humidification and insulation are desirable, their addition to older homes without vapor barriers in walls and ceilings may create moisture condensation problems. Where large differences exist between indoor and outdoor temperatures, pressure forces water vapor out through the walls.

In the uninsulated house this vapor usually moves to the outside without any problem. Where insulation is added, condensation often occurs within the insulation, causing wet insulation and siding; which can lead to fungus growth and rotting. In some instances where indoor relative humidities are low and the outside covering material allows moisture in the walls to escape readily, no moisture problems may result. However, mechanical humidification, in addition to normal moisture from cooking, bathing and respiration, amplifies moisture problems and may ruin the insulation. Vapor barriers in walls and ceilings reduce the rate of moisture movement into these areas, helping to control the moisture problems otherwise created by adding new insulation.

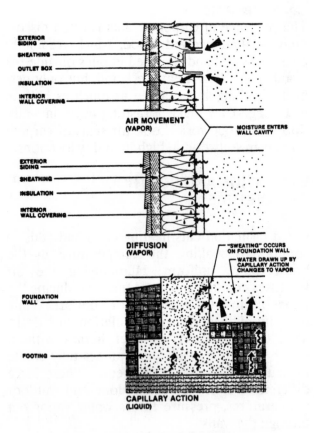

Figure 7—Moisture may enter the insulation cavity in a number of ways, causing decay and loss of insulation value.

high utilities probably indicate poor or nonexistent insulation.

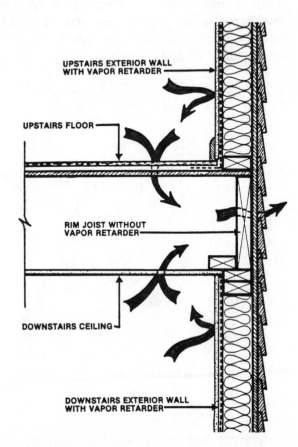

Figure 8—Water vapor can move through the rim joist when a vapor retardant is not installed.

Insulation

Look in the attic to determine the amount of ceiling insulation. The ceiling represents the greatest source of heat loss on cool days, as well as the greatest source of heat gain in warm days. At least 3 inches of insulation should be provided for homes in mild climates; 4 to 6 inches for those in cold climates. To find out if the walls are insulated, some siding and sheathing or interior covering must be removed. Obviously, most sellers will be reluctant to allow you to rip the siding off their home; so, you may have to deduce the insulation amount from energy usage. Ask for copies of utility bills for the past year. After taking into consideration the type of heating and cooling, unusually

Insulation in walls should be included as an item in any house rehabilitation in cold climates and in warm climates where summer cooling is essential. Insulation is also needed under the floors of crawl space houses in cold climates.

Vapor Barriers

Vapor barriers should be provided on the warm side of all insulation. Most houses built before the mid 1930s do not have vapor barriers. If the ceiling insulation is in blanket form with a covering around it, the covering material may resist the passage of moisture. If the ceiling insulation is loose fill, however, look under it for a separate vapor barrier of coated or laminated paper, aluminum foil or plastic film.

The same thing is true of insulated walls. The vapor barriers should be on the inside of the walls. Remove the covering of an electrical outlet or switch and look around the switch box for insulation, paper vapor coverings or pieces of plastic sheeting. Of course, make sure to turn off the power to the outlet first!

Check in crawl spaces for a vapor barrier laid on top of the soil. If there is none and the crawl space seems quite damp, a vapor barrier should be added.

There is no convenient way to determine if there are vapor barriers under floor slabs. If the floor seems damp most of the time, there probably is none. A new barrier or sealant would then have to be added on top of the slab, with a new finish floor applied over it, to have a dry finish floor.

Ventilation

The two major areas where good ventilation is required are the attic, or roof joist spaces in the case of a cathedral ceiling or flat roofed house, and the crawl space. The general adequacy of existing ventilation can be observed just from the degree of dampness in the home.

Moist air passes into the attic from the house and condenses as it cools or where it contacts the cold roof members. Both inlet and outlet vents must be located properly for good circulation of air through all the attic area. These vents not only help keep the attic dry in winter, but also keep hot air moving out from the attic during summer, helping keep the house cool.

Observe the size and location of crawl space vents. There should be at least four vents located near building corners for optimum cross ventilation and minimum dead air space.

MECHANICAL

Because many of the plumbing, heating and wiring systems in a house are concealed, it may be difficult to determine their adequacy. For the same reason it is difficult to make major changes without considerable cutting of wall surfaces and, in some situations, even structural members.

In a very old house the mechanical systems may have to be replaced. This is a major cost item. At the same time, however, properly installed new systems will be responsible to a large extent for comfort and convenience in the house. One bonus can be the dramatic recovery of space and improvement in the appearance of the basement when an old "octopus" gravity warm air heating system is replaced by a modern forced-air system.

Before contemplating any major heating and air changes, consult your local building and HVAC codes. Certain limitations such as clearances, duct sizes and heating loads may prevent you from making the change as envisioned.

PLUMBING

Water Supply System

Water pressure is important. Check several faucets to see if the flow is adequate. Low pressure can result from various causes. The pipe size may be too small or it may be reduced in diameter due to lime or mineral deposits. A 3/4-inch inside diameter service is considered adequate.

The main distribution pipes should be 3/4-inch in inside diameter, but branch lines may be only 1/2-inch in inside diameter. Below is a listing of the most common sizes of pipe. Measure first the outside diameter of your pipe. Then refer to the chart to determine its inside diameter.

Pipe	Diameter	
	Inside	Outside
Copper	1/2"	5/8"
	3/4"	7/8"
Galvanized	1/2"	7/8"
	3/4"	1-1/8"

The water supply pressure may be inadequate. If the house has its own water system, check the gauge on the pressure tank. This should read a minimum of 20, and preferably 40 to 50, pounds. Anything less will indicate, although unlikely, that the pump is not operating properly or the pressure setting is too low.

Check shutoff valves at the service entrance and at various points in the system to determine if they have become frozen with age or lack of use. Check on your property for leaks in the water supply system. Rusty pipes, white or greenish crusting of pipes or joints may indicate leaks.

Water hammer may also be a problem. This results when the water flow in the pipe is abruptly stopped by closing a faucet and a loud, thumping sound occurs. Air chambers placed on the supply lines at the fixtures usually absorb the shock and prevent water hammer. If you have water hammer, the air chambers may be clogged or filled with water. Simply clearing or draining these chambers should alleviate your problems. If you have no air chambers, they should be added.

Plumbing Drainage System

The drainage system consists of the sewer lateral, the underfloor drains, the drainage pipes above the floor and the vents. Pipes may have become clogged or broken or they may be of inadequate size. Venting, in particular, may be far below code requirements.

Flush the fixtures to see if your drains are sluggish. If so, check the following:

■ Old sewer laterals are commonly of vitreous bell tile. These may have been poorly installed or may have broken, allowing tree roots to enter at the breaks or through the joints. Roots can be removed mechanically, but this operation may have to be repeated every few years.

■ The underfloor drains may be of tile or even of steel and could be broken or rusted out. They may have become clogged. Simple cleaning should resolve the problem.

■ Vents may be inadequate or may have become clogged. In extreme cases they may cause the water in the traps to be siphoned out, allowing sewer gas to enter the house. Note any excessive suction when a toilet is flushed.

Required Additions

Additional supply and drain lines may be desirable in modernizing a house. New lines may be required for automatic washers, added baths, adequate sill cocks or reorganizing the layout. If you plan to add any of these amenities, make sure that present plumbing lines are accessible. Beware of plumbing lines cast in concrete slabs. The slab may have to be torn up to access present plumbing lines.

Water Heater

With a hot water heating system, water may also be heated satisfactorily for cooking, bathing and other personal needs. Old hot air furnaces have water heating coils; however, the hot water produced is seldom adequate. Furthermore, during summer months, when hot air heating is not needed, a separate system is required to provide hot water.

Most houses will be fitted with a gas or electric water heater. A gas heater should have at least a 30-gallon capacity. An electric water heater should have a capacity of at least 50 gallons, especially if it is one of the older slow-recovery types. Look for the capacity rating on a plate affixed to the side of the tank.

Plumbing Fixtures

Plumbing fixtures that are quite old may be rust stained and may require replacement. It may be desirable to replace them just for appearance sake alone. Washers and other parts may be so hard to find that replacement, rather than repair, is the best alternative.

HEATING

Heating system advances and current concepts of comfort outdate the heating systems in most old houses. Central heating, with heat piped to all rooms, is considered a necessity in all but very small houses.

The only way to satisfactorily check the adequacy of the heating system is through use. If the system is adequate for the desired degree of comfort, check the furnace or boiler for overall general condition.

Gravity Warm Air

Gravity warm air systems are common in older homes. Some gravity warm air furnaces may heat a house relatively well, but it is doubtful that the temperature control and heat distribution will be as good as with a forced circulation system.

If a warm air system is exceptionally dirty, there may be soot marks above the registers. This will indicate some repair work is in order. If the furnace is old, it may need to be replaced. In any event, rusty ducts may need replacement.

Gravity Steam

One-pipe gravity steam heating systems are common in older homes. The system is similar in appearance to hot water heaters. This is an extremely simple system and, if properly installed, it will provide adequate heat, but with no great speed or control. It can be modernized without basic changes merely by replacing standing radiators with baseboard heaters.

A one-pipe gravity steam system can be made more positive in action by converting it to a two-pipe system. This requires adding traps and return lines.

A two-pipe steam system can in turn be converted to a circulating hot water system. Circulating pumps must be added, but this results in greater speed of heat distribution and excellent control.

Radiant

Radiant heat from hot water flowing through coils embedded in concrete floors or plastered ceilings is less common, but may provide excellent heating. Such systems may become air-locked and require the services of an expert to restore proper operation. Breaks in ceiling coils can be repaired fairly easily, but repairing breaks in floors is extremely difficult. If floor breaks are extensive, the system will probably need to be replaced.

Electric Panel

The electric heating panels have no moving parts to wear out and should be in good condition unless a heating element has burned out.

ELECTRICAL

So many new electrical appliances have come into common use in recent years that old houses may not have adequate wiring to accommodate them, particularly if air conditioning is installed. The service level of your electrical system should be at least 100 amperes for the average three-bedroom house. If the house is large or if air conditioning is added, the service should be at least 200 amps. If the main distribution panel has room for circuits, additional circuits can be added to supply power where there is a shortage. Otherwise, another distribution panel may have to be added.

Examine electrical wiring, wherever possible. Some wiring is usually exposed in the attic or basement. Wiring should also be checked at several wall receptacles or fixtures. If any armored cable or conduit is badly rusted, or if wiring or cable insulation is deteriorated, damaged, brittle or crumbly, the house wiring should be replaced.

At least one electrical outlet on each wall of a room, and two or more on long walls, is desirable. Ceiling lights should have a wall switch. Rooms without a ceiling light should have a wall switch which controls at least one outlet.

Final Evaluation

After you have completely examined the house and listed all repair requirements, list all the pros and cons of the house on paper for evaluation. Some general guidelines for evaluating the information are presented here; however, judgment will be required to draw conclusions from these guides.

MAJOR REASONS FOR REJECTION

As stated above, some major reasons for rejection are:

■ The foundation may be completely irreparable. Houses are occasionally moved onto new foundations, but this is generally not economical unless the house is otherwise in extremely good condition.

■ If the entire frame of the house is badly out of square, or if the framing is generally decayed or termite infested, do not consider rehabilitation.

■ If there are numerous replacements, or major repairs and replacements combined, the suitability for rehabilitation is questionable.

Guideposts for the Final Decision

If the foundation and frame are in reasonable condition, and the repair and replacement items do not appear excessive, base a final decision on the following factors:

■ Cost
■ Location
■ Sentimental value

COST

If the cost of buying and rehabilitating the house does not exceed the fair market value of houses in the area, it is a sound investment. A general rule-of-thumb is that the rehabilitation cost should not exceed two thirds of the cost of a comparable new house. The cost can be determined in two ways:

A. If the work is to be done on a fixed price contract, the contractor's bid will give you a definite dollar amount. This figure should be increased by about 10 percent for unforeseen extras. Use the retail value of the renovations, not your cost.

B. If you plan to do most of the work yourself and are concerned with the economics of the project, get bids on those items that will be done by others. Then, figure the cost of all materials for the work you plan to do yourself. Finally, estimate your labor time and establish costs using a fair hourly rate. If you are not experienced in building construction, increase your labor estimate by at least 50 percent since much time will be lost in doing work a little at a time, stopping to read instructions and correcting mistakes. There is a strong tendency to underestimate your time and materials requirements.

LOCATION

A particularly good location would be justification for spending more; a generally undesirable or deteriorating location would indicate much less than two-thirds the new house cost should be spent.

SENTIMENTAL VALUE

Sentimental attachments are subjective; so, only you can value the rehabilitated house. Remember, however, that neither the finance company nor a prospective buyer will add anything to the value of the house for your sentimental attachments.

Cautions

Projects will go very slowly when you work only in your spare time. If the house is to be occupied immediately or at the earliest possible moment, do the necessary items at once and then plan to work on the list of "projects" one at a time with a breather space between them. Nobody wants to live in a mess continually and nobody can work continuously without having the project "go sour". Be as realistic as possible. It will increase the enjoyment of doing the work and the satisfaction of your finished home. Finally, don't be too rigid. Realize at the start that your ideas may change as your remodeling progresses and the final product begins to emerge. At the end of each phase, stop and evaluate the results of your efforts. Consult your plans of what remains ahead to ensure the plans are still consistent with what has transpired up to that point.

7. STRETCHING THE REMODELING DOLLAR

Once you have discovered the perfect remodeling "dream house", sit down and plan the complete scope of the remodeling task at hand. The size and type of remodeling projects will depend heavily on your future plans for the home. Is the home your last residence - your "palace" -- or are you planning the remodeling as an investment?

If you plan to live in the home permanently, you will obviously improve those areas which appeal to your needs. If you are buying the home for an investment or as a way to build home equity, then you must be very concerned about the monetary value of each and every improvement. It is so easy to become excited about the potential of your home that you fall into the trap of "over improving" the property. If you overdo your improvements, you may not be able to realize a return on your investment when you sell. Even if you choose to stay in the home indefinitely, wanton "over improvements" may catch up with you. How often have you had a career change or other incident that has forced you to move? Trying to sell an overbuilt home can take time and cost you money.

Once you have decided on the improvements you plan to make, prioritize the projects that bring the greatest return for the least investment. Do these projects first. Remodeling projects have a tendency to take longer to complete than planned. If you must sell ahead of schedule, your most productive improvements will have been done first.

Below is a list of remodeling projects ranked from the most productive project to the least:

1. Cosmetic improvements
2. Solving minor functional problems
3. Basement finishing
4. Attic conversion
5. Addition of a deck
6. Kitchen remodeling
7. Bath remodeling
8. Garage addition
9. Fireplace addition
10. Energy upgrade
11. Sunspace addition
12. Room addition
13. New siding
14. New roof
15. Solving major functional problems
16. New windows and doors
17. Swimming pool

THE IMPORTANCE OF COSMETIC IMPROVEMENTS

Nothing will increase the value of a home more than a cosmetic facelift. These include interior and exterior painting, new trim, new flooring, cleaning up of unsightly areas, landscaping and other items that damage the overall appearance of the home. Most people's impressions of a home are made in the first 5 minutes, and are always related to how the home "looks" and "feels".

Cosmetic facelifts are also primary do-it-yourself projects, which will increase their return on investment.

COLORS - PAINTING INSIDE AND OUT

Consumer marketing experts have long known the power of color and texture to influence the moods and perceptions of the buying public. That's why so many plain products are sold in fancy packaging. The proper use of paint can accomplish several goals:

- Making the home appear clean and fresh
- Eliminating "old house" odors
- Covering patches and imperfections in walls
- Making a room appear larger and brighter
- Setting the "mood" of the room

Try to choose exterior colors that complement the neighborhood and the period flavor of the house. Avoid interior colors that are too wild or bright. Allow accent pieces in the house to provide the bright colors.

LANDSCAPING

No true exterior facelift can be successful without an attractive yard. Many older houses are overgrown with large ragged foliage that obscures the house and may provide a dark and dreary atmosphere. Trim back large plants to expose the house. Adding small accent plants around the yard can make the yard appear more "groomed". If your lawn suffers from poor upkeep or bare spots, consider rock or foliage gardens to cover the affected areas.

Don't overspend, however, on your landscaping. A few landscaping dollars can go a long way. Excess landscaping will not increase the home value significantly. In fact, it can actually reduce home value if the buyer perceives hours spent in the yard grooming, cutting and pruning.

FLOORING AND TRIM

Like painting, the floor and trim are the most visible clues to a home's upkeep. Carpets can hold much of the "old house" odors that are hard to eliminate. If the carpet is in good shape, a simple steam cleaning may suffice. Older period flooring such as linoleum are best replaced when worn. There is no way to improve their appearance.

If you want to retain the period atmosphere of the home, examine the flooring carefully. Most older homes have solid wood floors under carpeting; the wood can be refinished much cheaper than laying new carpeting.

OVERCOMING FUNCTIONAL PROBLEMS

The second most profitable improvement is the elimination of design or physical limitations of the home. These limitations fall into two categories:

1. Physical problems with the structure
2. Functional obsolescence

PHYSICAL PROBLEMS

Physical repairs to the property can sometimes provide tremendous returns on your remodeling dollar. Your remodeling knowledge can convert directly into dollars in these cases. Many times the present owners are tired of the problems and are unaware of the costs to repair them. If you bargain wisely and from a position of strength, you can make your greatest profits on "ugly ducklings".

Obviously, any physical problems with the house, such as a leaking roof or basement or a sagging floor, demand immediate attention. Assuming that you bought the house at a reduced price, fixing these kind of problems will return the house to its former potential. Make sure to refer to these physical problems when bargaining for the best purchase price. In most cases the owner is probably eager to sell the house in order to avoid dealing with the problems. Make sure when buying an extensive fixup, that you know all the hidden costs of repair; or, you may find yourself inheriting someone else's albatross.

Whatever the physical problems, get these repairs out of the way first. Most physical repairs will require tearing up or removing existing material. You will want cosmetic changes to occur only after the structure is sound.

DEALING WITH FUNCTIONAL OBSOLESCENCE

Functional obsolescence refers to design problems with the house that may make it "obsolete" by today's living standards. These design flaws may make the home undesirable for modern homeowners. Examples of functional obsolescence include:

- A home with an outhouse!
- One bathroom
- Small kitchen
- Little or no insulation
- Insufficient electrical rating or outlets
- No garage
- Poor floor plan layout
- Very high ceilings
- A house with a dirt floor!

Floor plan layout

Traffic flow - Many old houses were designed around the fireplaces or heaters. Each bedroom had a space heater or fireplace with other rooms acting as heat buffer zones.. This design made for some unusual traffic patterns; traveling through a bedroom to get to the bathroom, for instance.

Examine your prospective house carefully to determine if you can solve these design problems. If you cannot, look for another house to buy! No matter how quaint a house may be, if the design is not practical for modern living, avoid it.

Floor Plan
Checklist

1. There should be unobstructed access to the kitchen from the garage.

2. All bathrooms should be accessible without traveling through another living area (bedroom).

3. The kitchen should be convenient to the the living and dining areas for entertaining.

Amenities
Checklist

1. There should be a location for a garage or carport.

2. There should be two bathrooms or the capability of adding one easily.

3. The house should have central air and heat or the ability to add them.

4. Kitchens and baths should be of modern design and have modern appliances or be conducive to being remodeled.

BASEMENT CONVERSION

Basement conversions provide an excellent opportunity to add space and amenities to the house for a minimum of cost and trouble. This space can solve many other problems in functional design by providing space for additional bedrooms, bathrooms and recreational areas. Basements are one of the lowest cost spaces in a home; hence, they offer a high return on your remodeling dollars.

Make sure to examine a basement carefully to determine its remodeling potential. Older basements are notorious for moisture and leakage problems; sewage connections may not be available without the use of a "flush up" toilet. New developments in waterproofing materials have made this job easier. Many parts of the country have partially enclosed basements built on sloping lots. These "walk-in" basements are particularly suited for bedroom and bath conversions and will bring a high return. Basements that are completely below ground will bring a much lower return due to the lack of suitable lighting.

ATTIC CONVERSIONS

Attics are another source of low cost conversion space and may enhance a house's value more than a basement conversion. This is because attics are free from the moisture and sewage problems inherent in basement conversions. As with the basement, attics already have the structural walls and ceiling present, making the job easier to complete. Make sure that structural roof members do not obstruct the location of walls. If the conversion is to be used for additional bedroom or recreational space, make sure to include a bathroom. This will ensure the greatest return on your remodeling investment.

If the roofline is too shallow for a conversion, you might consider removing the entire roof and adding another story to the structure. This option is especially attractive if the lot is small or the roof already needs extensive repair. Be aware, however, that the underlying structure must be structurally sound enough to bear the weight of the new floor.

DECKS

Decks have become increasingly popular in all parts of the country. They are easy to install and can greatly enlarge the entertainment area of the house. This addition has a greater return in the southern states where weather permits ample use of the deck. This is another good do-it-yourself project.

Many owners like to add additional amenities to their decks; such as, trellises, privacy walls and hot tubs. These devices make attractive selling devices, but may not return their full investment at selling time. This may be a minor point, however, since they add to your own enjoyment of the house.

KITCHENS

With the exception of baths, the kitchen has become one of the most popular areas in a modern house. Almost all kitchens in older homes are small and ill equipped for the "Yuppie gourmets" of modern times.

Minor kitchen remodeling can be quite cost efficient and may entail as little as new floor coverings and painting of the cabinets. Many manufacturers now offer refinishing kits that just replace the face and doors of the cabinets, leaving the old shelving intact. Minor facelifts can brighten up a kitchen, but will do little to solve major space or functional problems.

In many cases, a major kitchen overhaul will bring a greater return on investment than a minor facelift. A major overhaul will allow you to add new and more spacious cabinets, solve traffic flow problems and lighten up the kitchen with windows. A full facelift is expensive and may not return the full value of the investment; so, try to do yourself as much of the work as is possible. If your existing kitchen is out of date, consider the remodeling project a necessity.

BATHROOMS

Recent trends are toward lavish and spacious baths. The two-bath house has almost become a standard. Adding a second bath to a home may not return its full value, but it certainly eliminates a major obstacle in selling your home. This is true because buyers will be comparing your bath features to the ones present in new construction. Because of the high cost of tearing out old fixtures and installing new ones, consider doing much of the work yourself; however, bring in an experienced plumber for the final installation.

Tasteful decorating and a wise choice of fixtures will also add to your home's value without costing a fortune. Whenever possible, consider adding a bathroom to the master bedroom.

GARAGE

If your home does not include a garage or carport area, you should definitely consider adding a two-car garage. The garage will provide additional storage, as well as workshop, area. If your house also suffers from insufficient space, add your needed space at the same time as your garage project. When combined with a room addition, a garage will return all of its investment and more. Just make sure you don't overbuild for your neighborhood.

FIREPLACE

The fireplace adds quite a bit of charm to any home and fits in nicely with most older structures. Adding a masonry fireplace would be cost prohibitive and would require major structural adjustments; so, consider installing a prefabricated one. They are lower in cost, more energy efficient and much easier to install.

ENERGY UPGRADE

Energy efficiency improvements are more likely to save you money over the long run than bring you a high return on your investment; however, they *may* help you to get a better price for your home upon resale. Like most unseen benefits, energy efficiency will seldom bring a selling price covering its cost. Therefore, your decision to improve energy efficiency will largely depend upon your personal use of the property.

Minor energy improvements, though of low cost, can actually help you to sell the property. These improvements include weather stripping around doors, plastic films for windows and caulking. If insulation is poor, consider adding additional insulation to the attic first. It is the easiest to apply, costs the least and produces the

greatest efficiency gains. These improvements also have the benefit of being more visible to prospective purchasers.

SUNSPACE

Sunspaces are becoming more popular and can serve several functions, depending on their location in relation to the other rooms in the house. A sunspace off the kitchen, for example, can serve as an airy and attractive breakfast area, saving that space within the house for other uses. Sunspace additions, however, cannot be considered to produce great returns on investment unless done in conjunction with other improvements. Not only is the space quite expensive, but also the glass windows are an unavoidable expense even if you do the work yourself. In addition, the space is not usable all year round in most locales. A good compromise is to cut down on the exposed glass so that the heat gain/loss will decrease. Then the space can be used as regular living space all year round.

ROOM ADDITION

The value of a room addition will vary, depending on its use and the relative need for the space. You should look closely at the *utility* an addition can provide. If the addition adds a much needed bathroom or bedroom, it can add significantly to the value of the house. Just make sure that you are not overbuilding for the neighborhood. Remember, neighboring houses are usually of approximately the same size as yours. Your addition may make your home the largest in the neighborhood. Sometimes a better choice is to open up the existing space by knocking out walls. This option is much more cost effective than a room addition and can often yield superior results. Consult with a knowledgeable framing contractor before attempting this conversion; many walls are loadbearing and cannot be easily removed.

NEW SIDING

In most cases new siding is a poor investment; however, if the existing siding on the house is run down or cannot be refinished, then new siding can add significantly to the house's value. Refinishing the existing siding is a much lower cost alternative and will add the same value to the house if done properly. This is especially true if the original siding preserves the original flavor of the house. If you must put on new siding, consider doing it in conjunction with an energy upgrade. If you have the siding off the wall, the additional cost of wall insulation is minimal.

NEW ROOF

Nothing will scare a prospective buyer away faster than an unattractive, leaking roof. If the roof is in poor condition, you may have no choice but to replace it. But don't expect to add much value to the house. The roof is one of those "must do" maintenance items. If the roof is simply stained or unattractive, a steam cleaning can sometimes work wonders at a relatively low cost.

NEW WINDOWS AND DOORS

Replacing windows and doors is not a good short term investment unless the existing ones are beyond repair. However, if you plan to stay in the house for a long time, replacement can save later maintenance headaches. Consider double pane, vinyl clad windows for replacement. If you do the work yourself, the addition of patio or french doors can provide attractive, improved access to the outside at a reasonable cost.

SWIMMING POOL

This is the most popular of home improvements which seldom returns its investment. Obviously, people are installing pools for reasons other than investment return. Don't consider the addition of a swimming pool unless your home is in a high price bracket or you plan to be around for a while.

8. ESTIMATING THE REMODELING

Jumping into your first remodeling project without a realistic estimate of your costs could spell financial disaster. Spend a lot of time working on the cost aspect before continuing with your project. The information in this section should help you quite a bit.

Hidden Costs - Guessing at What You Can't See

Estimating a remodeling project can be a real challenge since many of the necessary repairs may be hidden behind walls and floor coverings. Examine your project with care and use deductive reasoning to find these hidden costs. If you are remodeling a room such as the bath, you will need to make a checklist of each item you intend to replace. If you are building a room addition, you will actually be estimating a small construction project having all the expenses associated with a full scale construction project.

The first thing you will want to do is sketch out the addition in detail. If you are building a structure from the ground up, you should get a draftsman or architect to draw up full scale blueprints. You can use these scaled blueprints to calculate your construction costs.

If you are not confident of your ability to estimate, ask other experts for help. One important source of information will come from the subcontractors you plan to use. These subs are familiar with the type of construction in your area and will be very knowledgeable in calculating the amounts of materials needed. In fact, most of your subcontractors will offer to calculate the amount of materials needed for you. This can be very valuable, especially for framing, because of the sheer number of different materials used.

Don't rely solely on your subcontractor's estimate! Make sure to also run your own figures for comparison; subs have a tendency to overestimate just to be on the safe side. If your estimate comes close to the subcontractor's, consider it to be a good starting point. Just make sure that you add at least a 5-10% waste factor to each estimate.

Another good source of estimating information is your local materials supplier. Suppliers used to do quite a bit of estimating for their customers. If you can find a supplier who still does, he is worth his weight in gold.

When figuring your takeoff, use the materials sheet as a checklist to make sure that you don't forget any necessary items. As you figure each item, enter it onto your purchase order forms, taking care to separate materials ordered from different suppliers onto different purchase orders.

Estimating New Construction

EXCAVATION

Excavation is usually charged by the hour of bulldozer or loader operating time. Larger loaders rent for higher fees. Determine whether clearing of the lot is necessary and whether or not refuse is to be buried on the site or hauled away. Below are approximate times per loader task. Remember, these are only approximations. Every lot is different and each may pose unique problems. Check with your grader; he may supply chain saw labor to cut up large trees.

One Half Acre Lot	Small loader	Large loader
Clearing trees	2-5 hrs.	1-4 hrs.
Digging trash pit	2-4 hrs.	1-3 hrs.
Digging foundation	2-3 hrs.	1-3 hrs.
Grading Site	1-5 hrs.	1-3 hrs.
Total	7-17 hrs.	4-13 hrs.

Larger loaders can be an advantage and can be cheaper in the long run, especially if the lot is heavily wooded or has steep topography. If your lot is flat and sparsely wooded, use the smaller loader.

CONCRETE

When calculating concrete, it is best to create a formula or conversion factor that will simplify calculations and avoid having to calculate everything in cubic inches and cubic yards. For instance, when pouring a 4" slab, a cubic yard of concrete will cover 81 square feet of area. This is calculated as follows:

1 Cubic Yard = 27 Cubic Feet = 46,656 Cubic Inches

1 Sq. Ft. of Concrete 4" thick = 576 Cubic Inches (12"x12"x4")

46,656 Cu.In./576 Cu.In. = 81 Sq. Ft. of Coverage for a 4" slab

By using this equation only once, you have a simple formula for calculating slabs 4" thick which you can use for driveways, basement floors and slab floors. For instance, to determine the concrete needed for a 1200 Sq. Ft. slab, simply divide by 81.

1200 Sq. Ft. / 81 = 14.8 Cu. Yds. of concrete

NOTE: Always make sure to add a 5 to 10% waste factor to all calculations.

Use this same principle to create simple formulas for footings, calculating blocks, pouring concrete walls, etc. Just remember to calculate your own set of formulas based on the building codes in your area.

Footings
Footing contractors should be hired to dig the footings and to supervise the pouring of the footings. Footing subs generally charge for labor only and will charge by the linear foot of footing poured. Pier holes will be extra. You must provide the concrete; the subs may charge more if they provide the forms. If you use a full service foundation company, they will charge you on a turnkey basis for footings, walls and concrete. This makes the estimating task much easier.

The footing generally must be twice as wide as the wall it supports; the height of the footing must be the same as the thickness of the wall. The footing contractor will know the code requirements for your area. Ask him for the dimensions of the footing and then figure an amount of concrete per linear foot. Here is a typical calculation for supporting an 8" block wall:

Footing dimension: 8" high x 16" wide

8" x 16" x 12"(1 ft. of footing) = 1536 Cu. In.

46,656 Cu. In. / 1536 Cu. In. = 30.38 lineal ft. of footing per Cu. Yd.

With this size footing, figure one cubic yard of concrete for every 31 lineal feet of footing (always round up to allow for waste). Make sure to include 4 extra feet of footing for every pier hole. Add 10% for waste.

Concrete Floors or Slabs
Use the conversion factor of 81 sq. ft. for 4" slabs or basement floors. If your slabs must be more or less than 4", make sure to formulate a new conversion factor.

Monolithic Slabs
Break a one-piece slab into two components: the slab and the footing sections. Then figure each item separately.

Block Foundations & Crawl Spaces

Concrete block comes in many shapes and sizes, the most common being 8"x8"x16". Blocks that are 12" thick are used to provide extra stability for tall block walls with backfill. Blocks 8" deep and 12" deep cover the same wall area; i.e., 888 sq. ft.

To calculate the amount of block needed, measure the height of the wall in inches and divide by 8" to find the height of the wall in number of blocks. The height of the wall will always be in even numbers of blocks plus a 4" cap block or 8" half block (for pouring slabs). Cap blocks are solid concrete 4"x8"x16" blocks used to provide a smooth surface on which to build. If you are building a basement wall, take the perimeter of the foundation and multiply by .75 (3 blocks for every 4 ft.). Then, multiply this figure by the number of rows of blocks. To calculate the row of cap block multiply the perimeter of the foundation by .75. Always figure 5-10% waste when ordering block.

If your foundation is a crawl space, your footing probably has one or more stepdowns, or bulkheads, as they are called. Stepdowns are areas where the footing is dropped or raised the height of one block. This allows the footing to follow the contour of the land. As a result, sections of the block wall will vary in height, requiring more or less rows of block. Take each stepdown section separately and figure 3 blocks for every 4 feet of wall. Multiply the total number of block by the total number of rows and then add all sections together for the total number of blocks needed.

Poured Concrete Walls

Your poured wall subcontractor will charge by the lineal foot for setting forms. Usually, the price quoted for pouring will include the cost of concrete; but, if not, you must calculate the amount of concrete needed. Determine the thickness of the wall from your poured wall sub and find the square foot conversion factor for the number of square feet covered per cubic yard. Divide this factor into the total square footage of the wall. Example:

8' Poured Concrete Wall x 12" x 12" = 1152 cubic inch per square foot of wall

46656 cubic. inch / 1152 cubic inch = 40.5 square foot per cubic yard of concrete

BRICK

To figure the amount of brick needed, figure the square footage of the walls to be bricked and multiply by 6.75. There are approximately 675 brick per 100 square feet of wall. Add 5-10% for waste.

Mortar

Mortar comes premixed in bags of masonry cement which consist of roughly one part portland cement and one part lime. Each bag requires about 20 shovels of sand when mixing. To calculate the amount of mortar needed for brick, figure one bag of cement for every 125 bricks. For block, figure one bag of cement for every 28 blocks. Make sure to use a good grade of washed sand for proper bonding of the mortar. Most foundations will require at least 10 cubic yards of sand.

FRAMING

Estimating your framing lumber requirements will be the most difficult estimating task and will require studying the layout and construction techniques of your house very carefully. Be sure to have a scaled blueprint of your home, as well as a scaled ruler for measuring. Consult with a framing contractor before you begin for advice on size and grade of lumber used in your area.

This is the time you will want to pull out your books on construction techniques and study them to familiarize yourself with the components of your particular house. Local building code manuals will include span tables for determining the maximum spans you are allowed without support. Your blueprints will also list the sizes of many framing members and may include construction detail drawings which can be especially helpful in determining the size and type of lumber needed for framing.

Floor Framing

Determine the size and length of floor joists by noting the position of piers or beams and by consulting with your framing contractor. Floor joists are usually spaced 16" on center. Joists spaced 12" on center are used for extra sturdy floors. If Floor Trusses are used, figure 24" on-center spacing. Calculate the perimeter of the foundation walls to determine the amount of sill and box sill framing needed.

Calculate the square footage of the floor and divide by 32 (the square footage in a 4 x 8' sheet of plywood) to determine the amount of flooring plywood needed.

Bridging between floor joists is used to reduce twisting and warping of floor members and to tie the floor together structurally. Bridging is calculated by taking the total number of floor joists and multiplying by three. This is the amount needed for one course of bridging. Most floors will require at least two courses of bridging; so, double this figure.

If you are using a basement or crawl space, you will probably be using a steel or wood beam to support the floor members. If floor trusses are used, these supports may not be needed since floor trusses can span much greater distances. Consult your local truss manufacturer for more information.

Wall Framing

When calculating wall framing lumber, add together the lineal feet of all interior and exterior walls. Since there is a plate at the bottom of the wall and a double plate at the top, multiply the wall length by three to get the lineal feet of wall plate needed. Add 10% for waste. If precut studs are used, there are many sizes; so, be sure to get the proper lengths. Allow one pre-cut stud for every lineal foot of wall and 2 studs for every corner. Count all door and window openings as solid walls. This will allow enough for waste and bracing.

Headers are doubled over all openings in load-bearing walls to add structural support. Add together the total width of all doors and windows and multiply by two. Check with your framing sub for the proper size header.

The second floor can be calculated the same way as the first floor, taking into consideration the different wall layouts, of course. The second floor of a two story house can be figured the same as a crawl space floor, with the exception that the joists will be resting on load-bearing walls instead of on a beam. This will require drawing a ceiling joist layout.

Roof Framing

If roof trusses are to be used, figure one truss for every two feet of building length. Then add one truss. If the roof is a hip roof or if it has two roof lines that meet at right angles, extra framing for bridging must be added.

To insure the proper fit, the roof truss manufacturer should calculate the actual size and quantity of roof trusses at the site or from blueprints. Ask him to present a bid and materials list during the estimating process.

A "stick built" roof is one that is built completely from scratch. It is much harder to calculate and requires some knowledge of geometry to figure all the lumber needed. The simplest way of finding the length of ceiling joists and rafters is to measure them from your scaled blueprints. All lumber is sold in even numbered lengths; so, always round up to the nearest even length.

When calculating ceiling joists, draw a joist layout with opposing joists always meeting and overlapping above a loadbearing wall. Figure one ceiling joist for every 16". Add 10% extra for waste.

Rafters are also spaced 16" on center. The length of the rafters can be determined by measuring from blueprints, making sure to allow for cornice overhangs. Where two roof lines meet, a valley or hip rafter is necessary. Multiply the length of a normal rafter by 1.5 to get the approximate length of this rafter.

Gable studs will be necessary to frame in the gable ends. The length of the stud should be equal to the height of the roof ridge. Figure one stud per foot of gable width. Add 10% for waste. This will be enough to do two gable ends since scrap pieces can be used in the short areas of the gable.

Decking for the roof usually consists of 1/2" CDX exterior plywood. Multiply the length of the rafter times the length of the roof to determine the square footage of one side of the roof. Double this figure to obtain total square footage area of the roof. Divide this figure by the square footage of a sheet of plywood (32). Add 10% waste. This is the number of sheets of plywood needed. Remember the square footage of the roof for figuring shingles.

ROOFING SHINGLES

Roofing shingles are sold in "squares"; i.e., the number of shingles necessary to cover 100 sq. ft. of roof. First, find the square footage of the roof, adding 1-1/2 square feet for every lineal foot of eaves, ridges, hips and valleys. Divide the total square footage by 100 to find the number of squares needed. Shingles come packaged in 1/3-square packages; so, multiply the number of squares by three to arrive at the total number of packages needed.

Roofing felt is applied under the roof shingles as an underlayment and comes in 500 sq. ft. rolls. Divide the total square footage of the roof by 500 and add 20% for overlap and waste to determine the number of rolls needed.

Flashing is required around any chimney or area where two roof lines of different height meet. It comes in 50-ft. rolls. Also measure the length of the ridge if you are installing roof ridge vents.

SIDING AND SHEATHING

Multiply the perimeter of the outside walls by the height to obtain the total square footage of outside walls. If gables are to be covered with siding, multiply the width of the gable by the height. This figure is sufficient for both gable ends. Add this number to the square footage of the outside walls. This figure is the total square footage of area to be sided.

Different types of siding are sold in different manners. Sheathing and plywood siding are sold in 4x8' sheets (32 sq.ft.). Divide this figure into the total square footage to determine the number of sheets needed. Add 10% for waste. Lap siding, on the other hand, is sold by squares or 1,000s.

When buying siding, make sure to ask if it is sold by actual square footage or by "coverage area" (the actual area to be covered). Add 10%, or 15% if lap siding is applied diagonally, for waste.

Most installed siding requires trim at the corners of the house. Corner trim boards are generally cut from 1x2 lumber. Figure two pieces for every inside and outside corner; the length equaling the height of the wall being sided.

CORNICE MATERIAL

To estimate cornice material, you must first determine the type or style of cornice and the trim materials to be used. Consult blueprints for any construction detail drawings of the cornice.

The following materials are generally used in most cornices:

- Fascia Boards - 1x6" or 1x8"
- Drip Mold (between fascia & shingles) - 1x4"
- Soffit - 3/8" exterior plywood
- Bed Mold - 1x2"
- Frieze mold - 1x8"

Calculate the total linear feet of cornice, including the gables, to find the total lineal feet of each trim material needed. Calculate the square footage of the soffit by multiplying the linear feet of the cornice by the depth of the cornice. Divide this by the square footage of a plywood sheet to determine the number of sheets needed.

INSULATION

Calculating the amount of wall insulation is easy. Batts of insulation are sold by square footage to be covered. Simply multiply the perimeter of the exterior walls to be insulated by the wall height to determine the total square footage to be insulated.

To calculate the amount of blown-in insulation needed, first determine the type of insulation to be used. Each type -- mineral wool, fiberglass and cellulose -- has its own R-factors per inch. This must be known in order to determine the required thickness of fill. Then multiply the depth in feet (or fraction thereof) by the square footage of the ceiling area to arrive at the cubic foot volume. Blown-in insulation is sold by the cubic foot. If batt insulation is used in the ceiling, it can be figured in the same manner as the wall insulation.

Most insulation subcontractors will quote a price, including materials and labor for installation. Ask the contractor to itemize the amount of insulation used. Compare his figures with yours.

DRYWALL

Gypsum wallboard is sold by the sheet (4x10, 4x12, etc.), but is estimated by square footage. To find the total amount needed for the walls, multiply the total linear feet of inside and outside walls by the wall height. Make sure to count each interior wall twice, since both sides of the wall will be covered. Count all openings as solid wall. Add 10% for waste. Some subs will charge by the square foot for material and labor, adding extra for tray ceilings and other special work.

For the ceiling, simply take the finished square footage of the house. Add 10% for waste. Then add the amount needed for the walls to arrive at the total amount of sheetrock needed. If the house has any vaulted or tray ceilings, extra sheetrock and labor must be added.

Joint finishing compound comes pre-mixed in 5-gallon cans; joint tape, in 250-ft. rolls. For every 1,000 sq. ft. of drywall, figure one roll of joint tape and 30 gallons of joint compound.

TRIMWORK

Base molding comes in many styles; the most common of which are clamshell and colonial. Basemolding is run along the bottom of the wall in every room. The lineal foot figure of walls used to calculate sheetrock is therefore equal to the lineal feet of baseboard trim needed. Add 10% for waste.

Make sure to measure the perimeter of any room that will require shoe molding or crown molding. Shoe molding (or quarter round) is usually used to cover the crack between the floor and wall in any room with vinyl or wood flooring. Crown molding around the ceiling may be used in any room, but it is most commonly used in formal areas such as foyers, living and dining areas. Calculate the amount of shoe or crown molding needed in exactly the same manner as the base molding.

DOORS

When ordering interior doors, you may want to purchase prehung doors with preassembled jambs. These doors are exceptionally easy to install and already have the jamb and trimwork attached. Study the blueprints carefully to be sure that the doors open in the proper direction and that they don't block light switches when opened. There are right-hand and left-hand doors. To determine which door to order, imagine standing in front of the door, and then walking through the doorway. If you must use your right hand to open the door, it is a right hand door. Most blueprints will have the size and type of each door marked in the opening.

FLOORING

Because of the complexity of laying flooring materials -- carpet, hardwood floors, vinyl or ceramic tile -- it is essential that a flooring contractor estimate the flooring quantities needed. An approximate measure is that amount equal to the square footage of the area to be covered plus 10% for waste. Carpet and vinyl are sold by the square yard; so, divide the area described above by 9 to determine square yardage. Keep in mind, however, that carpet and vinyl is sold in rolls 12' wide. This standard width may affect the amount of waste and therefore the amount to be added into the estimate.

MISCELLANEOUS COVERINGS

A wide variety of covering materials is now being used as floor coverings. These include ceramic tile for bathrooms or floors, parquet, slate for foyers or fireplaces and fieldstone for steps or fireplaces. Virtually all these materials are sold by the square footage of area to be covered. Subcontractors charge by the square footage to be installed; sometimes materials are included, sometimes not. Grouts and mortars used in installing these items (except rock) are premixed; the coverage expected is indicated on the container.

Paint

When hiring a painting contractor, the cost of paint should be included in the cost of the estimate, unless otherwise specified. If you should decide to do the painting yourself, you will need to know how much paint is needed. Simply calculate the square footage of the area to be covered and add at least 15% for waste and touchup. The coverage of different paint brands varies considerably; most paint containers state the area of coverage to be expected.

You must also figure the amount of primer needed. If your colors are custom mixed, make sure that you purchase sufficient paint to finish the job. It is sometimes difficult to get an exact match of a custom color if it is mixed again at a later date.

Wallpaper

One roll of wallpaper will safely cover 30 square feet of wall area, including waste and matching of patterns. The longer the repeat pattern, the more the waste will be. Some imported wallpapers may vary in coverage; be sure to check with your wallpaper supplier if you have any questions regarding coverage. When figuring the square footage of the walls of a room, count all openings as solid walls. Also, be careful to note if you are buying a single or double roll of wallpaper. Most wallpaper is sold in a roll that actually contains 2 true rolls of wallpaper, or 60 sq. ft. of coverage. Always buy enough paper to finish the job. Buying additional rolls at a later time can cause matching problems if some of the rolls are from a different dye lot. Look for the same lot numbers (runs) on all rolls purchased to assure a perfect match. Use only vinyl wallpaper in baths and kitchen areas for water resistance and easy cleanup.

CABINETS

Most blueprints include cabinet layouts. Use these plans if you are purchasing your own cabinets. If the cabinets are installed by a subcontractor, he will take care of the exact measurements. Make sure that included in his bid are painting, staining and installation.

MILLWORK AND MISCELLANEOUS

The ordering of windows, lights, hardware and other specialty items will not be covered here as they are very subjective. Once you decide on your preference, the purchase itself is straightforward. Other estimates, such as those for heating and air conditioning, plumbing, electrical and fixtures, must be obtained from the contractors themselves since they provide the materials and labor.

The following section outlines the way most subcontractors charge for their services. Some subs may or may not include the cost of materials in their estimates. Make sure you know exactly what is and is not included in your subcontractors bid.

Types of Subcontractors

Framing--Frame house, apply sheathing, set windows and exterior doors. Charge by the square foot of framed structure. including any unheated spaces such as the garage. Extras include bay windows, chimney chases, stairs, dormers and anything else unusual.

Siding--Apply exterior siding. Charge by the square of applied siding. Extras include diagonal siding, decks, porches and very high walls requiring scaffolding.

Cornice--(Usually the siding subcontractor) Apply soffit and fascia board. Charge by linear foot of cornice. Extras include fancy cornice work, dentil mold. Sometimes set windows and exterior doors.

Trim--Install all interior trim and closet fixtures and set interior doors. Charge a set fee for each opening or by linear feet of trim. Openings include doors and windows. Extras include stairs, rails, crown molds, mantels, book cases, chair rails, wainscoting and picture molding.

Footing--Dig footings, pour and level concrete, build bulkheads (for step downs). Charge by the linear foot. Extras include pier holes

Block--Lay block. Charge by the block. Extras include stucco & block.

Brickwork--Lay brick. Charge by the skid (1000 bricks).

Stonework--Lay stone. Charge by the square foot or by bid.

Concrete Finishing--Pour concrete, set forms, spread gravel and finish concrete. Charge by the square foot of area poured. Extras include monolithic slab and digging footing.

Roofing--Install shingles and waterproof around vents. Charge a set fee per square, plus surcharges according to pitch of roof. For example, $1 per square over pitch on a 6/12 pitch roof = $7/square. Extras include flashing, ridge vents and special cutout for skylights.

Wallpaper--Hang wallpaper which remodeler provides. Charge by the roll. Extras include high ceilings, wallpaper on ceilings, grass cloth.

Grading--Perform rough grading and clearing. Charge by the hour of bulldozer time. Extras include chainsaw operator, hauling away of refuse, travel time to and from site (drag time).

Poured Foundation--Dig and pour footings, set forms and pour walls. Charge by the linear foot of wall. Extras include bulkheads, more than four corners, openings for windows, doors and pipes.

Pest Control--Chemically treat the ground around foundation for termite protection. Charge a flat fee.

Plumbing--Install all sewer lines, water lines, drains, tubs fixtures and water appliances. Charge per fixture installed or by bid. For instance, a toilet, sink and tub would be three fixtures. Install medium grade fixtures. Extras include any special decorator fixtures.

HVAC--Install furnace, air conditioner, all ductwork and gas lines. Charge by the tonnage of A/C or on bid price. Extras include vent fans in bath, roof fans, attic fans, dryer vents, high efficiency furnaces and compressors.

Electrical--Install all switches and receptacles; hook up A/C compressor. Will install light fixtures. Charge by the receptacle. Extras include connecting dishwasher, disposal, flood lights, door bells.

Cabinetry--Build or install prefabricated cabinets and vanities and apply formica tops. Charge by the linear foot for base cabinets, wall cabinets and vanities. Standard price includes formica counter tops. Extras include tile or marble tops, curved tops, pull out shelves, lazy susans.

Insulation--Install all fiberglass batts in walls, ceilings, floors. Charge by square foot for batts, by cubic foot for blown-in.

Sheetrock--Hang sheetrock, tape and finish, stipple. Charge by the square foot of sheetrock. Materials are extra. Extras include smooth ceilings, curved walls, tray and vaulted ceilings and open foyers.

Septic Tank--Install septic tank. Charge fixed fee plus extra for field lines.

Landscaping--Level with tractor, put down seeds, fertilizer and straw. Charge fixed fee. Extras include trees, transplanted shrubs, pine straw, bark chips.

Gutters--Install gutters and downspouts. Charge by lineal foot, plus extra for fittings. Extras include half round gutters, collectors, special water channeling and gutters that cannot be installed from the roof.

Garage Door--Install garage doors. Fixed fee. Extras include garage door openers.

Fireplace--Supply and install prefabricated fireplace and flue liner. Extras include gas log lighter, fresh air vent and ash dump.

Painting and Stain--Paint and stain interior and exterior. Charge by square foot of finished house. Extras include high ceilings, stained ceilings, painted ceilings.

Ceramic Tile--Install all ceramic tile. Charge by the square foot. Extras include fancy bath-tub surrounds and tile counter tops.

Hardwood Floor--Install and finish real hard-wood floors. Charge by square foot. Extras include beveled plank, random plank and herringbone

Flooring--Install all carpet, vinyl, linoleum and prefinished flooring. Charge by the square yard. Extras include contrast borders and thicker underlayments.

GET BIDS WHENEVER POSSIBLE

Now that you know how detailed an estimate can be, look at the other side of the coin. You can spend a day calculating how many cubic yards of concrete you will need and how many approximate hours of labor it will take; or you can call up a full-service foundation company and nail down a bid. The moral here is to use bids whenever possible in completing your takeoff. The bottom line is what counts. If your estimate comes out to be $600 to tile a floor and your lowest bid is $750, you've obviously missed the boat - and wasted time.

COST ESTIMATE SUMMARY

	EST. COST	ACTUAL COST	OVER/UNDER
LICENSES AND FEES			
PREPARATION OF LOT			
FOOTINGS			
FOUNDATION			
ADDITIONAL SLABS			
MATERIALS (PACKAGE)			
FRAMING LABOR			
TRIM LABOR			
ROOFING			
HVAC			
ELECTRIC			
INTERIOR FINISH (SHEETROCK)			
PAINTING			
FLOOR COVERING			
WALKS, DRIVES, STEPS			
LANDSCAPING			
CABINETS AND VANITIES			
APPLIANCES AND LIGHTS			
INSULATION			
CLEANING			
DEVELOPED LOT COST			
CONSTRUC. CLOSING AND INTEREST			
SUPERVISORY FEE			
REAL ESTATE COMMISSION			
POINTS AND CLOSING			
CONTINGENCY (MISC. EXPENSES)			
SEPTIC			
FIREPLACE			
GUTTERS			
TOTAL			

NOTE: Use the Cost Estimate Checklist that follows as a guide when doing your "take-off". Additional blank forms are included in the Appendix for adding items that may not appear on the checklist.

COST ESTIMATE CHECKLIST

CODE NO. DESCRIPTION	QTY.	MATERIAL UNIT PRICE	TOTAL MAT'L	LABOR UNIT PRICE	TOTAL LABOR	SUBCONTR. UNIT PRICE	TOTAL SUB	TOTAL
LAYOUT								
STAKES								
RIBBON								
ROUGH GRADE								
PERK TEST								
WELL AND PUMP								
Well								
Pump								
BATTER BOARDS								
2 X 4g								
1 X 6								
Cord								
FOOTINGS								
Re-Rods								
2 X 8 Bulkheads								
Concrete								
Footings								
Piers								
FOUNDATION								
Block								
8"								
12"								
4"								
Caps								
Headers								
Solid 8's								
Half 8's								
Mortar Mix								
Sand								
Foundation Vents								
Lintels								
Portland Cement								
WATERPROOFING								
Asphalt Coat								
Portland Cement								
6 Mil Poly								
Drain Pipe								
Gravel								
Stucco								
FOUNDATION								
(Poured)								
Portland Cement								
Wales								
TERMITE TREAT								
SLABS								
Gravel								

TOTALS: ☐   ☐   ☐   ☐

COST ESTIMATE CHECKLIST (cont.)

CODE NO. DESCRIPTION	QTY.	MATERIAL UNIT PRICE	TOTAL MAT'L	LABOR UNIT PRICE	TOTAL LABOR	SUBCONTR. UNIT PRICE	TOTAL SUB	TOTAL
6 Mil Poly								
Re-Wire								
Re-Rods								
Corroform								
Form Boards								
2 X 8								
1 X 4								
Concrete								
Basement								
Garage								
Porch								
Patio								
AIR CONDITIONING								
House								
FRAMING SUB FL.								
I-Beam								
Steel Post								
Girders								
Scab								
Floor Joist								
Bridging								
Glue								
Plywood Sub Fl.								
5/8" T&G								
3/4" T&G								
1/2" Exterior								
Joist Hangers								
Lag Bolts								
Sub-Floor								
FRAMING-WALLS/PARTITIONS								
Treated Plate								
Plate								
8' Studs								
10' STuds								
2 X 10 Headers								
Interior Beams								
Bracing								
1 X 4								
1/2" Plywood								
Sheathing								
4 X 8								
4 X 9								
Laminated Beam								
Flitch Plate								
Bolts								
Dead Wood								

TOTALS:

COST ESTIMATE CHECKLIST (cont.)

CODE NO. DESCRIPTION	QTY.	MATERIAL		LABOR		SUBCONTR.		TOTAL
		UNIT PRICE	TOTAL MAT'L	UNIT PRICE	TOTAL LABOR	UNIT PRICE	TOTAL SUB	
FRAMING-CEILING/ROOF								
Ceiling Joist								
Rafters9								
Barge Rafters								
Beams								
Ridge Beam								
Wind Beam								
Roof Bracing Matl.								
Ceiling Bracing								
Gable Studs								
Storm Anchors								
Decking								
3/8" CDX Plywood								
1/2" CDX Plywood								
2 x 6 T&G								
Plyclips								
Rigid Insulation								
Felt								
15 #								
40 #								
60 #								
FRAMING-MISC.								
Stair Stringers								
Firing-in								
Chase Material								
Purlin								
Nails								
16DCC								
8DCC								
8" Glv.Roof.								
1 1/2" Glv. Rf.								
Concrete								
Cut								
ROOFING								
Shingles								
Ridge Vent								
End Plugs								
Connectors								
Flashing								
Roof to Wall								
Roll								
Window								
Ventilators								
TRIM-EXTERIOR								
Doors								
Main Entrance								

TOTALS: ☐ ☐ ☐ ☐

COST ESTIMATE CHECKLIST (cont.)

CODE NO. DESCRIPTION	QTY.	MATERIAL		LABOR		SUBCONTR.		TOTAL
		UNIT PRICE	TOTAL MAT'L	UNIT PRICE	TOTAL LABOR	UNIT PRICE	TOTAL SUB	
Secondary								
Sliding Glass								
Doors								
Windows								
Fixed Window								
Glass								
Window Frame								
Material								
Corner Trim								
Window Trim								
Door Trim								
Flashing								
Roof to Wall								
Metal Drip Cap								
Roll								
Beams								
Columns								
Rail								
Ornamental Iron								
NAILS								
16d Galv. casing								
8d Galv. casing								
4D Galv. Box								
LOUVERS								
Triangular								
Rectangular								
SIDING								
CORNICE								
Lookout Mat'l								
Facia Mat'l								
Rake mold								
Dentil mold								
Cont. Eave Vent								
Screen								
3/8" Plywood								
DECKS & PORCHES								
MASONRY, BRICK								
Face								
Fire								
MORTAR								
Light								
Dark								
Sand								
Portland cement								
Lintels								
Flue								

TOTALS:

COST ESTIMATE CHECKLIST (cont.)

CODE NO. DESCRIPTION	QTY.	MATERIAL		LABOR		SUBCONTR.		TOTAL
		UNIT PRICE	TOTAL MAT'L	UNIT PRICE	TOTAL LABOR	UNIT PRICE	TOTAL SUB	
Flue								
Ash dump								
Clean out								
Log lighter								
Wall ties								
Decorative brick								
Lime putty								
Muriatic acid								
Sealer								
Under-hearth								
block								
Air vent								
PLUMBING								
Fixtures								
Misc.								
Water line								
Sewer								
HVAC								
Dryer vent								
Hood Vent								
Exhaust vent								
ELECTRICAL								
Lights								
Receptacles								
Switches-single								
Switches-3 way								
Switches-4 way								
Range-one unit								
Range-surface								
Oven								
Dishwasher								
Trash compactor								
Dryer								
Washer								
Freezer								
Furnace-Gas								
Furnace-Elec.								
A/C								
Heat pump								
Attic fan								
Bath fan								
Smoke detector								
Water htr/Elec.								
Flood lights								
Door Bell								
Vent a hood								

TOTALS:

COST ESTIMATE CHECKLIST (cont.)

CODE NO. DESCRIPTION	QTY.	MATERIAL UNIT PRICE	TOTAL MAT'L	LABOR UNIT PRICE	TOTAL LABOR	SUBCONTR. UNIT PRICE	TOTAL SUB	TOTAL
Switched recept.								
150 amp service								
200 amp service								
Disposal								
Refrigerator								
Permit								
Ground fault								
Fixtures								
FIREPLACE								
Log lighter								
INSULATION								
Walls								
Ceiling								
Floor								
SHEETROCK								
Finish								
Stipple								
STONE								
Interior								
Exterior								
TRIM - INTERIOR								
Doors								
Bifold								
Base								
Casing								
shoe								
Window stool								
Window stop								
Window mull								
1x5 Jamb matl.								
Crown mold								
Bed mold								
Picture mold								
Paneling								
OS Corner mold								
IS Corner mold								
Cap Mold								
False Beam matl.								
STAIRS								
Cap								
Rail								
Baluster								
Post								
Riser								
Tread								
Skirtboard								

TOTALS:

COST ESTIMATE CHECKLIST (cont.)

CODE NO. DESCRIPTION	QTY.	MATERIAL UNIT PRICE	TOTAL MAT'L	LABOR UNIT PRICE	TOTAL LABOR	SUBCONTR. UNIT PRICE	TOTAL SUB	TOTAL
Bracing								
LOCKS								
Exterior								
Passage								
Closet								
Bedroom								
Bath								
Dummy								
Pocket door								
Bolt single								
Bolt double								
Flush bolts								
Sash locks								
TRIM MISC.								
Door bumpers								
Wedge shingles								
Attic stairs								
Scuttle hole								
1x12 shelving								
Shelf & rod br.								
Rod Socket sets								
FINISH NAILS								
3D								
4D								
6D								
8D								
Closet rods								
Sash handles								
SEPTIC TANK								
Dry well								
BACKFILL								
DRIVES & WALKS								
Form boards								
Rewire								
Rerods								
Expansion joints								
Concrete								
Asphalt								
Gravel								
LANDSCAPE								
PAINT & STAIN								
House								
Garage								
Cabinets								
WALLPAPER								

TOTALS: ☐ ☐ ☐ ☐

COST ESTIMATE CHECKLIST (cont.)

CODE NO. DESCRIPTION	QTY.	MATERIAL UNIT PRICE	TOTAL MAT'L	LABOR UNIT PRICE	TOTAL LABOR	SUBCONTR. UNIT PRICE	TOTAL SUB	TOTAL
TILE								
Wall								
Floor								
Misc.								
GARAGE DOORS								
GUTTERS								
Gutters								
Downspouts								
Elbows								
Splash blocks								
CABINETS								
Wall								
Base								
Vanities								
Laundry								
GLASS								
SHOWER DOORS								
MIRRORS								
ACCESSORIES								
Tissue holder								
Towel Racks								
Soap Dish								
Toothbrush holder								
Medicine Cab.								
Shower rods								
FLOOR COVERING								
Vinyl								
Carpet								
Hardwood								
Slate or stone								
MISCELLANEOUS								
CLEAN UP								
HANG ACCESSORIES								
FLOOR COVERING								
Vinyl								
Carpet								
Hardwood								
Slate or stone								

TOTALS:

COST ESTIMATE CHECKLIST

CODE NO. DESCRIPTION	QTY.	MATERIAL		LABOR		SUBCONTR.		TOTAL
		UNIT PRICE	TOTAL MAT'L	UNIT PRICE	TOTAL LABOR	UNIT PRICE	TOTAL SUB	

TOTALS:

9. WHEN TO USE THE EXPERTS

Once you have decided to move forward with a remodeling project, you must decide how much of the work to do yourself. The more work you do, the greater the profit you will make. You will save less money and, hence, reduce your return when you contract with others to do the work.

Using a Remodeling Contractor

If you contract a "remodeling specialist", whether a company or an individual, you will be paying retail costs. This "specialist" will either do the work himself or function as the general contractor on the project. The purpose of the contractor is to coordinate the work of carpenters and subcontractors, getting materials and labor to the remodeling site at the right time. A competent contractor can get the work completed quickly and with a minimum of frustration.

Many full service remodeling contractors will mark up costs as much as 50-100% on most jobs, and well they should, because they are incurring significant risk. This risk is high because it is so difficult to estimate exactly what is needed to complete a remodeling project. Many problems may be hidden from view until the project is started. The high prices you pay for a project may be to provide "insurance" in case the remodeler incurs hidden costs.

The quality of these professionals vary considerably, so shop carefully. Remodeling contractors are easily found in the yellow pages, in the classifieds or posted at local home improvement centers. If you are starting your first remodeling project and are worried about having limited personal time to put into the project, the remodeling professional may be the best alternative. Watch the professionals in action and learn their secrets. You will be much better prepared for the next project.

Doing the Work Yourself

By doing the work yourself, you can eliminate much of the markup added by the remodeling professional. The amount saved will depend upon your degree of involvement. Some of the savings you can expect are:

Contracting fees	15-30%
Labor costs	20-30%
Material costs	5-15%

Total	40-75%

Material costs can be saved by taking time to shop for bargains in materials and by coordinating your project to use the least amount of materials possible. The remodeler will seldom take this time since he is passing the costs on to you, the consumer.

Your level of participation in the project will fall into two categories:

1. Serving as the contractor
2. Providing the labor yourself

SERVING AS THE CONTRACTOR

Working as your own contractor will provide significant savings and can easily be done while working full time. Most scheduling can be done on the phone in the evenings. By scheduling other subcontractors to perform the work, you will depend on their expertise to complete the project properly. If your own remodeling experience is limited, rely on these professionals on the first few jobs.

PROVIDING THE LABOR YOURSELF

You can save a great deal more money by providing much of the labor. This can be a lot of fun, but be honest with yourself. Do you have the time it takes to do the work? Is your time worth more than the money you would save?

If you have another full-time job, any work you do will be after hours. If you do remodeling work yourself, make sure that you are saving more than the cost to hire a subcontractor. There are two main reasons why you shouldn't get carried away with doing too much of the work yourself:

■ There are many jobs you shouldn't even consider doing. Remember, where special skills are needed, they serve an important purpose: accomplish professional results and save you from injury, expensive mistakes, frustration and wasted time. Certain jobs may only appear easy. You can ruin your health sanding hardwood floors or drywall. You can ruin a den trying to put up raised paneling and crown molding.

■ Work can distract from your more important job of overseeing the work of others. Your most valuable skill is that of BOSS - scheduler, inspector, coordinator and referee. Saving $50 performing a small chore could cost you even more in terms of problems caused by oversight elsewhere on the site. Doing the work yourself invariably extends your project time table. It will typically take you 2-3 times longer to do the work than a seasoned professional.

JOBS TO CONSIDER DOING YOURSELF:
- Painting and sanding
- Hanging Wallpaper
- Installing doors and light fixtures
- Light landscaping
- Light trimwork
- Cleaning up

JOBS BETTER LEFT TO PROS:
- Framing
- Masonry
- Electrical
- HVAC
- Roofing
- Cabinetry
- Plumbing
- All others not listed

Remodeling an Occupied Home

Remodeling an occupied home can be a real challenge and sometimes quite dangerous. Be prepared for dirt, sawdust, interruptions of electrical and water service, noise and general inconvenience. Don't underestimate the psychological toll this will take on your personal life. If you remodel homes as an investment, consider remodeling your own house first. Only then, will you have a full awareness of what your tenants would have to tolerate during remodeling.

Keep children and pets away from workmen during the project. Make sure to cover all exposed furniture fully. Make arrangements with friends or neighbors in the event that water or electrical services must be turned off. Projects never go as smoothly as expected; so, plan for delays.

If the renovation requires major changes to the structure of the house or changes to the only bathroom or kitchen, consider moving into a temporary residence. This will expedite the project, as well as make life much more bearable.

10. WORKING WITH SUBCONTRACTORS

If you decide to use a remodeling contractor for most of your remodeling, you will avoid many of the hassles of working with subcontractors. This can be one of the main reasons to use a professional. You may be more than happy to incur the extra expense of a remodeler if you do not have the time to manage the project effectively. On the other hand, if you decide to do the work yourself, you will need to be part negotiator and part manager; but your financial rewards will be much greater.

The subcontractors you use are in business for themselves and withhold their own taxes. Your subs may consist of workers who supply labor only (such as framers and masons) or businesses that provide materials and labor (such as heating and air contractors). Use contractors whenever possible to avoid the paperwork headaches that go along with payroll accounting. The IRS may require you to file a "1099" form on your subs. This form shows how much you have paid your subs so that the IRS can be sure that they are paying their share of taxes. Check with the IRS or your accountant to obtain the necessary forms.

LOCATING SUBCONTRACTORS

Finding good subs and labor is an art. The following is a "sure fire" list of sources for locating subs and for helping you determine the best combination of skill, honesty and price:

- **Job Sites** - This is an excellent source because you can see their work.

- **The Yellow Pages** - Look under specific titles. Most major remodeling subs advertise here. Expect to be charged a bit more for these subcontractors.

- **Classified Ads** - Many advertisers in the classifieds are part timers or moonlighters. Their rates can be very competitive.

- **On the Road** - Look for phone numbers on trucks. Busy subs are normally good subs.

- **Material Supply Houses** - Many supply houses keep a bulletin board on which subs can leave their business cards.

- **References from Builders and Other Subcontractors**

REFERENCES

References are essential in the homebuilding business. Nobody should earn a good reputation without showing good work and satisfied customers. Insist on at least three references one of which should be their last job. If their last reference is four months old, it may be their last good reference.

Some people feel that companies which use a person's name as the title, such as "A. J. SMITHS's ROOFING", will tend to be a "safe" choice as compared to "XYZ ROOFING". The premise is that a man's name follows his reputation, but this obviously cannot be taken at face value. Contact references and inspect the work. You may even wish to ask the customer what he paid for the job, although this may sometimes be awkward.

Acquiring reference information should be a rule. It is not a bad idea to have your "candidate" sub-contractors fill out a brief form in order for you to find out a little about them. By asking the right questions, you can get a fairly good idea of what type of character they are.

ACCESSIBILITY

It is important to be able to reach your subs. Try not to hire subs that live too far away. If they need to make a quick visit to fix something, if may not be worth their time. Your subs must have a home phone where they can be reached.

PAYING SUBS

When you have your checkbook out to pay your subs, remember LESTER'S LAW - "The quality of a man's work is directly proportional to the size of his investment." If you want your subs to defy human nature and do the best job possible, then give them motivation. *DO NOT PAY ANY SUBCONTRACTOR UNTIL YOU ARE COMPLETELY SATISFIED WITH HIS WORK AND MATERIALS.* Once you have paid him, you have killed all incentive for him to perform for you - do not expect to see him again. Subs make money by getting lots of jobs done, not by taking lots of time on one job. Make each of your subs earn his pay. Below is a suggested schedule for payment:

- 45% after rough-in.

- 45% after finish work complete and inspected.

- 10% retainage held for about two weeks after finish work. This is to protect yourself if something is detected a bit later.

Set the terms of payment in writing before you "seal the deal".

PAYING CASH

Paying with cash gets results. Telling a sub that "you will pay him in cash upon satisfactory completion of his job" should be ample incentive for him to get the job done. It may motivate him to do a good job to boot! Make sure when obtaining cash to pay for any work done that you keep documentation for the IRS! Write a check in the sub's name and have him co-sign it. Then, cash the check. In this way you will have

an "audit trail" to prove that you paid the sub for work done.

Be fair with money. Pay the amount you promised. However, be discretionary in your payment schedule. Pay your subs and any contract labor as work is completed. Not everyone can go a week or two without a little money. It is customary to pay major subs, (such as plumbers, HVAC subs and electricians) 40% after rough-in and the remaining 60% after final inspection and approval. This "keeps the pot sweet". If you pay subs too much too early, their incentive to return to complete the work satisfactorily may diminish. If he doesn't return, you'll have to pay another sub a healthy sum to come in and finish the job. Some subs may not even guarantee work they didn't do completely. The moral of the story is clear -- *Never pay subs for more than the work that has already been done.* Give them a reason to come back.

SPECIFICATIONS

REMEMBER: NOT WRITTEN, NOT SAID. Don't count on getting anything you don't ask for in writing. A list of detailed specifications reduces confusion between you and your sub and will reduce call-backs and extra costs. Different subs have different ways of doing things. You are paying; so, make sure they do it YOUR way.

PAPERWORK

Many subs live from week to week and despise paperwork. You will have difficulty getting some subs to present bids or to sign affidavits. Many are stubborn and believe that "their word is their bond". You must use discretion in requiring these items. Generally, your more skilled trades such as HVAC, electrical and plumbing subcontractors will be more business-like and will cooperate more fully with your accounting procedures. These trades are the most important from which to get affidavits because they purchase goods from other suppliers which become a permanent part of your house. Labor-only subs need not sign affidavits, if you make sure that they provide you with an invoice for work done and marked "PAID IN FULL". This practice will save you many headaches later.

LICENSES

Depending upon who does your work, you may want them to furnish a business license. If required, make sure that plumbers, electricians, HVAC subs and other major subs are licensed to work in your county. If they have not obtained the required license, have them do so, or get another sub who is licensed..

ARRANGEMENTS FOR MATERIALS

Material arrangements must be agreed upon in a signed, written job order. All arrangements must be spelled out in detail whether your sub is providing all or just some of the materials. If a sub is supposed to supply materials, make sure he isn't billing the materials to your account, expecting you to pay for them later. If you are to supply the materials, make sure they are at the site ahead of time and that there is sufficient material to do the job. This will be appreciated by the subs and will encourage additional cooperation in the future not to mention a savings to you because less wasted time will result.

KEEP YOUR OPTIONS OPEN

Don't count on any one subcontractor for any task. Have at least one or two back-up subs who can fill in when the primary one doesn't show up or does not please you. It is best to be up front with your primary subcontractors; let them know that you plan to count on them and expect them to live up to their word. If they can't be there to do the work, skip to your second-string subs without delay.

BE FLEXIBLE WITH TIME

Because of variables in weather, subs and their work, expect some variation in work schedule. Chances are they are doing four or five other jobs at the same time. Expect some problems in getting the right guy at exactly the right time.

EQUIPMENT

Your work specifications should specify that subs are to provide their own tools including extension cords, ladders, scaffolding, power tools, saw horses, etc. Before hiring a sub, make sure he has all the tools. Don't plan on furnishing them. Defective tools which you supply can make you liable for injuries incurred when using them. If you don't have sawhorses available for your framing crew and if they didn't bring any, count on them spending their first ten minutes cutting up your best lumber to make a few.

WORKMENS COMPENSATION

Make sure your sub's workmen's compensation policy is up to date before the job is started. Get a copy of the insurance binder. Call the carrier to make sure the coverage is still in effect. If the sub doesn't have workmen's compensation, make it clear to him that you intend to withhold a portion of his payment to cover the expense. This can be a sore spot later if you forget to arrange this in advance.

THE BIDDING PROCESS

The steps below apply to the process of reaching final written agreements with your subs:

■ **Review** your project scrapbook and locate potential subcontractors.

■ **Finalize** all design and material requirements affecting each subcontractor.

■ **Prepare** standard specifications for each remodeling job.

■ **Contact** the sub-contractor and discuss plans. Mention any forms to be completed and specify the deadline.

■ **Select** the best three bids, based on price and your personal assessment of the sub.

■ **Compare** the bids against your budget.

■ **Negotiate** with prospective subs. Ask them what their best "CASH" price is. When you can't get the price any lower, ask for more services for the same amount of cash.

■ **Select** the subs you plan to use. Make it clear to them that now that they have been selected, they must commit to a specific time frame for completion of your job. Explain that you will be fair with payments but that you expect timely, quality work according to the written agreement.

■ **Contact** subs well in advance of their job and tell them when you expect them at the site. Follow them closely or you will lose them. If your building schedule changes, let the subs know as soon as possible so that they can make other plans. This courtesy will be appreciated and will be returned when you or the subs have last minute changes.

11. WORKING WITH MATERIAL SUPPLIERS

Saving Money on Materials

Remodeling provides you with the opportunity to shop around for material bargains. Since most remodeling projects can be planned ahead of time, you will have ample opportunity to accumulate your materials as bargains present themselves. Make sure that all items you choose will work properly together and will provide a uniform and planned look. Remodeling is a huge industry; materials can be purchase from a host of different sources.

RETAIL CHAINS

Most large retail chains carry a diverse inventory of remodeling supplies. Many of these supplies are called "professional supplies". Unfortunately, they seldom perform up to the consumer's expectations. If you want true professional quality, purchase from suppliers who service the professional community.

LARGE BUILDING MATERIAL SUPPLIERS

These include consumer-oriented and "trade" oriented stores, such as Lowe's or Wickes. These stores increasingly cater to a mixed clientele of professionals and amateurs. Because of this, good material bargains can be found at these outlets.

Dealing with larger companies offers the advantage of greater savings because of their ability to purchase material in volume. Larger companies may also offer wider selections than their smaller counterparts.

PRODUCT MANUFACTURERS

Deal directly with manufacturers when possible. Companies which specialize in windows, doors, carpet, bricks or other such items may provide you with merchandise at close to wholesale prices. Be prepared to pick many of these purchases up yourself since delivery may be costly or unavailable.

USE A LIMITED NUMBER OF SUPPLIERS

In order to reduce confusion and accounting, limit the number of vendors with whom you deal. An added benefit of few vendors may be special volume discounts due to larger purchase volumes.

SET UP CONTRACTOR ACCOUNTS

Open contractor accounts at your suppliers. Most suppliers offer special discounts for builders and professional contractors. You are now a remodeling contractor so ask for these discounts! Most large material supply houses have special contract sales personnel in the back of the store.

Use "float" techniques as much as possible. Contractor accounts often allow special payment schedules. For example, payment of the open balance may not be due until the first of each month. In this case it would be to your advantage to purchase your materials early in the month and gain a full month's use of them before having to pay for them. The time value of money is on your side.

Paying accounts within a specified period is a sure fire way to earn early payment discounts. Many suppliers give a percentage discount if full payment is made by the end of the month, the beginning of the month or within 30 days of purchase. Make sure you take advantage of these discounts; they can really add up. They're money in your pocket.

SHOP CAREFULLY

GET SEVERAL BIDS on all expensive items or whenever you feel you could do better. The old saying, "Only one thing has one price: a postage stamp", is alive and well in the building material business. Shop around and chances are, you'll find a better price. Check with the local builders in your area and ask them where they buy their materials.

SOURCES OF BARGAINS

If you plan to remodel on a regular basis, keep a constant eye out for close-out sales, yard sales and scratch and dent sales. Many surplus shops buy discontinued items direct from the manufacturers. Oftentimes, these items are still in new condition and can be purchased at tremendous savings if picked carefully.

Place an ad in the classifieds for any items you need for a project. Many renovations of older homes require unusual or discontinued items. Quite often, the only way to find these items will be to find other individuals who have collected them.

Drive by any projects where older buildings are being demolished. Many older styles of trim, hardwood and antique brick can be salvaged from these projects at little or no cost.

Handling Material

Inspect material as it arrives on site and determine what is returnable. If something is damaged or just doesn't look right, insist on having it returned for exchange or credit. This is normal and expected; you're paying good money and should expect quality material in return. Indicate returned items on the bill of lading as proof of return to prevent having to pay for them later.

In the normal course of construction, you will probably order too many of certain items accidentally (or on purpose to avoid delays due to shortages). Find out what overages can be returned to suppliers. For your protection, ask for written return policies. Certain cardboard cartons, seals, wrapping or steel bands may have to be intact for an item to be returnable. There may be minimum returnable quantities; for example, bricks may have to be returned in full skids (1000 units). Restocking charges may also be incurred when returning materials.

USE PURCHASE ORDERS

Manage your purchases with purchase orders. Explain to your suppliers up front that you plan to control purchases with "P.O.s" and that you will not pay any invoice without a purchase order number on it. Purchase orders ensure that you receive and pay for exactly what you ordered, but no more than you ordered. Make sure to use two-part forms. This makes it impossible for someone to create or alter a form. Prenumbered, multipart purchase orders are available at most local office supply stores.

MINIMIZE INVENTORY

Schedule your material deliveries carefully, to avoid excess materials on site. This is easier said than done. Minimizing the materials on site minimizes your investment and exposure to theft or damage. Most material suppliers will be glad to store purchased items for you and deliver them when you are ready for them. Fragile materials such as drywall and windows should not be left lying around too long. These are easily damaged and are the prime targets of theft. Make sure to lock up all movable items in a storeroom or basement.

Have materials dropped close to where they will be used in order to save time and effort. Bricks, loads of sand and gravel are good examples. Require delivery men to move plywood, drywall and other heavy items up to the second floor if that is where they will be used. Again, make sure to write your delivery instructions and directions to the site on the purchase order.

Keep materials protected from weather by covering them with plastic or keeping them inside whenever possible. Lumber, especially plywood, is susceptible to water damage. Lumber should be covered with heavy duty plastic and should be ordered shortly before it will be used. Rocks, brick or scrap wood should be used to hold the plastic down on windy days.

SECTION II:
IMPLEMENTATION

12. STARTING THE RENOVATION

Introduction

This part of the handbook presents some information on the materials and methods commonly used in rehabilitating an older dwelling. Obviously, detailed planning cannot begin until after your home's suitability for rehabilitation has been determined, the procedures for which were discussed in the Appraisal section of this book.

Our approach here is to discuss rehabilitation in a way that will be applicable to a broad range of individual interests and capabilities. Some people may be able to do the entire job themselves; others may want to learn only enough so that they can formulate an intelligent plan, contract the necessary labor and supervise the project knowledgeably. And those in between these two extremes may perform substantial amounts of work themselves, calling in consultant "experts" as needed for specialized assistance

In assessing the renovation, what must be done, and how to do it, expert guidance may be required from architects, engineers, contractors, decorators or skilled craftsmen. This could be especially true when updating critical structural features, no matter how minor, or when making major structural changes. Likewise, other specialists may be required for electrical, plumbing or heating work. With the proper help, rehabilitation can be made much easier.

Upgrading the Layout

After the house has been examined and determined to be suitable for rehabilitation, plans should be made to improve the layout, provide more space, add modern conveniences and improve appearance. If your house requires no changes and only needs restoration to its original condition, you are indeed fortunate -- and in the minority! Usually, some degree of struc-

tural change or stabilization is necessary; not to mention the fact that over the years changes in living patterns, conveniences and concepts of comfort make some degree of remodeling desirable. Be creative and use your imagination in designing the desired layout. Take your time -- the layout will form the basis for your remodeling project, the result of which will be an increase in the value of your home and the continued benefits of convenience and livability.

The general layout of your home should provide separate zones for various family functions and good traffic circulation through and between these areas. In the moderate-cost rehabilitation project this may not be practical. Even where money is no object, you will probably have to make compromises in your layout. All discussion here is of goals for which to aim when practical; inability to implement all changes should not prevent the restoration of your home to as sound and comfortable a condition as is possible.

Remember, after formulating your plan and before commencing your project, check with your local building department to obtain a building permit, if required.

ZONED LIVING

The layout of your house should be zoned to provide three major family functional areas -- one each for relaxation, working and privacy. The relaxation zone will include recreation, entertaining and dining areas. In a small house all three functions may be performed in one room, but larger homes may have separate living rooms, dining rooms, family rooms, dens, studies and recreation rooms. The last is frequently in the basement.

The working zone includes the kitchen, laundry room or utility room. It may also include an office or work shop.

The privacy zone consists of bedrooms and baths; it may include the den which can double as a guest bedroom. In some layouts a master bedroom and bath may be located away from, and even on a different level from, the rest of the bedrooms. So, a home can actually have two separate privacy zones.

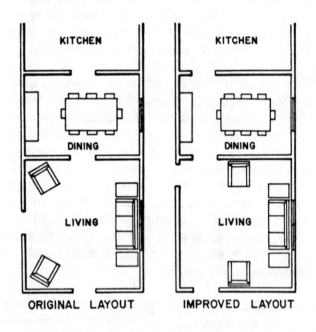

Figure 9--Relocation of doors to direct traffic to one side of rooms.

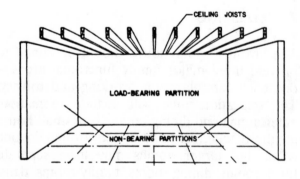

Figure 10--Load-bearing and nonload-bearing partitions. (A second-floor load may place a load on any partition.)

Zones within the home should be located for good visibility and accessibility to the outdoors.

If the backyard is the primary outdoor area used, perhaps your living room should be at the back of the house. The working zone should have good access to the garage, dining room and outdoor work areas. The main entrance to the house should have good access to the driveway or usual guest parking area, which may be located in front of, in back of or on either side of the house. In considering where to locate rooms and entrances, past convention should not be the overriding consideration. Let your personal preferences, convenience and comfort mandate your remodeling layout. After all, you are the person who will be living in the home -- you would not be undertaking the remodeling unless the present layout did not meet your needs. Modify the layout to suit you! Aren't you the customer to be satisfied in this instance?

TRAFFIC CIRCULATION

One of the most important, yet most over-looked, items in layout design is traffic circula-tion. Ideally, there should be no traffic through any room. This is difficult to accomplish in living and work areas. A more feasible plan is to keep traffic from cutting through the middle of the room.

Many older homes have doors centered in the wall of a room; this not only directs traffic through the middle of the room, but also cuts the wall space in half, making furniture arrangement difficult. Study the plan and observe where a door might be moved from the middle of a wall space to the corner of the room. Also consider where doors might be entirely eliminated. Remember, however, that moving doors is costly and should be limited in the moderately-priced remodeling project. The following figure shows examples of improvements in layout through relocation of doors.

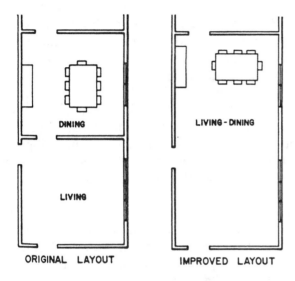

Figure 11--Removal of partition for better space utilization.

CHANGING PARTITIONS

Often room partitions must be moved in order to achieve rooms of the desired size. This is not difficult if the partition is nonloadbearing and plumbing, electrical or heating services are not concealed within it. It is possible to move even loadbearing partitions by adding a beam to support the ceiling.

To determine whether a partition is loadbearing or not, check the span direction of ceiling joists. If joists are parallel to the partition, the partition is usually nonloadbearing. It may be supporting a second floor, however; so, remember to check this as well. In most structures where the second floor joists are perpendicular to the partition, they require support and are loadbearing. An exception occurs with trusses. If trusses span the width of the building, all partitions are nonloadbearing.

Although removal of a nonloadbearing partition will not require a structural modification, the wall, ceiling and floor will require repairs where the partition intersected them.

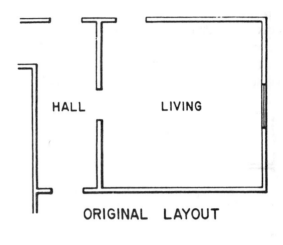

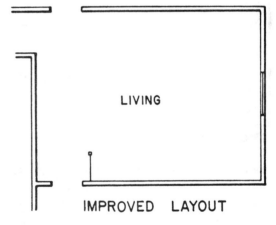

Figure 12--Removal of partition for more spacious feeling.

If rooms are small, it may be desirable to remove partitions to gain a more open, spacious feeling. A partition between living and dining rooms can be removed to make both seem larger and to gain a dual purpose space. In some instances, unneeded bedrooms adjacent to the living area can be converted into additional living area. In some remodeling projects, removing a partition between a hallway and a room may give a more spacious feeling, even though the traffic flow continues through the area.

SPACED WINDOWS

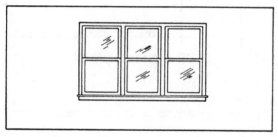

GROUPED WINDOWS

Figure 13--Improved window placement through grouping.

WINDOW PLACEMENT

Windows influence the general arrangement of both your layout and your furniture; so, consider them carefully when planning your remodeling project. Although the moving of windows is costly -- involving changes in studs, headers, interior and exterior finishes and trim -- properly placed windows can enhance the livability of a house, to say nothing of its visual appeal. Where possible, avoid small windows scattered over a wall; they cut up the wall space and make it unusable. Attempt to group windows into one or two large areas and thus leave more wall space undisturbed.

Where there is a choice of outside walls for window placement, southern walls rank first in cold climates. Winter sun shines into the room through a southern window and heats the house, but in the summer the sun is at a higher angle so that even a small roof overhang shades

the window. In extremely warm climates, northern windows may be preferable to southern windows in order to avoid heat gain even in the winter. Western windows should be avoided as much as possible because the late afternoon sun is so low that there is no way of properly shading the window. Eastern windows are usually preferred for breakfast nooks and other areas used primarily in the morning. The morning sun, while bright and cheery, does not impart the heat of a noonday or setting sun.

Windows provide three major functions. They admit daylight and sunlight, allow ventilation of the house and provide a view. Points to consider in planning for each of these three functions are discussed below.

Some general practices to ensure adequate light are:

1. Provide glass areas in excess of 10 per cent of the floor area of each room.

2. Place principal window areas toward the south, except in warm climates.

3. Group window openings in the wall to eliminate undesirable contrasts in brightness.

4. Screen only those parts of the window that open for ventilation.

5. Mount draperies, curtains, shades and other window hangings above the head of the window and to the side of the window frame so that the entire glass area is revealed when the window coverings are drawn back.

To insure good ventilation, some practices to follow are:

1. Provide ventilation in excess of 5 per cent of the floor area of a room.

2. Locate the ventilation openings to take full advantage of prevailing breezes.

3. Locate windows for the greatest flow of air across the room and within the level where occupants sit or stand. Ventilation openings should be located in the lower part of the wall unless the window swings inward, directing airflow downward.

To provide a good view:

1. Minimize obstructions in the line of sight of those sitting or standing in the room.

2. Determine sill heights on the basis of room use and furniture arrangement.

CLOSETS

An item sometimes overlooked in planning your layout is closet space. Most older houses have few, if any, closets. Plan for a coat closet near both the front and rear entrances. There should be a cleaning closet in the work area, and a linen closet in the bedroom area. Each bedroom also requires a closet. If bedrooms are large, it will be a simple matter to build a closet across one end of the room. The small house will present more difficulty. Look for wasted space, such as the end of a hallway or a wall offset. If the front door opens directly into the living room, a coat closet can sometimes be built beside or in front of the door to form an entry.

In the story-and-a-half house, closets can often be built into the attic space where headroom is too limited for occupancy.

Closets used for hanging clothes should ideally be at least 24 inches deep, but shallower closets are also practical. Other closets can vary in depth depending on their use, but a depth greater than 24 inches in any closet other than a walk-in is usually impractical.

Where existing closets are narrow and deep, rollout hanging rods can make them very usable. To make the best use of closet space, plan for a full-front opening.

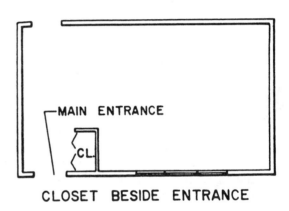

CLOSET BESIDE ENTRANCE

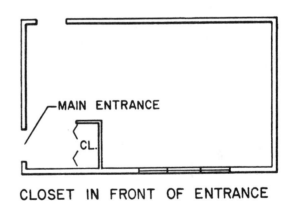

CLOSET IN FRONT OF ENTRANCE

Figure 14--Entry formed by coat closet

In many remodeling situations, plywood wardrobes may be more practical than conventional closets that require studs, drywall, casing and doors. More elaborate closets can be built by dividing the wardrobe into a variety of spaces for various types of storage and installing appropriate doors or drawers.

PORCHES

Porches on older houses are often very narrow, with sloping floors. They do not lend themselves well to the type of outdoor living, such as dining and entertaining, usually desired today; however, these porches are very difficult to enlarge. It is often found preferable to tear off the old porch and completely rebuild a new one.

Appearance

Many older houses possess desirable qualities of appearance that should be retained. Many new house designs copy styles of the past in an attempt to capture the dignity of the two-story Colonial, the quaintness of the Victorian house, the charm of the old English cottage, the look of solid comfort of the Midwestern farmhouse, or the rustic informality of the ranch house. If a house possesses any of these or other desirable qualities, avoid drastic changes in appearance during your remodeling project. To retain the character of the house, choose the materials for all additions, new windows and doors carefully. Make sure they blend into the present character of your home.

Figure 15--Preserve traditional styling of house to provide uniformity of design.

If in your remodeling project you want to give your home a completely new "look" and break from the past, plan all changes in appearance carefully. The two key considerations are unity and simplicity. To achieve unity and simplicity, make rooflines continuous, where possible. Make all windows the same type and use only one or two siding materials. Avoid trim that appears stuck onto the house without serving any purpose; remove such trim where it does exist. The result is not only simplicity, but also a reduction in maintenance costs. An exception to this treatment of trim is the historically or architecturally significant "gingerbread" found in some older homes. This trim, if restored, requires added maintenance on an ongoing basis to ensure its preservation. In two-story houses, windows are generally lined up and placed over each other on the first and second floors. Relocation of a window on either floor could destroy the unity and simplicity of the home's lines.

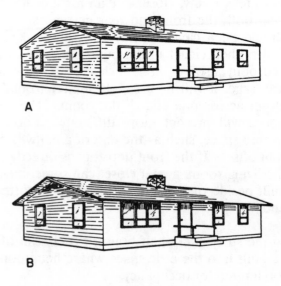

Figure 16--Improved appearance by adding roof overhang: A, without overhang; B, with overhang.

One of the most common causes of poor appearance is a lack of roof overhang. There should be a roof overhang of at least 1 foot, preferably 2 feet, all around the house. Not only does the proper amount of roof overhang improve the appearance of a house, but also it performs a vital function -- the protection of your siding and windows. The addition of a roof overhang will pay for itself in reduced maintenance.

For the house that is exceptionally plain, one of the best places to add interest is at the main entrance. This is the natural focal point of your home. An attractive door, a raised planter or interesting steps can do much to enhance the overall appeal of your home. One word of caution -- Keep the entrance in scale and in character with the house at large; avoid an overly grand appearance.

The house that looks too tall can often be improved by adding strong horizontal lines; such as, the addition of a porch or strong carport rooflines. Painting the first and second story different colors can also produce a lower appearance. Color can be used in many ways to affect the apparent size of your home. A light color makes a house appear large; whereas, a dark color will make it appear much smaller.

Interior appearance should also be considered before finish materials are selected. The most convenient materials to apply do not always produce the desired character. Ceiling tile that is attractive in a recreation room may not be suitable in a living room. Paneling comes in various types and qualities, lending different degrees of dignity and charm to a room. Always keep the desired effect in mind when plans are made and materials are chosen.

Getting Started

After you have thoroughly examined your home and have formulated the complete remodeling plan, the actual rehabilitation process begins.

In locations where termites are a particular problem and are prevalent in and around the house, soil poisoning may be advisable before the work begins. Local information on termites may be available from your County Extension Office.

The order in which components of the house are reconditioned will vary with each situation; however, the first step in rehabilitation should be to level the house and floor system. A level base from which to work is essential. Roof repairs and changes in windows and exterior doors should be made before interior work begins. All changes in plumbing, electrical wiring and heating should also be completed before interior finish work is started.

Certain general information will be useful in reconditioning wood-frame construction:

(1) Recommended moisture content of framing material is 15 per cent for most areas in the United States. It should never exceed 19 per cent.

(2) Recommended moisture content for interior finish woodwork varies from 6 to 11 percent depending on the area of the United States.

(3) Plywood should be exterior grade anywhere it will be exposed to moisture during construction or in use.

(4) Recommended nailing patterns for assembly of framing and application of covering materials varies, depending on the type of materials and their use.

(5) Actual lumber sizes have changed and new lumber may not be fully compatible with that of old framing. Some older homes may have been constructed using full thickness lumber; so, allowance must be made for size differences.

13. KITCHEN

Planning the Renovation

Before undertaking the remodeling of your kitchen, evaluate carefully how you and your family use that room. Besides the usual -- cooking and cleaning -- do you use that room to eat, to congregate around the table and converse, to chat on the phone, to study, to pay bills, to write? When you entertain, do you like to have your guests help with food preparation or at least visit with you in the kitchen while you add the finishing touches to the meal? Are you the kind of host(ess) who prefers not to be hidden away in the kitchen, away from your guests and their conversation, but wants the kitchen to be just as integral a part of the house as the living room, allowing both for food preparation and visiting with guests? Or, do you prefer that the kitchen be isolated so that food preparation can be done in private and so that guests cannot see the kitchen in disarray following and during food preparation?

After you have carefully analyzed how you now -- and how you would like to in the future -- use your kitchen, you are then ready to start a detailed analysis of your present kitchen and what will be necessary to convert it into your ideal.

The factors to consider when undertaking such an analysis are its present floorplan, discernible traffic patterns, available counter space, storage needs, appliances, surfaces of all areas (floor, walls, ceilings, counters), necessary lighting and your personal style preference. Each of these factors will be taken in turn so that you can see how dissecting the evaluation of your present and future kitchen can lead to an orderly, successful remodeling job, the results of which will be exactly as you have dreamed.

The best way to perform this analysis is to purchase some simple graph paper. If the paper you use has a 1/2-inch scale, then each square represents 1 foot. If the paper has a 1/4-inch scale, then 2 squares represent 1 foot. It is important to remember these dimensions when drawing your kitchen. Only by maintaining a uniform scale can you make sure that the analysis of your present kitchen is accurate, the plans for your remodeled kitchen are indeed complete and function as planned, with everything fitting and working just as you imagined.

Present Floorplan

The first step in graphing the layout of your kitchen is to graph the perimeter. Measure the basic width and length of the kitchen. Be sure to indicate the position and width of all doors and windows, placing them on your plan in the exact location in which they are found in your kitchen. After you graph the entire perimeter of the kitchen and any adjacent areas which will be involved in your remodeling, draw a second line, parallel to and outside the line you have just drawn. Shade the area between these lines. This area represents the normal 4-inch walls found in today's houses. If you are remodeling an older home whose walls are of 6 inches or some other width, indicate the dimension on your plan.

The next step in developing your floorplan is to indicate how doors and windows open and close. If the door swings inward, indicate this by a solid line measuring the width of the door and drawn from the door hinges to the point where the door would be in the open position. Then, to show the door's path, draw a quarter circle from the door's open position to its closed position. If some of your doors swing both ways, draw a semicircle as above showing the path of the door when opened to its widest position on one side of the wall to the open position on the opposite side of the wall. For sliding doors, show the stationary half by a single line and then draw the moving half on the outside or inside of the stationary door (whichever is appropriate for your particular set of doors) in the half-open position. For pocket doors, show them in the half-opened position by single lines which begin within the double lines representing the wall and ending one-quarter into the doorway from each side. For bifold doors, draw little W's the depth of each panel. Repeat the above steps for all windows, drawing them in the half-opened position and showing all opening and closing paths as you did for each door.

Depending on the age of the house you are remodeling, the size of all openings -- doors and windows -- as well as the depth of the walls may vary greatly from present day norms. These variances should be indicated on your plan so that structural changes which may be necessary can be identified and so that when purchasing doors or windows the proper sizes can be ordered.

The next items which must be drawn in on your plan are the cabinets. First, draw in your base cabinets. Today's standard depth is 24 inches; however, older homes often have cabinets which are shallower by varying amounts. So, be sure that you measure all cabinets carefully. After you have drawn in your base cabinets, indicate your wall cabinets by a dotted line through the base cabinet drawing to represent how far the wall cabinets overhang onto the base cabinets. Again, such as was the case with the base cabinets, the usual amount of overhang is 12 inches; however, older homes may vary. Be sure that you do not assume the standard, but actually measure each cabinet.

Should you have a pantry or other storage area which accesses from the kitchen, draw it as you have the rest of the kitchen. Draw its width and depth to scale and draw the door and its path just as you were instructed above. If the kitchen contains an eating area, draw it in precisely, even if it is not a built-in unit. Draw in the size and shape of the table, followed by the number and size of the chairs. Place the eating area on the floorplan exactly as it is in your kitchen. With the chairs, indicate how far into the floor they are usually pushed in order to sit at and get up from the table.

TRAFFIC PATTERN

Now, you are ready to plan the common traffic pattern in your kitchen. Draw in with arrows the usual traffic flow by family members and guests from each door into the kitchen and out again. You are now ready to draw in your work triangle.

A work triangle is the triangle created by connecting the three major kitchen appliances -- the sink, the stove and the refrigerator. An efficient kitchen is on with a work triangle having sides of no more than 4 to 7 feet. By graphing your work triangle, some present inefficiencies may immediately become obvious. Often, it is found that what you feel is an unworkable kitchen, and one needing major remodeling, is really only a kitchen whose work triangle is too large or too uneven. If this is the case, you may be able to achieve an efficient work area by simply relocating the major appliances rather than undergoing costly changes in cabinetry, appliances and other structures such as walls and doors.

The four generally recognized arrangements for kitchens are the "U", "L", corridor and sidewall types. The arrangement selected depends on the amount of space, the shape of the space and the location of the doors. If you are adding a new kitchen, select the layout preferred and plan the addition in accordance with that. The work triangle is smallest in the "U" and corridor layouts. The sidewall arrangement is preferred where space is quite limited and the "L" arrangement is used in a relatively square kitchen which must include a dining table.

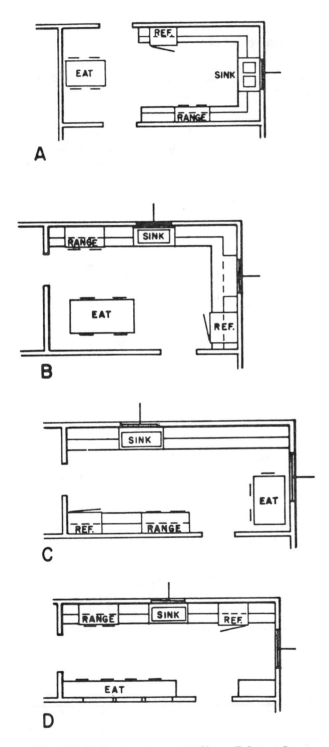

Figure 17--Kitchen arrangements: A, U-type; B, L-type; C, corridor; D, sidewall.

APPLIANCES

Now, draw in all appliances in the kitchen. Measure their widths and depths and plot them exactly as they appear in your present kitchen. On the outline of your base cabinets, draw in your sink opening and cooktop, indicating the exact size and placement of each burner, vent or barbecue grill, if your range includes these features. After you have drawn in all appliances, draw a dotted line to indicate the position of each appliance's door in its fully-opened position. After doing this, often the traffic jam created by overlapping doors becomes painfully obvious. Just as obvious can be the fact that a great deal of your workflow problems can be eliminated by simply moving one appliance or another a few inches or feet. Often, this can be done without even having to run new plumbing or wiring lines.

If your laundry area opens into the kitchen, draw the washer and dryer and their enclosure. If your heating, air conditioning and water heater units are in the kitchen area, draw them and their enclosures. Do not forget to draw each enclosure's door and its path.

At this time, you must draw in all plumbing and wiring. Trace all lines and indicate each shut-off. Mark supply and waste lines separately. For electrical wiring, mark each outlet and its voltage. Indicate with arrows which outlets govern the electricity to what appliances and light fixtures. Older homes often have only 110-volt wiring which must be updated. If you do not feel confident in assessing your present wiring and future needs, please consult a registered electrician. Failure to do so can result in anything from overload nuisances to fires.

COUNTERS

Next, measure each counter area. If your counters include separate tiled and butcher-block areas, draw each one separately. The purpose of this exercise is to assess your present work surfaces. Do you have enough room next to the cooking area for placement of heated cooking utensils. If so, is the surface heat resistant? Do you have enough room next to the sink for jobs like chopping and grinding which are more appropriately conducted near the sink for easy cleanup? Do you have an area suitable for rolling out dough and other baking functions? Do you have counter space adjacent to the refrigerator so that grocery bags can be placed there for ease of unloading? Are your present counters long enough, but too shallow? After placing cannisters, small appliances and other decorative pieces on your counters, have you a workable space remaining?

Often, you will find simply by graphing your present counter space that you do have enough counter space in terms of width and depth; however, the countertops are not of the proper surface for the tasks performed on them. In other words, those counter surfaces nearest the range may not be of heat resistant material. Or, they might be of heat resistant material, but still not able to withstand the direct heat of a pan taken directly from the burner? If this is the case, simply changing the countertop materials may achieve workable work surfaces. In terms of cost and convenience, merely changing countertop surfaces is certainly preferable to tearing apart and rearranging your cabinets.

ELEVATIONS

The next graphs you must draw are the elevations, or facings of each of the walls in your kitchen. Stand back from the wall and graph exactly what you see. Draw in each opening, window covering, cabinet, appliance, hanging light fixture and any other item which can be seen; such as, tables, chairs, hutches. You must prepare one drawing to scale for each wall in the kitchen. You will use these drawings to assess symmetry, suitable color combinations,

suitable wall covering patterns, window coverings and cabinetry.

Now, identify and draw in your storage needs; i.e., the space needed for utensils, pots and pans, boxed foods, spices, tall oil bottles, etc. Compare these needs to what you presently have. Simple rearranging of shelves may satisfy your needs and preclude the purchase of new cabinetry.

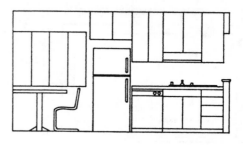

Figure 18--Kitchen elevation.

Design

Now that you have fully graphed you present kitchen, it is time to identify all the changes you would like to make. Remember, remodeling gives you the chance to not only have the kitchen of your dreams, but also to solve your present structural or design inadequacies. The success or failure of your remodeling effort rests not only on the accuracy of your layout, but also on how well you analyze your results and incorporate your design ideas. Approach this combined task in an orderly fashion.

First, put your completed floor plan and the elevation drawings in front of you. Review each one carefully, making a list of all the changes you feel necessary. Make another list of changes which are not necessary, but would be nice as an alternative. In this way, if your original list proves to be too costly or if major structural changes must be made to effect some of your changes and you do not wish to undertake such a major remodeling task, you have already identified other alternatives and can easily move from one remodeling choice to another. This is true of all aspects of the remodeling job -- from new cabinets to a choice between paint or wall paper.

To do this, take the basic floor plan you graphed and make copies of it. Experiment on the copies by moving appliances, changing cabinets, adding work surfaces, adding an island, changing or adding an eating nook. This is your time to dream; make any changes you want. Make as many drawings as you like. Slowly, you will begin to see a pattern emerge of your predominant preferences in placement of appliances, work surfaces, storage needs and desired traffic patterns. This will help you refine your "needs" and "wouldn't it be nice" lists.

Once this is completed, it is time to evaluate your style preference. Often, your choice in color scheme does not result in the "feel" you wished to create. The combination of color, cabinets, appliances, window or wall coverings can end up being an assault on your senses rather than the cozy room you envisioned. So, the best way to avoid costly mistakes and to evaluate the overall effect of your remodeling ideas is to draw and color them on copies of the wall elevations.

First, on your elevations, draw vertical and horizontal lines, connecting the lines of the window and door openings, appliances and cabinets. Too many lines confuse the eye and, no matter how well-coordinated the color scheme, that flaw cannot be masked. It is a simple, time-saving technique to draw vertical and horizontal lines on a copy of your elevation drawings, ensuring all door and window rims, appliance and cabinet edges are aligned. Often the only change needed is extending a counter, moving a cabinet or an appliance. If these simple measures cannot effect the change, then often a decorative addition, like a wall-hung

spice rack can be used to fill in an obvious gap and align with the bottom edge of a window and/or cabinet.

After you have ensured your kitchen's clean lines, look at the color scheme you have chosen and the overall "feeling" you are trying to create. Do you want a warm and cozy kitchen? Do you want a sterile, efficient appearance? Or, are you trying to use color to mask a ceiling that is too high, a room that is too small or a room that is too large to appear cozy? It is well known that colors can be used to achieve just about any effect you wish. If you would like some additional professional guidance, there are interior designers who specialize just in kitchen design.

Basically, colors fall into two main categories -- warm and cool. Colors in the blue family are considered cool and tend to enlarge a room. Colors in the red/yellow/orange family are warm and tend to make a room smaller and "cozier". It has always been a good rule of thumb to avoid dark colors in a very small room so that the room does not appear even smaller. Lighter hues tend to make a room appear larger. Experiment with dark and light hues of whatever color scheme you have chosen. On copies of your elevations, shade in the colors you have chosen, making the walls dark and the ceilings light, and vice versa. Try varying the tints used from wall to wall. Try painting two walls one color and the other two either a contrasting one or a different hue. Go through this same exercise with several different color schemes. You will quickly begin to see which combination you find aesthetically pleasing.

Do not forget the color of the appliances. If their color no longer fits your design scheme, but you do not wish to purchase new appliances, have a new enamel finish baked on at your nearest automobile paint shop. Most new appliances, however, have removable color panels to make decorative changes even easier.

Once you have decided what color scheme you prefer, color it in on several elevation drawings and begin to experiment with cabinet fronts and counter surfaces. Attack one at a time. Draw in the grain on the cabinets and any discernible pattern; such as, horizontal or vertical strips of wood, cabinet hardware and its placement. Then, add the pattern and color of your countertops and wall coverings. Do not forget the smallest item, like the sink backsplash. When combining all these features on one elevation, you will be able to quickly see if your ideas, when put together, create the effect you desire. You can then make the necessary changes on paper, instead of making costly errors by proceeding to effect the changes and then realizing that you do not like the result.

Now is also the time to draw and color in any major decorating and/or color accents you think will be effective. Chances are that, if they do not produce the desired effect on the drawings, they will not do so when you have installed them. Always remember to start with and to work around any features which you consider essential; such as, an heirloom cabinet or a special wall covering. Build your new kitchen around the feature you most want to accent, ensuring your remodeling efforts will highlight, rather than detract from, your "treasure" -- be it a piece of furniture or simply a striking wall covering.

After you have narrowed your ideas down to those you wish to implement, look at your overall plan and analyze your lighting needs. You may like the new track lighting fixtures or tiffany hanging lamps; however, evaluate their light beams and the shadows they will cast on your work surfaces. Make sure that you have ample under-the-counter lighting to illuminate your work area without casting shadows. If you still have your heart set on track lighting, make sure that the individual lights are aimed at your work surface from your side, rather than from

your back. Or better yet, why not utilize track lighting for decorative lighting of cabinets or wall decorations and install under-the-counter incandescent or fluorescent lighting for efficient food preparation and cleaning. If you prefer a kitchen in which at least one light is left illuminated at night, dimmer switches can be installed for varied lighting effects.

Cabinets

If the cabinet space in your kitchen is adequate and well arranged, updating the cabinets may be the only change you will need to make. New doors and drawer fronts can be added to the old cabinet framing. Even refinishing or painting the old cabinets and adding new hardware can sometimes do much to improve an old kitchen. If your kitchen has adequate cabinets, the single improvement that will most update it is new counter tops. Tops should be fabricated and installed by a good custom counter shop. Plastic laminate over particle board backing is commonly used.

Doorways should be located to avoid traffic through the work triangle. Generally doorways in corners should be avoided and door swings should avoid conflict with the use of appliances, cabinets or other doors. If swinging the door out would put it in the path of travel in a hall or other activity area, consider using a sliding or folding door. Sliding doors and their installation are expensive, but in certain situations they may be well worth it.

Windows should be adequate to make the kitchen a light, cheerful place. The current trend toward indoor-outdoor living has fostered the "patio kitchen," with large windows over a counter which extend to the outside and provide a "pass-through" or an outdoor eating counter. This is particularly useful in warmer climates, but it also has merit for summer living in any climate.

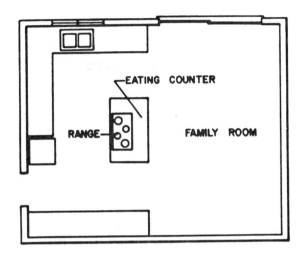

Figure 19--Island counter dividing kitchen and family room.

The placement of the sink in relation to windows is a matter of personal preference. Many women like to look out the window while they are at at the sink, but installing the sink along an interior plumbing partition is usually less costly than on an outside wall.

If your kitchen is quite large, it may be convenient to use part as a family room. The combined kitchen-family room concept can also be achieved by removing a partition to expand the kitchen or by adding on a large room. One method of arranging workspace conveniently in such a room is by using an island counter, which can also serve as an eating counter for informal dining.

EXISTING CABINETS

The existing kitchen cabinets in your house may be out of style and may be arranged quite inconveniently; however, new hardware and door fronts may do much for the appearance of old cabinets. For a natural finished wood, new doors and drawer fronts can be used on the old cabinet frame. Moldings can be added to achieve the desired character.

Repair of Existing Cabinets

If existing cabinets are adequate and well arranged, certain repairs may be in order. One of the usual problems is latches which no longer operate. These are easily replaced. One of the popular types is the magnetic catch. The magnetic part is attached to a shelf or the side of the cabinet and a complementary metal plate is attached to the inside face of the door. New door and drawer pulls to match any decor can also be easily added.

New door and drawer fronts can be added where more extensive facelifting is desired. All framing can be completely concealed by using flush doors with concealed hinges. Doors are fitted closely edge to edge to give a continuous panel effect. Finger slots in the bottom edge of the door can be used for a simple modern design, or door pulls can be added for any desired character.

New Cabinets

Kitchen cabinets can be custom made or purchased in units as stock items. Stock cabinets can be purchased in widths varying in 3-inch increments between 12 and 48 inches. These units are fastened to the wall through cleats located at the back of each cabinet. Wall-hung cabinets should be attached with long screws that penetrate into each wall stud.

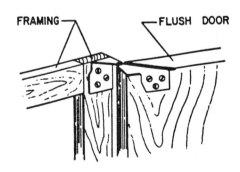

Figure 20--Concealed hinge used with flush cabinet door.

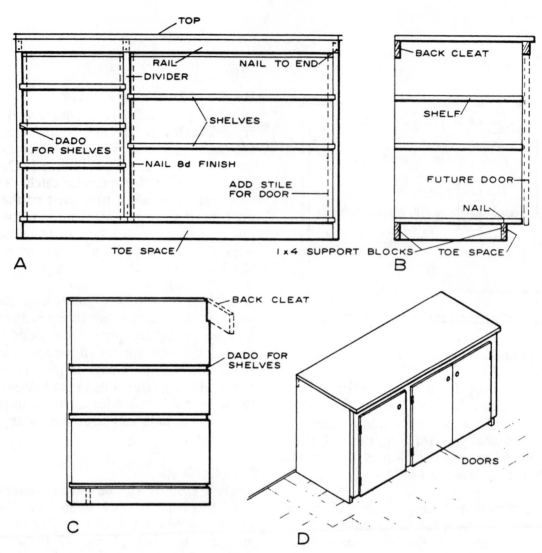

Kitchen cabinet base unit. A, front view; B, section; C, end from interior; D, overall view.

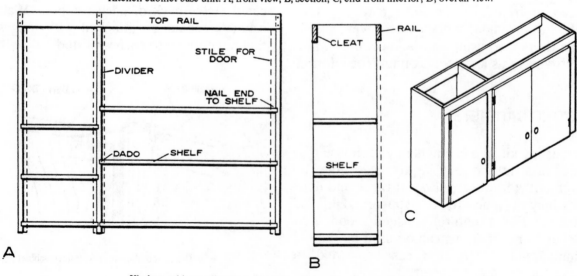

Kitchen cabinet wall unit: A, front view; B, section; C, overall view.

Figure 21

While a range of sizes is shown, the standard counter height is usually 36 inches; counter width, 25 inches.

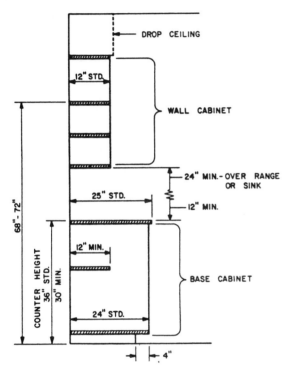

Figure 22--Kitchen cabinet proportions.

Counter Tops

Where cabinets are adequate, the best way to update a kitchen is to apply new counter tops.

Custom shops will measure, fabricate and install them. The most common type is plastic laminate.

Several sheet and roll materials which can be glued to clean, smooth backing are available. These include laminated melamine, laminated polyester, vinyl and linoleum. They are normally applied to 3/4-inch exterior-type plywood and are flexible enough to be shaped to a coved backsplash. Other materials can only be applied flat; so, the backsplash is covered separately and a metal strip is used to cover the joint between the backsplash and the countertop.

Marble is shop-fabricated, self-edged and requires no backing material. It must be precut to size in the shop because special tools are required. Marble is hard and costly; so, it is usually limited to bath counters.

Ceramic tile can be set in a mortar bed or applied with adhesive. It is the only material that must be applied at the building site rather than in a shop or factory. It is available in a variety of sizes. The smaller 1-inch-square tiles are often preassembled on a mesh backing in 1-foot-square units. It was once very popular and is quite attractive, but it is quite hard for kitchen counters and the joints are a maintenance problem.

KITCHEN LAYOUT SHEET
(1/4" square = 1 foot)

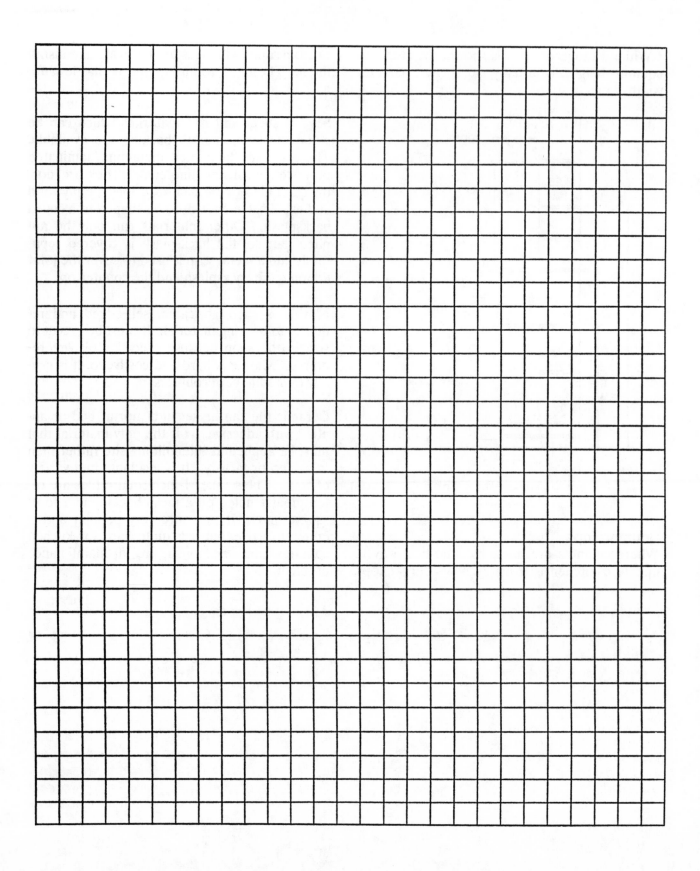

14. BATHS

Remodeling the Bathroom

Remodeling the bathroom can have one of the most significant effects on your home's value. Like the kitchen, the bathroom can be dated just by the style and technology of the fixtures. Modern bath appliances have changed considerably over the past few years, making older units obsolete in both appearance and function.

While upgrading the rest of the house may simply consist of applying a new coat of paint, bath renovations usually require extensive changes. Bath areas also show wear faster because of their concentrated use and the effects of moisture on older materials.

Modern values have changed the bathroom from a purely functional design to a romantic escape where you can steam away the aches and pains of modern living in a sauna, enjoy the pristine view of a Japanese garden from a soaking tub or participate in romantic interludes with the partner of your choice. These visionary images put a lot of demand on the limited space and access of older baths. Turning these old caves into modern Roman baths without spending a fortune will require creative energy and extensive research.

Since remodeling the bathroom is so important, you should take care to plan out the renovation thoroughly. Work out all of your plans on paper first, looking at space requirements, costs and your floor plan. In this way you can make maximum use of your remodeling dollar, as well as make a more functional design.

Shop thoroughly for materials and decorating ideas. Write off for remodeling ideas from bath accessory manufacturers. These brochures can be a veritable gold mine of ideas, providing inventive and up-to-date creative suggestions.

Remember, the idea is to provide the maximum effect for the minimum cost. Examine the relative condition of each fixture in the bathroom. If they work properly, you may not wish to change them; however, fixtures are an important part of the bathroom decor. Make sure the present fixtures blend with your new decorating scheme. While some old plumbing fixtures, such as the old fashioned cast iron bathtubs, can be preserved for atmosphere, most fixtures seldom meet the needs of present day bathers. Many old sink fixtures have separate hot and cold faucets -- an unacceptable modern day inconvenience.

Sometimes a fresh coat of paint, new wallpaper or a decorative mirror can do wonders without the expense of a major remodeling project. Select paint and wallpaper samples and check to see if they match current fixtures. You may be surprised at the change light pastels can have on the brightness of an existing bathroom.

Minor remodeling would consist of the following items:

- Fresh coat of paint
- New wallpaper
- New towel racks and fixtures

A more complete rehabilitation might include:

- New plumbing fixtures on sink and tub
- New sink and cabinet
- New tile floor, vinyl floor covering or carpet
- Converted shower enclosure
- New mirror or lights above the sink
- New or refinished tub

NOTE: Tub refinishing has become a new industry that involves recoating the existing tub with a new durable finish that rivals the original porcelain finish. Not only can it work wonders on old antique tubs that have mineral stains or chips from age, but also it costs less than a new tub.

Match new styles and colors to existing fixtures for a consistent style. If you plan to retain many old fixtures, choose colors and accessories that will accent them. Use brass fixtures or natural wood to emphasize victorian styling. If you plan to modernize all fixtures, you will have greater artistic freedom in choosing colors and styles.

Shop around for specials on fixtures. Many stores run specials on old models, odd lots or discontinued lines. Shopping specials can save you a considerable amount of money and possibly allow you to upgrade to higher quality fixtures.

Major renovations

The most expensive remodeling job requires structural changes to the bathroom such as tearing out an old tub or expanding the size of the bathroom. Avoid this option if possible; structural remodeling is costly and is less likely to provide maximum return on your investment. Most structural changes require rerouting the plumbing of the bath; this may be very difficult without tearing out additional walls to gain access to the plumbing. If your house is situated on a crawl space or basement foundation, locating plumbing will be much easier. If your house is located on a concrete slab, adding new baths or fixtures may require tearing up the floor and recasting concrete. In homes with slab construction, try to tap off of existing plumbing or consider the addition of an entire room.

If you plan to relocate plumbing yourself, investigate the use of CPVC or polybutylene plastic pipe. CPVC is a stiff plastic pipe made of chlorinated polyvinyl chloride which is easier to install and less costly than copper pipe.

Polybutylene is also a new plastic compound that is easy to use, quick to install and very inexpensive. In many ways it outperforms its copper cousins. Polybutylene is an inert plastic which does not accumulate mineral deposits from the water passing through it. Its flexibility makes it easy to snake around framing with a minimum of joints and makes it very resistant to freezing and water hammer (a thumping sound caused by the sudden shutting off of the water supply). Many do-it-yourself stores are switching from CPVC to Polybutylene because of its many advantages, but you may still have to shop around to find it.

If the tub or shower needs replacing or repositioning, take a look at the new ready to assemble kits. These kits consist of acrylic or fiberglass panels that can be readily assembled after fitting the parts through the door of the bathroom.

TACKLING MAJOR REVISIONS

Major revisions can require a good deal of skill and time to accomplish. If this is your only bathroom, major overhauls can make the normal task of bathing a major challenge. Plan ahead so that fixtures are not all out of service at one time, or arrange with neighbors to use their facilities.

You might consider using a designer or remodeling contractor to accomplish your bathroom remodeling task, but their fees will add considerably to the cost of your project. Make sure to get several written estimates with firm start and completion dates. You may be shocked at the variance in bids; so, make sure to have included in your bids as many specifics about materials and workmanship as you can. Plumbing work generally includes quite a bit of markup. If you feel confident in doing the job yourself, you can save a considerable amount of money.

MAKING USE OF SPACE

Extra bathrooms and powder rooms can add considerable value to your house and can be fitted into surprisingly small spaces. If you need an additional bathroom, look carefully to see if you can steal space from a bedroom, closet or other bath. Extra small showers can be fitted into areas that were once closets. Extra deep tubs as short as 42" can be used in tight spaces. Extra small sinks can be purchased that will fit into corners.

Even when your bath area is smaller than you like, you can make confined spaces seem larger with the use of decorative techniques. Use light colors for wallpaper and tile. Add a skylight or window garden to give the space a more open feel. Sometimes the best wall covering is not wallpaper, but mirrors. They expand the perspective and perceived space of the room, as well as provide an easy-to-clean, durable surface.

Floor Plans

Before beginning your bathroom project, plan your changes thoroughly on paper. From a drafting store, purchase an architectural template which includes most common bath fixtures. These fixtures are to scale and can be drawn on drafting paper. This will help you to plan your space efficiently, just as you did with the kitchen.

Adding a Bathroom

If you are remodeling an older house, it will probably suffer from a shortage of bathrooms. Improved bathroom facilities should be one of your priorities in the planning stages of remodeling.

Finding a convenient location for the addition of a bath in an existing house is often quite difficult. Adding a room onto the house is seldom a good solution because it is usually preferable to to have bathroom access from a bedroom hallway. A half-bath near the main entrance or in the work area is desirable.

One consideration in locating a bath economically is to keep all piping runs as short as possible. Also, all fixtures on one plumbing wall can use a common vent.

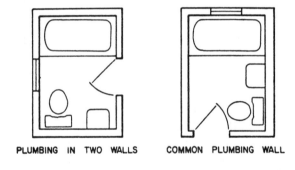

PLUMBING IN TWO WALLS   COMMON PLUMBING WALL

Figure 23--Minimum size bathroom (5 ft by 7 ft).

If your challenge is to find room for an additional bath or two, the best sources, in order of preference, are:

1. **The "wet wall" between the current bathroom and the new bathroom.** This is the wall which houses all current plumbing. By using this wall, you can tie your new fixtures into the existing plumbing with a minimum of effort and cost.

2. **The current bathroom location.** If the present bathroom is large enough and has access to it from more than one side, split it into two bathrooms. Many times the space will be just a bit too small for this ploy. If so, check the possibility of cantilevering the present bathroom over the outside wall. This can add up to four feet of length to the bath area, without

requiring alteration of the foundation. You can now use this expanded area to create two baths from one.

3.   **An existing laundry room.** This area is perfect for a conversion because the plumbing is already present in the wall. With careful planning, you may be able to combine the laundry room with a bathroom by enclosing the washer and dryer behind folding doors. If your new bath area is not large enough for the washer and dryer, investigate the new stackable washer and dryer combinations. These extra-small appliances will handle a standard laundry load, but they take up less than half the wall space of conventional units.

4.   **Adjoining closet areas.** Closets that back up to existing bathroom areas can be merged into the new bath area. The closet location usually allows private access to the new bath from the bedroom; a valuable feature.

5.   **Room additions.** This is the least desired location for new baths since it requires a major structural remodeling of the building structure. Bathroom structural additions will seldom return their invested value because the cost of adding to an existing structure is so much greater than the increased value of the house. If you add space to the house for a new bath, consider adding other living spaces as well. You have already incurred the major costs of engineering, foundation work, alteration of the exterior walls and framing; so, why not add value to your project by also adding a laundry room, bedroom extension or playroom? This makes the investment much more worthwhile.

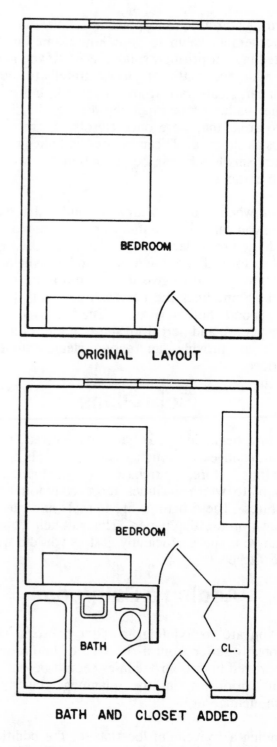

Figure 24--Portion of a large bedroom used to add a bath.

One common mistake in adding a bath to an older home has been to place it in any unused space without, regard to the convenience of the location. Consequently, many bathrooms have been placed in what was formerly a pantry, a large closet or under a stairway. This usually means the only access to the bathroom is through the kitchen or bedroom, or that the bathroom is totally removed from the bedroom area. If this mistake has been made in your home, it is important to add another bath in a good location.

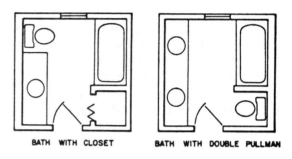

BATH WITH CLOSET   BATH WITH DOUBLE PULLMAN

Figure 26--Moderate size bathrooms (8 ft. by 8 ft.)

The minimum size for a bathroom is 5 feet by 7 feet; larger sizes are certainly desirable. Increasing the size slightly would make the bath less cramped and could provide space for a storage closet for towels, cleaning equipment or supplies. If you plan to add only one bath, consider making it an area with compartments for use by more than one person at a time. Two baths can be most economically built with fixtures placed back to back, but do not sacrifice a convenient location to accomplish this. Bathrooms built on both floors of a two-story house are most economically built with the second-floor bath directly over the first-floor bath.

Bathroom fixtures vary in size; so, be sure to obtain the dimensions of the fixtures you plan to use prior to drawing your detailed plan.

COMPARTMENTED BATH AREAS

A compartmented bathroom is designed to permit several persons to use the space at the same time. It uses more space than a standard bathroom, but it has several unique properties which make it appropriate for many remodeling jobs:

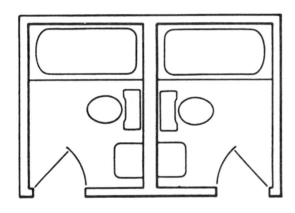

Figure 25--Two bathrooms with economical back-to-back arrangements.

In a house with large bedrooms, a portion of one bedroom can be taken for a bath. Such a bedroom should have at least one dimension of at least 16 feet. If the bedrooms are all small and needed, there may be no choice but to build an addition. It may be more advantageous to make a small bedroom into a bath (or two baths) and add on another bedroom that to add on the bathroom. A possibility in the 1-1/2 story house is to add a bath in the area under the shed dormer. When this is done, remember that the wall containing the plumbing must have a wall below it on the first floor through which piping can run. The same is true of two-story homes.

1.   Existing space can be more easily adapted to the new bathroom floor plan

since it can consist of several small spaces which are not congruous.

2.   Fewer plumbing fixtures are used for the number of people accessing the bathroom. This can save a considerable amount of expense, since the fixtures and the installation of them are the most expensive parts of the bathroom.

3.   Compartmenting makes the bath area available to more than one person at the same time.

4.   Each user's privacy is enhanced.

Avoid using this technique unless the design of your house requires innovative use of space. Compartmentalized bathrooms use as much space as two separate ones; they also require more extensive remodeling of existing space and replumbing of existing fixtures. Don't make your job more difficult than it has to be!

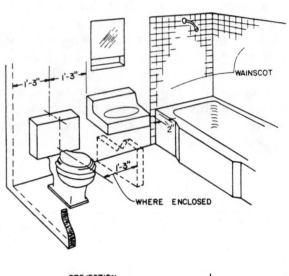

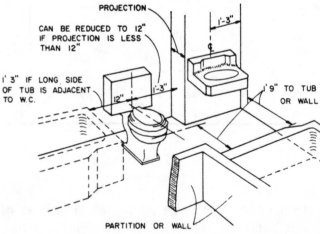

Figure 28--Recommended dimensions for fixture spacing.

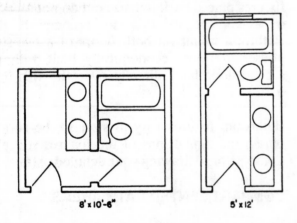

Figure 27--Compartmented bathroom.

BATHROOM LAYOUT SHEET
(1/4" square = 1 foot)

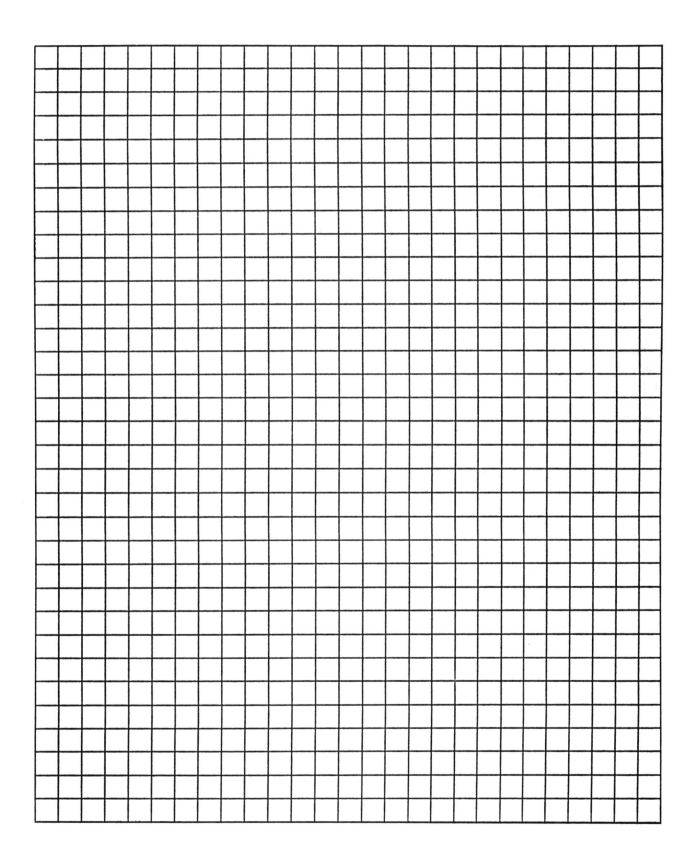

15. ADDING SPACE

Expanding Within the House

Regardless of the size of the house, there always seems to be a need for more space. Seldom is there enough storage space. Work space for a shop or other hobbies is almost always needed. More recreational and informal living spaces are usually desired. Family rooms are seldom found in older houses. Furthermore, in some houses rooms may be small or additional bedrooms may be needed. Many older houses have only one bathroom; so, bathroom additions are often required. Often possibilities for expansion abound -- existing unfinished space such as the attic, basement or garage. If expansion into these areas is not practical, an addition can be built.

ATTIC

The house with a relatively steep roof slope may have some very usable attic space going to waste. It can be made accessible for storage space by the addition of fold-down stairs. If this space is usable as a living area and if it has good access, it may be a prime candidate for use as additional bedrooms, a den, a study, a hobby room or an apartment for a relative.

Where the attic is at the third-floor level, local codes should be checked. Some codes do not permit use of the third floor for living areas; others require a fire escape.

The headroom requirements for attic rooms are a minimum ceiling height of 7 feet 6 inches over at least one-half the room and a minimum ceiling height of 5 feet at the outer edges of the room. The space with a lower ceiling height could be used for built-in furniture or storage space.

If there is sufficient headroom only in a narrow strip at the center of the attic, consider building a large shed dormer to increase the usable space. Dormers, though not needed for increasing usable space, may be required for the addition of windows.

It is crucial that consideration be given to insulation, vapor barriers and ventilation when finishing attic space. Attics are particularly hot in the summer. Insulate your attic space well; install vapor barriers around all walls and the ceiling of the finished space; ventilate the attic space above and on each side of the finished space. Provide good cross ventilation through the finished area.

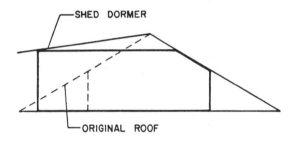

Figure 29--Shed dormer for additional attic space.

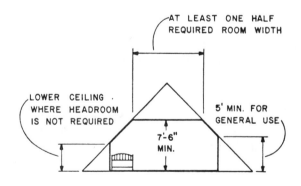

Figure 30--Headroom requirements for attic rooms

An item sometimes overlooked in expanding into the attic area is a stairway. The usual straight-run stairway requires a space 3 feet wide and at least 11 feet long, plus a landing at both top and bottom. There must also be a minimum overhead clearance of 6 feet 8 inches at any point on the stairs. If space is limited, spiral stairs may be the solution. Some spiral stairs can be installed in a space as small as 4 feet in diameter; however, code limitations should be checked. While spiral staircases are quite serviceable, they are a little more difficult to ascend or descend. This makes them unsuitable for the elderly. Also, be advised that they will not accommodate large or bulky pieces of furniture. So, determine what the access will be for moving furniture in and out of the attic space. This may be the determining factor when deciding how to use that area.

Finishing the Attic

Making an attic usable may be a simple matter of installing finish ceiling, wall and floor coverings; however, it will often require adding a shed or gable dormer for more space or for natural light and ventilation. Furthermore, the existing joists may not be adequate to support a floor load. It may be best to get professional advice on this unless tables are available that show allowable joist and rafter spans. If the joists are inadequate, the best solution is usually to double existing joists.

Gable Dormer

Where light and ventilation, rather that additional space, are the main requirements, gable dormers are often used. They are more attractive in exterior appearance than shed dormers; however, due to the roof slope, they are usually limited to a small size. They are also more complicated to build than shed dormers.

The roof of the gable dormer usually has the same pitch as the main roof of the house. The dormer should be located so that both sides are adjacent to an existing rafter. The rafters are then doubled to provide support for the side studs and short valley rafters. Tie the valley

rafter to the roof framing by a header. Frame the window and apply interior and exterior covering materials as described in other sections herein.

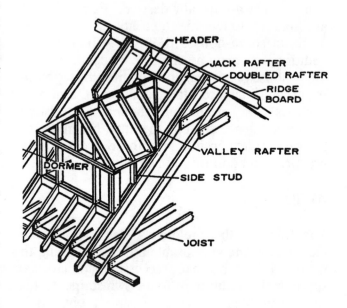

Figure 31–Framing for gable dormer.

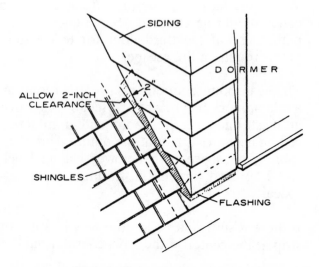

Figure 32–Flashing at dormer walls.

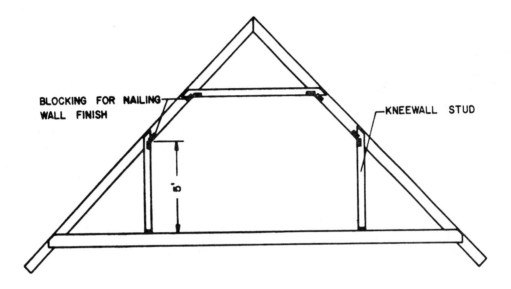

Figure 33--Installation of knee walls and blocking

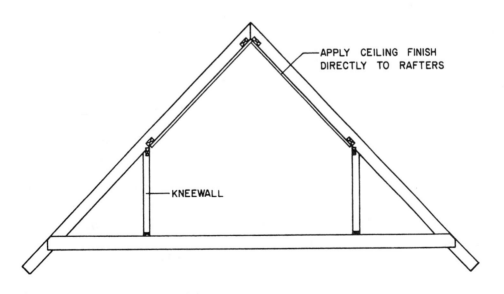

Figure 34--Attic finished with a cathedral ceiling.

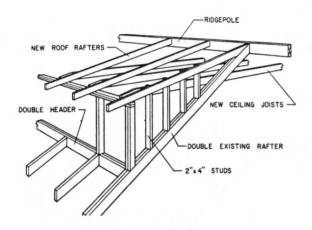

Figure 35--Framing for shed dormer

One of the most critical items in dormer construction is proper flashing where the dormer walls intersect the roof of the house. When roofing felt is used under the shingles, it should be turned up the wall at least 2 inches; shingle flashing should be used at this junction. This flashing consists of tin or galvanized metal shingles bent at a 90-degree angle to extend a minimum of 4 inches up the side of the wall over the sheathing. Use one piece of flashing at each shingle course, lapping successive pieces in the same manner as shingles. Apply siding over the flashing, allowing about a 2-inch space between the bottom edge of the siding and the roof. Cut ends of siding should be treated with water-repellent preservative.

Shed Dormer

Shed dormers can be made any width and are sometimes made to extend across the entire length of the house. They are less attractive than gable dormers and, for this reason, are usually placed at the back of the house. Sides of the shed dormer are framed in the same manner as the gable dormer; so, the sides should coincide with existing rafters. The low-slope roof has rafters framing directly into the ridgepole. Ceiling joists bear on the outer wall of the dormer, with the opposite ends of the joists nailed to the main roof rafters. The low

slope of the dormer roof means that the requirements of roofing application will be different from those of the main roof. Shingle sizes and exposures should conform to those shown.

Knee Walls

Sides of the attic rooms are provided by nailing 2-by-4- or 2-by-3-inch studs to each rafter at a point where the stud will be at least 5 feet long. Studs should rest on a soleplate in the same manner as other partitions. Nail blocking between studs and rafters at the top of the knee wall to provide a nailing surface for the wall finish.

Ceiling

Nail collar beams between opposite rafters to serve as ceiling framing. These should be at least 7-1/2 feet above the floor. Nail blocking between collar beams and between rafters at their junction to provide a nailing surface for the finish wall and ceiling materials.

An alternate method of installing the ceiling is to eliminate the collar beams and to apply the ceiling finish directly to the rafters. This results in what is commonly called a cathedral ceiling. If the dormer is wide, cross partitions or some other type of bracing is required for stability.

Chimney

If a chimney passes through the attic, it must either be hidden or worked into the decor. Never frame into the chimney; keep all framing at least 2 inches from the chimney. Where framing is placed completely around the chimney, fill the space between the chimney and framing with noncombustible insulation.

BASEMENT

An unfinished basement may be one of the easiest places for expansion, although certain conditions must be met if it is to be made habitable. A habitable room is defined as a space used for living, sleeping, eating or cooking. Rooms not included and, therefore not bound by the requirements of habitable rooms, include bathrooms, toilet compartments, closets, halls, storage rooms, laundry rooms, utility rooms and basement recreation rooms. The average finished-grade elevation at exterior walls of habitable rooms should be no more than 48 inches above the finished floor. Average ceiling height for habitable rooms should be no less than 7 feet 6 inches. Local codes should be checked for exact limitations. Other basement rooms should have a minimum ceiling height of 6 feet 9 inches.

Figure 36--Large basement window areaway with sloped sides.

Dampness in the basement can be partially overcome by installing vapor barriers on the floor and walls if they were not installed at the time of original construction. In an extremely damp basement, plan to use a dehumidifier for summer comfort.

One of the main disadvantages of basement rooms is the lack of natural light and of a view. If the house is on a sloping lot or graded in a manner to permit large basement windows above grade, it is much more usable than in the house where the basement has only a few inches of the top of the wall above grade. Even the completely sunken basement, however, can have natural light if large areaways are built for windows and the walls of the areaways are sloped so that sunlight can easily reach the windows. At least one window large enough to serve as a fire exit is recommended, and often

required by code. It may be convenient to extend the areaway to form a small sunken garden, but in so doing be sure to provide adequate drainage.

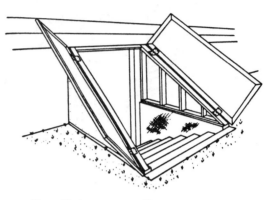

Figure 37--Areaway type of basement entrance.

The usefulness of the basement may also be increased by adding a direct outside entrance. This adds to fire safety by giving an alternate exit. It is particularly desirable if the basement is to be used as a shop or for storing lawn and garden equipment. If an outside stairway is provided, try to place it under cover of a garage, breezeway or porch in order to protect it from ice, snow and rain. Otherwise, use an areaway-type entrance with a door over it.

Finishing the Basement
Basements can be finished to any desired style or degree, depending on the investment required and the use to be made of the finished space. This may vary from insulated walls with quality paneling, wood floors and acoustical ceiling, to merely painting the existing concrete walls and floors. Keep in mind that basement areas, even where the grade is low, tend to be damp; dehumidification, therefore, may be required. Basements may also be cooler; so, the rooms may be uncomfortably cool in periods of light heating. A small amount of auxiliary electric heat can partially correct this. Insulation of below-grade concrete or masonry walls is also crucial.

Figure 38–Sunken garden forming large basement window areaway.

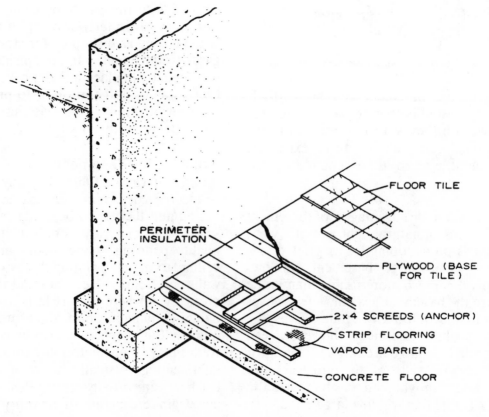

FLOOR TILE

PERIMETER
INSULATION

PLYWOOD (BASE
FOR TILE)

2 x 4 SCREEDS (ANCHOR)

STRIP FLOORING

VAPOR BARRIER

CONCRETE FLOOR

Figure 39–Installation of wood floors in a basement.

Floors

If a concrete floor is dry most of the year, it indicates that a vapor barrier was probably applied under the slab at the time it was constructed. In such a basement, resilient tile or indoor-outdoor carpeting could be applied directly to the smooth slab. Any protrusions from the slab should be chipped off and smoothed. Extension unevenness in the slab indicates that an underlayment over sleepers should be used as a base for the tile or carpet.

Install the tile as described under the section on "Floors", following the manufacturer's recommendations on adhesives and installation. Carpeting is usually just cut to size and laid flat, with only double-faced tape at the edges and seams.

A very low-cost floor can be achieved by merely applying a deck paint. It should be a latex paint to avoid chipping or peeling. Although painting may not give the finished appearance provided by a floor covering, it does brighten the basement and produce a smooth surface that is easily cleaned. Painting the basement floor is particularly suited to shops, utility rooms and playrooms.

Where a concrete floor is desired, but the existing floor is cracked, uneven or damp, a vapor barrier can be laid over the existing floor and a 2- to 3-inch topping of concrete fill can be added.

Where a vapor barrier is required and finished flooring is planned, apply an asphalt mastic coating to the concrete floor, followed by a good vapor barrier. This can serve as a base for tile; however, the use of furring strips with finish floor applied over them may produce a better end result. Wood flooring manufacturers often recommend that preparation for wood strip flooring consists of the following steps:

1. Mop or spread a coating of tar or asphalt mastic on the concrete, followed by an asphalt felt paper.

2. Lay 2-by-4s flatwise in a coating of tar or asphalt, spacing the rows about 12 inches apart; start at one wall and end at the opposite wall.

3. Place a 2-foot width of insulation around the perimeter, between 2-by-4s where the outside ground level is near the basement floor elevation.

4. Install wood-strip flooring across the 2-by-4s.

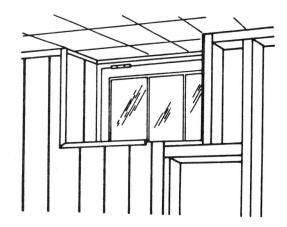

Figure 40--Framing around basement window of a wall finish application.

A variation of this preparation for flooring consists of laying a good-quality vapor barrier directly over the slab and anchoring the furring strips to the slab with concrete nails. Insulation and strip flooring are then applied in the manner described above.

Plywood, 1/2- or 5/8-inch thick, can also be applied over furring strips to provide a base for resilient tile or carpet.

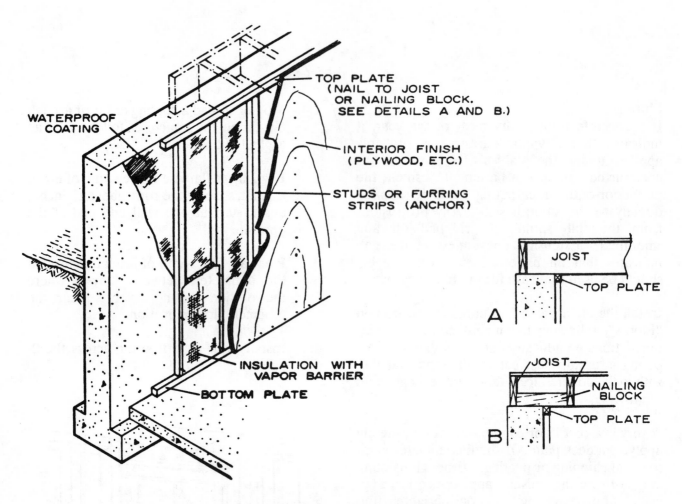

WATERPROOF COATING

TOP PLATE
(NAIL TO JOIST
OR NAILING BLOCK.
SEE DETAILS A AND B.)

INTERIOR FINISH
(PLYWOOD, ETC.)

STUDS OR FURRING
STRIPS (ANCHOR)

INSULATION WITH
VAPOR BARRIER

BOTTOM PLATE

JOIST

TOP PLATE

A

JOIST

NAILING
BLOCK

TOP PLATE

B

Figure 41--Basement wall finish over framing.

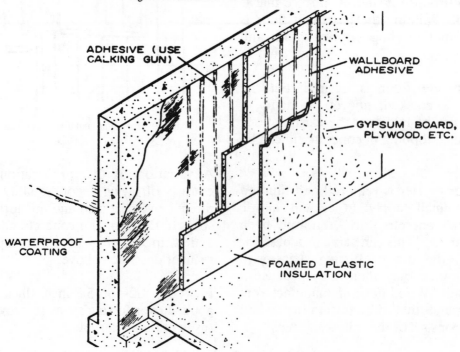

ADHESIVE (USE
CALKING GUN)

WALLBOARD
ADHESIVE

GYPSUM BOARD,
PLYWOOD, ETC.

WATERPROOF
COATING

FOAMED PLASTIC
INSULATION

Figure 42--Basement wall finish over rigid insulation.

Walls

Where basement walls were waterproofed on the outside, there should be no problem in applying most kinds of wall finish. If there is any possibility of water entry, however, it is important to apply a waterproof coating to the inner surface. Numerous coatings of this type are available commercially; however, they cannot be applied over a painted surface.

If a more finished appearance is not essential, walls can simply be painted for a bright, clean appearance. If a better interior finish is desired, it is applied over furring strips or rigid insulation.

Furring strips, 2-by-2 inches or larger, are used on the walls in preparation for the interior finish. Strips should be pressure treated for decay resistance, especially if the walls are not waterproofed. Anchor a 2-by-2-inch bottom plate to the floor at the junction of the wall and floor. Fasten a 2-by-2-inch or larger top plate to the bottom of the joists above, to nailing blocks or to the wall. Then, fasten 2-by-2-inch or larger furring strips at 16- or 24-inch spacing vertically between top and bottom plates. Concrete nails are sometimes used to anchor the center of the furring strips to the basement wall.

Before proceeding any farther with the finish wall, install all required electrical conduit and outlet boxes between furring strips. Place blanket-type insulation with vapor barrier on the inside face in each space between furring strips. The wall is then ready to receive the interior finish. Almost any dry wall material can be applied in the manner described under "Interior Wall Finish".

Wall finish material is sometimes applied over foamed plastic insulation, which is applied directly to basement walls without the use of furring strips. For this method, walls must be smooth and level without protrusions so that the sheets of foam insulation can be secured to the walls with beads of adhesive.

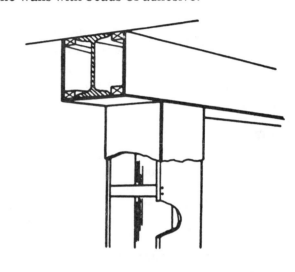

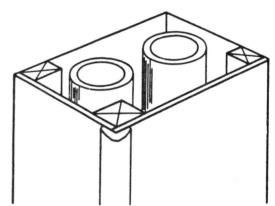

Figure 43--Application of paneling to cover columns, beams and pipes.

Use dry wall adhesive to secure the wall finish to the insulation. Follow manufacturer's recommendations on adhesives and methods of installation for both the foam insulation and the dry wall. Select a foam insulation with good vapor resistance to eliminate the need for a separate vapor barrier.

Basement partitions are made in much the same manner as on the main floor. The only difference is in securing the soleplate to the slab with concrete nails or other types of concrete anchors.

Finishing walls should include concealing unsightly items such as steel beams, columns and exposed piping. These items can be covered by building a simple box around them and paneling over the box.

Ceilings

The ceiling finish can be applied using the same materials and techniques described in the section on "Ceilings". In many basements, a suspended ceiling system will be best. It can be placed below piping and electrical conduit, and panels are easily removed for repair or changes in utilities. In considering the use of a suspended ceiling, make certain that at least 7 feet will still be available from floor to ceiling. It may be necessary to apply the ceiling directly to the bottom of floor joists and box around or paint to match the ceiling.

Before installing any ceiling, insulate cold-water pipes. When the basement has a high relative humidity, water condenses on the cold pipes and this condensation drips down on the ceiling under the pipes. Molded insulation made specifically for wrapping around pipe is commercially available.

GARAGE

Another place for expansion is the garage built as an integral part of the house. If the garage is well built, the only work required is finishing; this is much less costly than adding onto the house. The main consideration is whether the additional finished space is needed more than the garage is needed. Since the garage is often adjacent to the kitchen, it is an ideal candidate for conversion to a large family room. It could also be used for additional bedrooms, possibly another bathroom.

The walls and ceiling of the garage can be finished in any conventional manner. The floor will probably require a vapor barrier, insulation and a new subfloor. It may be convenient to use the existing garage door opening to install large windows or a series of windows; otherwise, the door opening can be completely closed and windows added at other points. Methods of adding the floor and applying other finishes are presented under "Reconditioning Details".

Finishing the Garage

The garage which was built integrally with the house can be used as living space simply by insulating it and adding floor, wall and ceiling finishes. There may be some additional requirements for windows and for heating.

Floors

The new finish floor is applied directly over the existing concrete slab or, where headroom is sufficient, over new floor framing above the slab. Where the ceiling of the finished garage is at the same elevation as the house ceiling, new floor framing can be installed to place the new floor at the same level as the house floor. The framing may rest on the foundation wall or may be supported on ledgers nailed to the wall studs. Consult joist tables to determine the correct size for the required span. The floor is merely installed as a conventional floor, as described under "Floor System"; insulated in the same manner as a crawl-space house, as described under "Insulation".

The garage roof is often lower than the house roof; so, the floor must be placed directly on the concrete slab one or two steps below the house floor. Finish floor can be installed using the same materials and techniques as for a basement slab. If the garage floor is near ground level, insulation is required. If the finished floor is on sleepers over the concrete, place insulation between sleepers.

Another method of insulating is to dig the soil away from the foundation and to apply rigid insulation to the outer face of the foundation wall to the depth of the footing. It must be a moisture-proof insulation, such as polystyrene or polyurethane, and should be attached with a mastic recommended by the insulation manufacturer. The insulation should be covered with a material suitable for underground use; such as, asbestos-cement board or preservative-treated plywood. When subterranean termites are a threat, soil can be poisoned during the backfill, the procedure for which was herein explained.

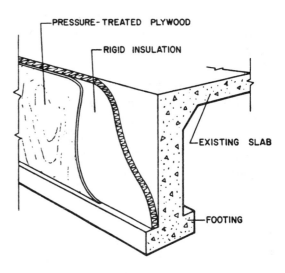

Figure 45--Application of insulation to outer face of garage foundation wall.

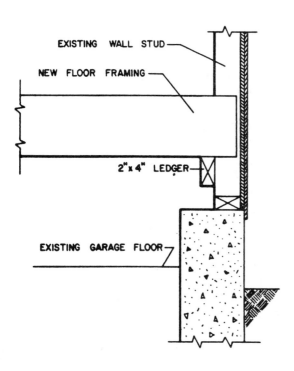

Figure 44--Framing to bring new garage floor to the level of the house floor.

Walls

The garage walls are not usually insulated; so, blanket insulation with a vapor barrier on the inside face should be installed in the space between studs. Then, apply any type of dry wall in the manner described under "Interior Wall Finish".

Frame any additional doors and windows following the instructions given under "Doors" and "Windows". It may be convenient to use the existing garage door opening for a sliding glass door or a window wall. If it is not to be used for either purpose, fill it in, using conventional 2-by-4-inch framing; install covering materials

Ceiling

The ceiling can be installed as described under "Ceilings". Be sure to insulate and ventilate well the attic space.

AN ADDITIONAL FLOOR

If you are contemplating a major renovation of the structure and the existing roof is in disrepair, consider adding an additional floor. This is accomplished by completely removing the existing roof and then building an additional floor and new roof on top of the existing floor.

This is a difficult procedure and should not be undertaken without the help of a trained carpenter. You must make sure that the existing walls can support the weight of the new floor. If the existing walls meet modern construction standards and are in good condition, this option is feasible.

SUNROOM

Sunrooms can be added to the house as a completely new structure or as a conversion from existing structures. If the house already has a porch or deck, consider enclosing them with glass. This area can provide quality heated living space which can open up an otherwise drab interior.

Additions to the Existing House

If space requirements are not fulfilled after utilizing available attic, basement or garage space, the only alternative left is to construct an addition. Before proceeding with additions, investigate all minimum setback regulations to ensure that your plan does not violate any regulations.

Use additions for your most critically needed space. If you need more bedrooms, but you would also like a much larger living room, maybe the present living room can be used as a bedroom and a large living room can be added. If the main requirement is a large modern kitchen, add on a new kitchen and use the old kitchen as a butler's pantry, utility room, bathroom or hobby room.

The important thing to remember when adding on to your home is that the addition should be

in keeping with the style of the rest of the house. Rooflines, siding and windows should all match the original structure as closely as possible.

One of the most difficult problems encountered in building additions to your home is the actual connecting of the addition to the original structure. In some constructions it might be best to use the satellite concept. With this approach, the addition is built as a separate building. It is then connected to the original house by a narrow section which serves as an entryway or mudroom. One of the disadvantages of this approach is the resultant large exterior wall, with its corresponding heat loss and exterior maintenance.

MATCH THE EXISTING HOUSE STYLE

Make sure that any additions to the house match or blend in with the existing structure. Other sections herein describe methods for installing windows, doors and covering materials. Most of these instructions also apply to new construction. The main item peculiar to additions is making the connection between the addition and the existing structure.

Where the addition is to be made by extending the length of building, the structure as well as the siding and roofing must match the existing portion. To accomplish this, a complete roofing job may be necessary. Where existing shingles can be matched, some of the shingles near the end must be removed in order to lap the saturated felt underlayment. The new shingles are then worked into the existing shingle pattern. Short pieces of lap siding must also be removed so that the new siding can be toothed into the existing siding with end joints offset.

If the addition is to be perpendicular to the house, the siding can either match or contrast with the existing siding. The roofing material, however, should match.

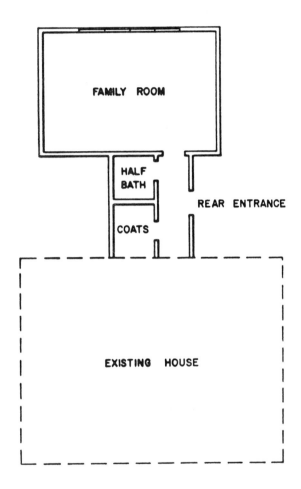

Figure 46--Addition using the satellite concept.

16. FOUNDATION

Because a good foundation, or one able to be repaired, is a crucial prerequisite for rehabilitation, massive repairs or replacement will not be discussed.

SOIL POISONING AROUND FOUNDATION

Subterranean termites are the only wood-destroying insects that may require measures beyond those provided by sound construction practices. Generally, the most widely recommended form of supplementary treatment against termites is soil poisoning. This treatment is also an effective remedial measure.

Studies made by the U. S. Department of Agriculture show that certain chemicals added to the topsoil under buildings or around foundations will prevent or control termite infestation for many years. Specific chemicals to be used for control should be those registered by the Environmental Protection Agency. Every precaution should be taken when using chemicals. You do not want to risk the good health of your family and friends by indiscriminately or improperly applying chemicals to the soil around your home. Be sure to use chemicals exactly in the manner and in the strengths indicated on the container. When you can, it is advisable to have these chemicals applied by a professional exterminator.

Slab construction - The treatment of soil under slab-on-ground construction is difficult. One method of treatment consists of drilling holes about a foot apart through the concrete slab, adjacent to all cracks and expansion joints and injecting a chemical into the soil beneath the slab. Another method is to drill through the perimeter foundation walls from the outside and force the chemical just beneath the slab along the inside of the foundation and along all cracks and expansion joints.

Crawl space houses - To treat buildings having crawl spaces, dig trenches adjacent to and around all piers and pipes and along the sides of foundation walls. Around solid concrete foundations the trenches should be 6 to 8 inches in depth and breadth. Chemical is poured into the trench and, as the excavated soil is put back into the trench, it is also treated. The soil is tamped and the trench filled to a level above the surrounding soil to provide good drainage away from the foundation.

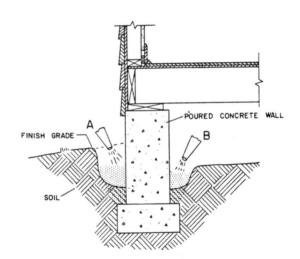

Figure 47–Application of chemical to crawl space construction soil treatment: A, along outside wall; and B, inside foundation wall.

In brick, hollow-block or concrete foundations that have cracked, dig the trench to, but not below, the footing. Then, as the trench is refilled, treat the soil. Treat voids in hollow-block foundations by applying the chemical to the voids at or near the footing.

Basement houses - Application of soil poisoning for this type of construction is much the same as for slab-on-ground and crawl-space construction. Treat the basement floor in the same way as a slab-on-ground house.

Figure 48--The northern limit of damage in the United States by subterranean termites, line A; by dry wood or nonsubterranean termites, line B.

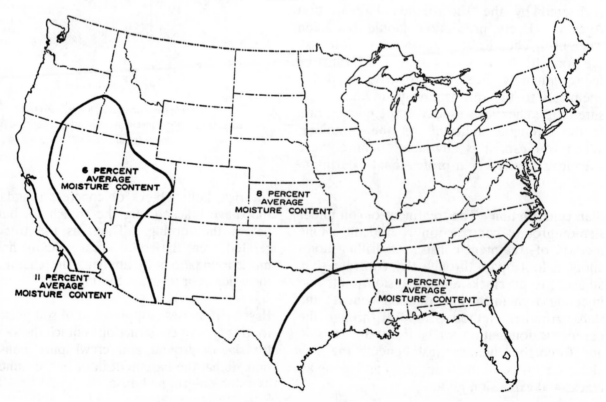

Figure 49--Recommended average moisture content for interior finish woodwork in different parts of the United States.

Precautions - Chemicals for termite control are poisonous to people and animals. Be sure to use them properly and safely. Here are some basic safety rules:

1. Carefully read all labels and follow directions.

2. Store insecticides in labeled containers out of reach of children and animals.

3. Dispose of empty containers.

4. Wash contaminated parts of your body with warm, soapy water immediately after exposure.

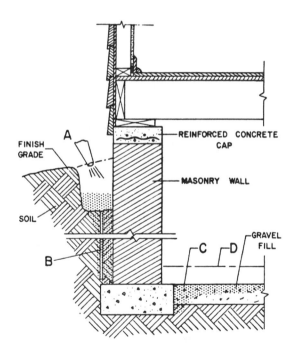

Figure 50--Application of chemical to the soil in and around a full basement: A, soil treatment along outside of the foundation; B, pipe and rod hole from bottom of trench to the top of the footing to aid distribution of the chemical; C, drill holes for the treatment of fill or soil beneath a concrete floor in basement; D, position of concrete slab.

CRACKS IN CONCRETE FOUNDATION

Minor hairline cracks frequently occur in concrete walls during its curing process and usually require no repair. Open cracks should be repaired, but the type of repair depends on whether the crack is active or dormant and whether waterproofing is necessary. One of the simplest methods of determining if the crack is active is to place a mark at each end of the crack and observe at future dates whether the crack extends beyond the marks.

If the crack is dormant, it can be repaired by routing and sealing. Routing is accomplished by following along the crack with a concrete saw or chipping with hand tools to enlarge the crack near the concrete surface. The crack is first routed 1/4 inch or more in width and depth; then, the routed joint is rinsed clean and allowed to dry. A joint sealer such as an epoxy-cement compound should then be applied in accordance with the manufacturer's instructions.

Working cracks require an elastic sealant. Sealants vary greatly in elasticity; so, a good quality sealant that will remain pliable should be used. The minimum depth and width of routing for these sealants is 3/4 to 1 inch. The elastic material can then reform with movement of the crack. Strip sealants which can be applied to the surface are also available, but these protrude above the surface and may therefore be objectionable. When applying sealants, always remember to follow closely the manufacturer's instructions.

CRUMBLING MORTAR

Where masonry foundations or piers have crumbling mortar joints, these should be repaired. First, chip out all loose mortar and brush the surface thoroughly to remove all dust and loose particles. Before applying new mortar, dampen the clean surface so that it will not absorb water from the mixture. Mortar can be purchased premixed. It should have about the consistency of putty and should be applied like a caulking material. For a good bond, force the mortar into the crack to contact all depressions. Then, smooth the surface with a trowel. Provide some protection from sun and wind for a few days to keep the mortar from drying out too fast.

must be used to raise the floor girder off the post in question. This releveling must be done slowly and carefully to avoid cracking the plaster in the house walls. Steel jack posts are convenient replacements for the post removed. If a wood post is used, a pedestal should be built to raise the base of the post slightly above the floor surface. This allows the end of the post to dry out if it becomes wet.

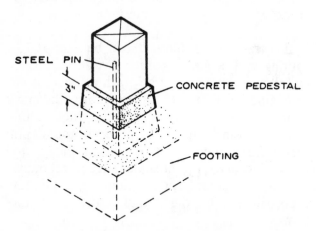

Figure 51—Basement post on pedestal above the floor.

UNEVEN SETTLEMENT

Uneven settlement in a concrete foundation due to poor footings, or no footings at all, usually damages the foundation to a point which precludes repair. In a pier foundation the individual pier or piers could be replaced or, if the pier has stopped settling, blocking could be added on top of the pier to level the house. In either situation, the girder or joists being supported must be jacked and held in a level position while the repairs are being made.

BASEMENT POSTS

Any type of basement post may have settled due to inadequate footings; wood posts may have deteriorated due to decay or insect damage. To correct either problem, a well-supported jack

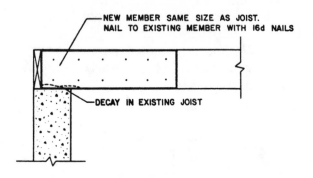

Figure 52—Repair of joist with decay in end contacting the foundation.

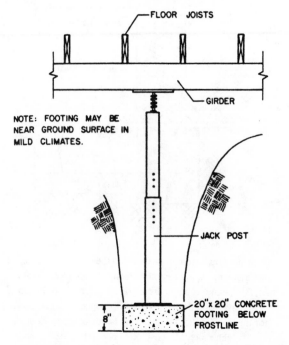

Figure 53—Jack post supporting a sagging girder in a crawl space house.

17. FLOOR SYSTEM

REPLACEMENT OF FRAMING MEMBERS

If examination of the floor framing revealed decay or insect damage in a limited number of framing members, the members affected will have to be replaced or the affected sections repaired. Large-scale damage would probably have resulted in classifying the house as not worthy of rehabilitation. Damaged members should be replaced with preservative-treated wood if exposure conditions are severe. To accomplish this, the framing supported by the damaged member must be temporarily supported by jacks in a crawl-space house or by jacks with blocking in a basement house. A heavy crossarm on top of the jack will support a width of 4 to 6 feet. Where additional support is necessary, more jacks are required. Raise the jacks carefully and slowly, and only enough to take the weight off the member to be removed. Excessive jacking will pull the building frame out of square. After the new or repaired member is in place, gradually take the weight off the jack and remove it.

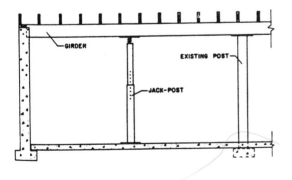

Figure 54--Jack post used to level a sagging girder in a basement house.

Sometimes decay may exist in only a small part of a member. An example might be the end of a floor joist supported on a concrete foundation wall; it could contain decay only where the wood contacts the concrete. After applying a brushed-on preservative to the affected area, jack the existing joist into place and nail a short length of new material to the side of the joist.

LEVELING THE FLOOR

After the foundation repairs have been properly made, the support points for the floor should be level; however, the floor may still sag. Where the floor joists have sagged excessively, permanent set may have occurred and little can be done except by replacement of the floor joists. A slight sag can be overcome by nailing a new joist alongside alternate joists in the affected area. If the new joists are slightly bowed, place them crown up. Each joist must be jacked at both ends to force the ends to the same elevation as the existing joist. This same treatment can be used to stiffen springy floors.

Girders that sag excessively should be replaced. Excessive set cannot be removed. Jack posts can be used to level slightly sagged girders or to install intermediate girders; however, unless the space is little used or jack posts can be incorporated into a wall, they are generally in the way.

When jack posts are used to stiffen a springy floor or to carry light loads, they can be set directly on the concrete floor slab. Where they are used to support heavy loads, a steel plate may be necessary to distribute the load over a larger area of the floor slab. The jack post should not be used for heavy jacking. Where heavy jacking is involved, use a regular jack to carefully lift the load, and then put the jack post in place.

ELIMINATION OF SQUEAKS

Squeaks in flooring frequently are caused by movement of the tongue of one flooring strip in the groove of the adjacent strip. One of the simplest remedies is to apply a limited amount of mineral oil to the joints.

Sagging floor joists often pull away from the subfloor and result in excessive deflection of the floor. If this is the cause of squeaks, squeeze construction mastic into the open joints. An alternate remedy is to drive small wedges into the spaces between joists and subfloor. Drive them only far enough for a snug fit. This method of repair should be limited to a small area.

Undersized floor joists that deflect excessively are also a major cause of squeaks. The addition of girders to shorten the joist span is the best solution to that problem.

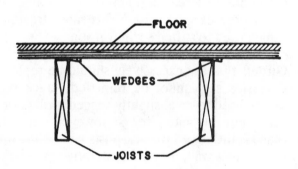

Figure 55--Wedges driven between joists and subfloor to stop squeaks.

Strip flooring installed parallel to the joists may also deflect excessively. Solid blocking nailed between joists and fitted snugly against the subfloor will prevent this deflection if it is installed at relatively close spacing.

One of the most common causes of squeaking is inadequate nailing. To correct this, drive a nail through the face of the flooring board near the tongue edge into the subfloor -- preferably also into a joist. Set the nail and fill the hole. A less objectionable method from the standpoint of appearance is to work from under the floor using screws driven through the subfloor into

the finish floor. This method will also bring warped flooring into a flat position.

NEW FLOOR COVERING

Floor covering is available in a variety of materials. These include wood in various forms -- asphalt, vinyl, vinyl asbestos, rubber and cork tile; ceramics; linoleum; sheet vinyl; carpeting; and liquid seamless flooring. The material selected depends on existing conditions, the planned use of the floor and your budget.

Before any floor is laid, a suitable base must be prepared. Unless existing wood flooring is exceptionally smooth, it should receive a light sanding to remove irregularities before any covering is put over it. If a thin underlayment or no underlayment is being used, wide joints between floor boards should be filled to avoid showthrough on the less rigid types of finish floor. An underlayment of plywood or wood-base panel material installed over the old floor is required when linoleum or resilient tile is used for the new finish floor.

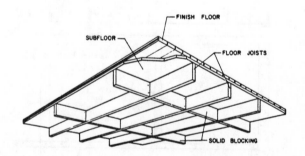

Figure 56--Solid blocking between floor joists where finish floor is laid parallel to joists.

Where underlayment is required, it should be in 4-by-4-foot or larger sheets of untempered hardboard, plywood or particle board 1/4" or 3/8" inches thick. Some underlayments cannot be used with certain floor coverings; so, be sure to check the manufacturer's recommendation before forging ahead with perhaps the wrong underlayment for the floor covering being installed. Avoidance of this precaution could nullify the warranty received when your floor covering was purchased.

Underlayment grade of plywood has a sanded, C-plugged or better face play and a C-ply or better immediately under the face. It is available in interior types, exterior types and interior types with exterior glue. The interior type is generally adequate, but one of the other two should be used where there is possible exposure to moisture. Underlayment should be laid with 1/32-inch edge and end spacing to allow for expansion. Nail the underlayment to the subfloor using the type of nail and spacing recommended by the underlayment manufacturer.

Installation over existing flooring - Wood flooring, sheet vinyl with resilient backing, seamless flooring and carpeting can all be installed directly over the old flooring after major voids have been filled and the surface sanded relatively smooth. These coverings can also be installed over old, firmly cemented resilient tile.

Wood flooring may be hardwood or softwood. Grades, descriptions and types are herein provided.

Hardwood flooring is available in strip or block and is usually tongued, grooved and end matched, but it may be square-edged in thinner patterns. The most widely used pattern of hardwood strip flooring is 25/32 by 2-1/4 inches with a hollow back. Strips are random lengths varying from 2 to 16 feet. The face is slightly wider than the bottom so that tight joints result.

Softwood flooring is also available in strip or block. Strip flooring has tongued-and-grooved

edges; some types are also end matched. Softwood flooring costs less than most hardwood species, but it is less wear-resistant and shows surface abrasions more readily. It can, however, be used in light traffic areas.

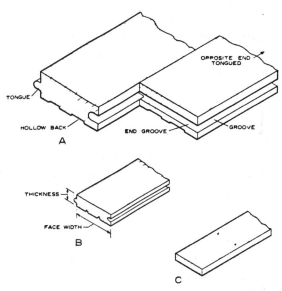

Figure 57--Strip flooring, A, side and end matched; B, side matched; C, square edged.

Bundles of flooring should be broken and kept in a heated space until their moisture content is that of your interior finish.

Strip flooring is normally laid crosswise to the floor joists; however, when laid over old strip flooring, it should be laid crosswise to the existing flooring. Nail sizes and types vary with the thickness of the flooring. For 25/32-inch flooring, use eightpenny flooring nails; use sixpenny flooring nails for 1/2-inch flooring; and use fourpenny casing nails for 3/8-inch flooring. Other nails, such as the ring-shank and screw-shank types, can be used, but it is always wise to check the flooring manufacturer's recommendations. Flooring brads with blunted points which prevent splitting of the tongue are also available.

Begin installing matched flooring by placing the first strip 1/2 to 5/8 inch away from the wall to allow for expansion along with changes in moisture content. Nail straight down through the board near the grooved edge. The nail should be close enough to the wall to be covered by the base or shoe molding; it should be driven into a joist when the flooring is laid crosswise to the joists. The tongue should also be nailed, with consecutive flooring boards nailed through it only. Nails are driven into the tongue at an angle of 45 degrees to 50 degrees and are not driven quite flush, to prevent damaging the edge by the hammer head. The nail is then set with the end of a large nail set or by laying the nail set flatwise against the flooring. Contractors use nailing devices designed especially for flooring. These drive and set the nail in one operation.

Select lengths of flooring boards so that butts will be well separated in adjacent courses. Drive each board tightly against the one previously installed. Crooked boards should be forced into alignment or cut off and used at the ends of a course or in closets.

The last course of flooring should be left 1/2 to 5/8 inch from the wall, just as the first course was. Face-nail it near the edge where the base or shoe will cover the nail.

Square-edged strip flooring must be installed over a substantial subfloor and can only be face-nailed. The installation procedures relative to spacing at walls, spacing of joints and general attachment are the same as those for matched flooring.

Most wood or wood-base tile is applied with an adhesive to a smooth base such as underlayment or finished concrete with a properly installed vapor barrier. Wood tile may be made up of a number of narrow slats held together by a membrane, cleats or tape to form a square; or, it may be plywood with tongued-and-grooved edges. To install wood tile, an adhesive is spread on the concrete slab or underlayment with a notched trowel and the tile laid in it. Follow the manufacturer's recommendation for adhesive and method of application.

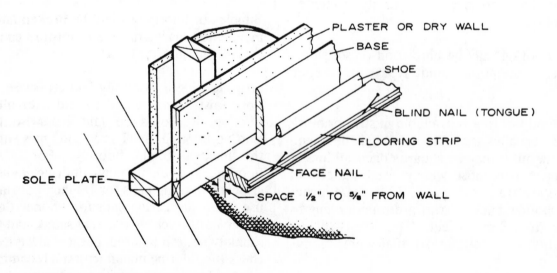

Figure 58--Installation of first strip of flooring.

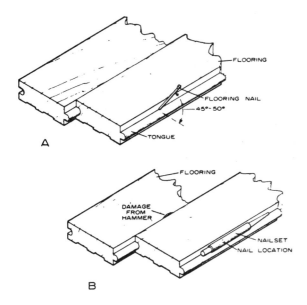

Figure 59--Nailing of flooring; A, angle of nailing; B, setting the nail without damage to the flooring.

Wood block flooring usually has tongues on two edges and grooves on the other two. It is usually nailed through the tongue into a wood subfloor. It may be applied on concrete with the use of an adhesive. The effects of shrinkage and swelling are minimized by changing the grain direction of alternate blocks.

Particleboard tile is installed in much the same manner as wood tile, except it should not be used over concrete. Manufacturer's instructions for installation are usually quite complete. This tile is usually 9-by-9-by-3/8 inches in size, with tongued-and-grooved edges. The back is often marked with small saw kerfs to stabilize the tile and provide better adhesion.

Sheet vinyl with resilient backing smooths out minor surface imperfections. Most vinyl will lay flat; so, no adhesive is required. Double-faced tape is used at joints and around the edge to keep the covering from moving. So that entire rooms can be covered without seams, most sheet vinyls are available in widths of 6, 9, 12 and 15 feet. This permits a fast, easy installa-

tion. The material is merely cut to room size using scissors and taped to the floor.

Seamless flooring consisting of resin chips combined with a urethane binder can be applied over any stable base, including old floor tile. This is applied as a liquid. Apply several coats, allowing each to dry before applying another. Complete application may take from 1/2 to 2 days, depending on the brand used. Manufacturer's instructions for application are quite complete. This floor covering is easily renewed by additional coatings; damaged spots are easily patched by adding more chips and binder.

Carpeting lends itself well to use in remodeling. It can cover a multitude of sins. It is easily installed over almost any flooring that is level, relatively smooth and free from major surface imperfections. Carpeting is now available for all rooms in the house, including the kitchen where close weaves are used so that spills stay on the surface and are easily wiped up. The cost of carpeting may be two or three times that of a finished wood floor; its life, however, is much shorter. On the other hand, some advantages of carpeting include less maintenance, sound absorption and resistance to impact.

Installation over underlayment - Both linoleum and resilient tile require a smooth surface -- either an underlayment or a concrete slab -- on which to be bonded with adhesive. Linoleum, unlike most resilient tiles, should not be laid on concrete slabs which are directly on the ground; such as, those found in basements.

Linoleum is available in a variety of thicknesses and grades and is usually in 6-foot-wide rolls. It is laid in accordance with manufacturer's directions, being rolled to ensure adhesion to the floor.

One of the lower cost resilient coverings is asphalt tile. Because most asphalt tile is damaged by grease and oil, it should not be a material of choice for kitchens. Asphalt tile is about 1/8-inch thick and either 9- or 12-by-12 inches in size. It is attached with adhesive which is applied with a notched trowel, according to the manufacturer's directions.

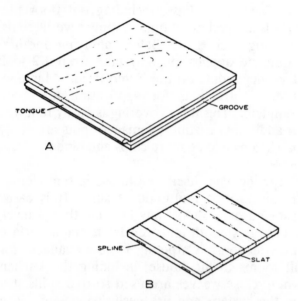

Figure 60--Two types of wood block flooring.

Other types of tile, such as vinyl, vinyl-asbestos, rubber and cork, are available in 9-by-9 or 12-by12 inch sizes, and even sometimes larger.

It is important that tile be laid in such a manner that its joints do not coincide with the joints of the underlayment. The manufacturer's directions usually include instructions on laying baselines near the center of the room and parallel to its length and width. The baselines are then used as a starting point in laying the tile.

18. SIDING

Solving your wood siding problems often involves corrective measures in other parts of your home. Failure of paint is frequently not the fault of the siding, but can be attributed to moisture moving out through the walls or to water washing down the face of the wall. Corrective measures are discussed under sections on "Vapor Barriers" and "Roof System." After adopting these corrective measures, siding may need only refinishing as discussed in the section on "Painting and Finishing."

Even some of the "permanent" sidings that require no painting may cause other serious problems. Moisture can be trapped in the wall, creating a decay hazard. It is imperative, therefore, that the siding you choose is one which allows water vapor to escape from inside the wall.

If new horizontal wood or nonwood siding is used, it is best to remove the old siding. Vertical board and panel-type siding may be successfully applied over the old.

The main difficulty in applying new siding over existing siding is in adjusting the window and door trim to compensate for the added wall thickness. The window sills on most houses extend far enough beyond the siding so that new siding should not affect them; however, the casing may be nearly flush with the siding and require some type of extension. One method of extending the casing is by adding an additional trim member over the existing casing. When this is done, a wider drip cap may also be required. The drip cap could be replaced, or it could be reused with blocking behind it to hold it out from the wall a distance equal to the new siding thickness.

Another method of extending the casing would be to add a trim member to the edge of the existing casing, perpendicular to the casing. A wider drip cap will also be required. Exterior door trim can be extended by the same technique used for the window trim.

Any of the conventional siding materials can be used for rehabilitation, but some may be better suited to this application than others. Panel-type siding is probably one of the simplest to install and one of the most versatile. It can be applied over most surfaces, helping to smooth out unevenness in the existing walls.

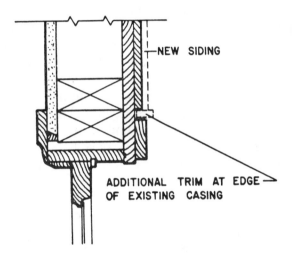

Figure 63--Top view of window casing extended for new siding by adding trim at the edge of existing casing.

PANEL SIDING

Panel-type siding is available in plywood, hardboard and particleboard, as well as numerous nonwood materials. The most popular of these are probably plywood and hardboard. Always specify exterior type for both; the hardboard must be tempered. The grade of plywood depends on the quality of finished surface desired.

Plywood panel siding is available in a variety of textures and patterns. Sheets are 4 feet wide and are often available in lengths of 8, 9 and 10 feet. Rough-textured plywood is particularly suited to finishing with water-repellent preservative stains. Smooth-surfaced plywood can be stained, but it will not absorb as much stain as rough-textured plywood. The finish, therefore, will not be as long lasting. Paper-overlaid plywood is particularly good for a paint finish. The paper overlay not only provides a very smooth surface, but also minimizes expansion and contraction due to moisture changes. Most textures can be purchased with vertical grooves. The most popular spacings of grooves are 2, 4 and 8 inches. Battens are often used with plain panels. They are nailed over each joint between panels and can be nailed over each stud to produce a board-and-batten effect.

In new construction, plywood applied directly over framing should be at least 3/8-inch thick for 16-inch stud spacing and 1/2-inch thick for 24-inch stud spacing. Grooved plywood is normally 5/8-inch thick with 3/8-by-1/4-inch-deep grooves.

For installation over existing siding or sheathing, thinner plywood can be used; however, most of the available sidings will be in the thicknesses listed above. Nail the plywood around the perimeter and at each intermediate stud, using galvanized or other rust-resistant nails spaced 7 to 8 inches apart. Use longer nails than those used for applying the siding directly to the studs.

Some plywood siding has shiplap joints. These should be treated with a water-repellent preservative and the siding nailed at each side of the joint. Square-edge butt joints between plywood panels should be caulked with a sealant, with the plywood nailed at each side of the joint. Where battens are used over the joint and at intermediate studs, nail them with eightpenny galvanized nails spaced 12 inches apart. Longer nails may be required where thick existing siding or sheathing must be penetrated.

Nominal 1-by-2-inch battens are commonly used.

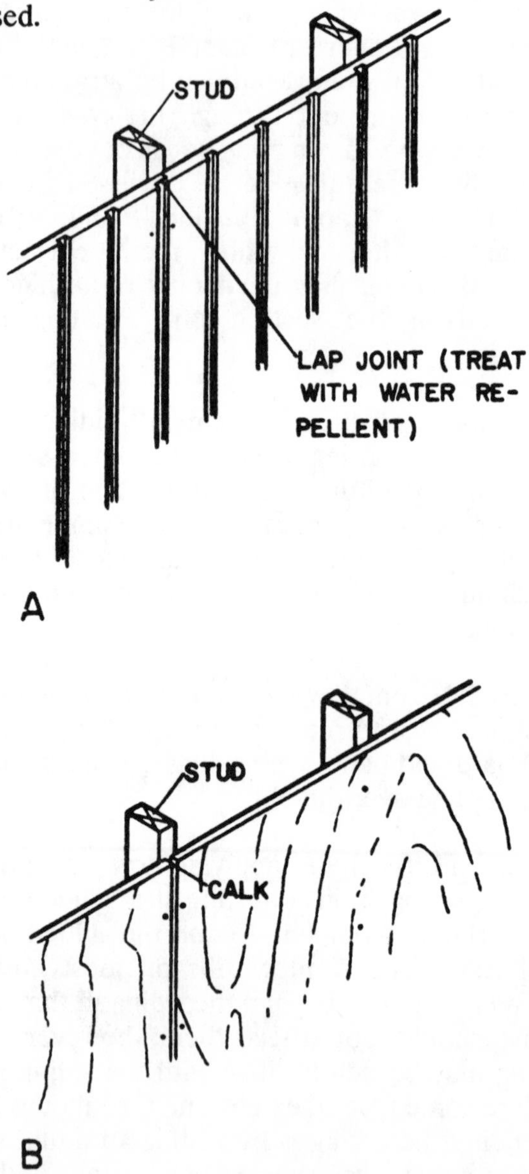

A

B

Figure 64--Joint of plywood panel siding: A, shiplap joint; B, square-edge joint.

If existing siding on gable ends is flush with the siding below the gable, some adjustment will be required in applying panel siding in order to have the new siding extend over the siding below. This is accomplished by using furring strips on the gable. The strips must be the same thickness as the new siding applied below. Nail a furring strip to each stud and apply the siding over the furring strips in the same manner as applying it directly to studs.

Plywood siding can be purchased with factory-applied coatings which are relatively maintenance free. While initial cost of these products is higher than uncoated plywood, savings in maintenance may compensate for this. Such coated siding is usually applied with special nails or other connectors in accordance with the manufacturer's instructions.

and finished coats of paint are applied after installation.

Corners are finished by butting the panel siding against corner boards as shown. Use a 1-1/8-by-1-1/8-inch corner board at interior corners and 1-1/8-inch-by 1-1/2- and 2-1/2-inch boards at outside corners. Apply caulking wherever siding butts against corner boards, window or door casings and trim boards at gable ends.

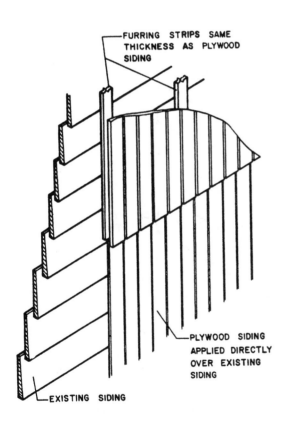

Figure 65--Application of plywood siding at gable end.

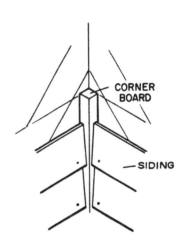

Figure 66--Corner bead for application of horizontal siding at interior corner.

HORIZONTAL WOOD SIDING

Bevel siding has been one of the most popular sidings for many years. It is available in 4- to 12-inch widths. The sawn face is exposed where a rough texture is desired and a stain finish is planned. The smooth face can be exposed for either paint or stain. Siding boards should have a minimum of 1-inch horizontal lap. In application, the exposed face should be adjusted so that the butt edges coincide with the bottom of the sill and the top of the drip cap of window frames.

Hardboard siding is also available in panels 4 feet wide and up to 16 feet long. It is usually 1/4-inch thick, but may be thicker when grooved. Hardboard, applied in the same manner as plywood, is usually factory-primed

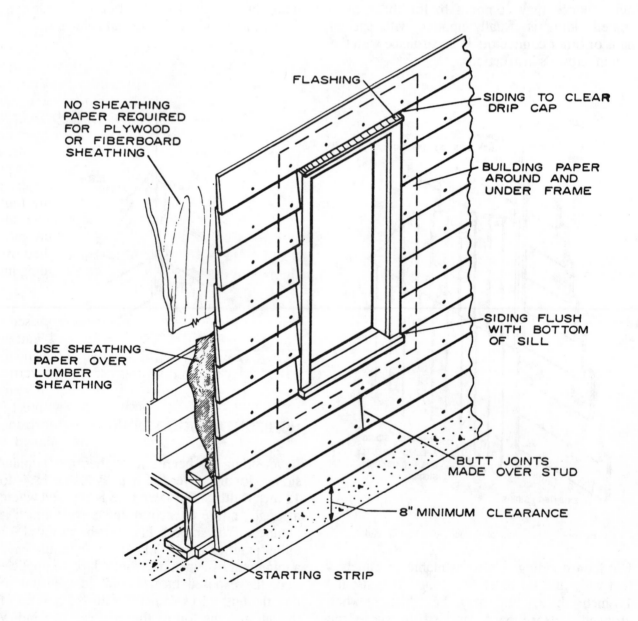

Figure 67--Single course application of shingle siding.

Horizontal siding must be applied over a smooth surface. If the old siding is left on, it should either be covered with panel sheathing or have furring strips nailed over each stud. Nail siding at each stud with a galvanized siding nail or other corrosion-resistant nail. Use sixpenny nails for siding less than 1/2-inch thick and eightpenny nails for thicker siding. Locate the nail to clear the top edge of the siding course below. Butt joints should be made over a stud. Interior corners are finished by butting the siding against a corner board 1-1/8 inches square or larger, depending on the thickness of the siding. Exterior corners can be mitered, butted against corner boards 1-1/8 inches or thicker and 1-1/2 and 2-1/2 inches wide or covered with metal corners.

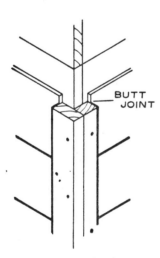

Figure 68--Corner boards for application of horizontal siding at exterior corner.

Strips of plywood or hardboard can be applied horizontally. In this application, the strips are lapped just as bevel siding, but a starting strip is required at the base and a shingle wedge is required at each vertical joint. The starting strip should be the same thickness as the siding. Nail the siding at each vertical joint in the same manner as bevel siding. Some manufacturers supply special clips for applying the siding. When these are used, follow the instructions provided.

VERTICAL WOOD SIDING

Vertical siding is available in a variety of patterns. Probably the most popular is matched (tongued-and-grooved) boards. Vertical siding can be nailed to 1-inch sheathing boards or to 5/8- and 3/4-inch plywood. Furring strips must be used over thinner plywood because the plywood itself will not have sufficient nail-holding capacity. When the existing sheathing is thinner than 5/8-inch, apply 1-by-4-inch nailers horizontally, spaced 16 to 24 inches apart vertically. Then, nail the vertical siding to the nailers. Blind-nail through the tongue at each nailer with galvanized sevenpenny finish nails. When boards are 6 inches or wider, also face-nail at midwidth with an eightpenny galvanized nail. Vertical siding can be applied over existing siding by nailing through the siding into the sheathing.

Another popular vertical siding is comprised of various combinations of boards and battens. The "board" consists of a wide vertical board, and the "batten" consists of a narrow vertical board that covers the seam between each board; providing vertical shadowlines. It also must be nailed to a thick sheathing or to horizontal nailers. The first board or batten should be nailed with one galvanized eightpenny nail at center or, for wide boards, two nailers spaced 1 inch each side of center. Close spacing is important to prevent splitting if the boards shrink. The top board or batten is then nailed with twelvepenny nails, being careful to miss the underboard and nail only through the space between adjacent boards. Use only corrosion-resistant nails. Galvanized nails are not recommended for some materials; so, be sure to follow the siding manufacturer's instructions.

WOOD SHINGLE AND SHAKE SIDING

Some architectural styles may be well suited to the use of shakes or shingles for siding. They give a rustic appearance and can be left unfinished, if desired, to weather naturally. They may be applied in single or double courses over wood or plywood sheathing. Where shingles are applied over existing siding which is uneven or over nonwood sheathing, use 1-by-3 or 1-by-4-inch wood nailing strips applied horizontally as a base for the shingles. Spacing of the nailing strips will depend on the length and exposure of the shingles. Apply the shingles with about 1/8- to 1/4-inch space between adjacent shingles to allow for expansion during rainy weather.

siding application. Second-grade shingles can be used because only one-half or less of the butt portion is exposed.

The double-course method of laying shingles consists of applying an undercourse and nailing a top course directly over it with a 1/4- to 1/2-inch projection of the butt over the lower course shingle. With this system, less lap is used between courses. The undercourse shingles can be of lower quality; such as, third grade or the undercourse grade. The top course should be first grade because of the shingle length exposed.

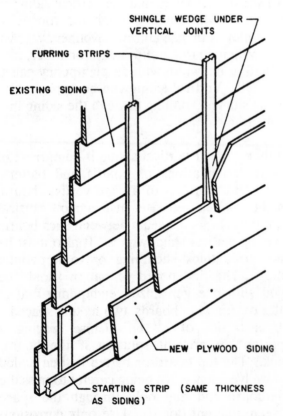

Figure 69--Application of plywood as lap siding.

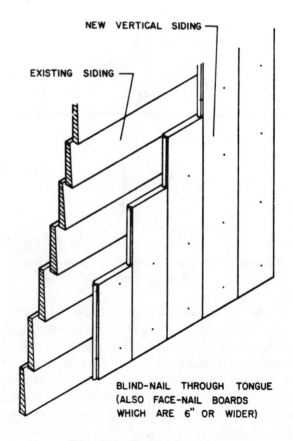

Figure 70--Application of vertical siding.

The single-course method consists of simply laying one course over the other similar to lap

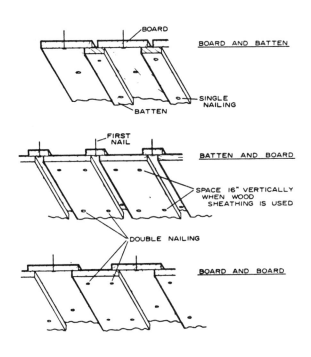

Figure 71--Application of vertical wood siding.

Regardless of the method of applying the shingles, all joints must be broken so that the vertical butt joints of the upper shingles are at least 1-1/2 inches from the undershingle joint.

Use rust-resistant nails for all shingle applications. Shingles up to 8 inches wide should be nailed with two nails. Wider shingles should be secured with three nails. Threepenny or fourpenny zinc-coated "shingle" nails are commonly used in shingle-coursing. Zinc-coated nails with small flat heads are commonly used for double coursing where nails are exposed. Use fivepenny nails for the top course and threepenny or fourpenny for the undercourse. When plywood sheathing less than 3/4-inch thick is used, threaded nails are required to obtain sufficient holding power. Nails should

be 3/4-inch from the edge. They should be 1 inch above the horizontal butt line of the next higher course in the single-course application and 2 inches above the bottom of the shingle or shake in the double-course application.

MASONRY VENEER

Where brick or stone veneer is used as siding, mortar may become loose and crumble or uneven settlement may cause cracks. In either case, new mortar should be applied both to keep out moisture and to improve appearance. Repair is accomplished in much the same manner as for masonry foundations, except that more attention to appearance is required. After removing all loose mortar and brushing the joint to remove dust and loose particles, dampen the surface. Then apply mortar and tamp it well into the joint for a good bond. Pointing of joints should conform to existing joints. Particular care should be exercised in keeping mortar off the face of the brick or stone unless the veneer is to be painted.

Brick or stone veneer should be cleaned gently --with soft bristled brushes and water under low pressure. When a chemical cleaner is required, the services of a professional masonry cleaner are recommended.

NON-WOOD SIDING

Nonwood sidings, such as aluminum, steel or vinyl, are available in a variety of styles and colors. They are often applied by contractors who specialize in one of these products. The manufacturer's literature usually gives complete instructions for application and maintenance. If you are doing your own work, follow these instructions closely.

19. ROOF SYSTEM

The first steps in repairing a roof system are to level sagging ridge poles and to straighten sagging rafters. Then, the new roof covering can be applied to a smooth, flat surface.

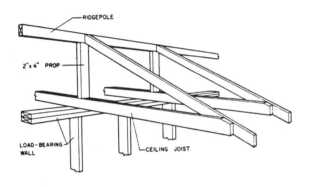

Figure 72--Prop to hold sagging ridgepole in level position.

FRAMING

The sagging ridgepole can sometimes be leveled by jacking it at points between supports and installing props to hold it in a level position. When this is done, the jack must be located where the load can be traced down through the structure so that the ultimate bearing is directly on the foundation. Where there is no conveniently located bearing partition, install a beam under the ridge and transfer load to bearing points. After the ridge pole is jacked to a level position, cut a 2-by-4 just long enough to fit between the ceiling joist and ridgepole or beam; nail it at both ends. For a short ridgepole, one prop may be sufficient. Additional props should be added as needed. In some repairs the addition of collar beams may be sufficient without requiring props. Where rafters are sagging, nail a new rafter to the side of the old one after forcing the new rafter ends into their proper position. Permanent set in the old rafters cannot be removed.

SHEATHING

Sheathing may have sagged between rafters, resulting in a wavy roof surface. Where this condition exists, new sheathing is required. Often the sheathing can be nailed right over the old roofing. This prevents your having to remove and dispose of the old roofing. Wood shingles which show any indication of decay should be completely removed before new sheathing is applied. Where wood shingles are excessively cupped or otherwise warped, they should also be removed. Wood shingle and slate roofs of older houses were often installed on furring strips rather than on solid sheathing.

Sheathing nailed over existing sheathing must be secured with longer nails than would normally be used. Nails should penetrate the framing 1-1/4 to 1-1/2 inches. Nail edges of plywood sheathing at 6-inch spacing and to intermediate framing members at 12-inch spacing. Apply the plywood with the length perpendicular to the rafters. For built-up roofs, if the plywood does not have tongued-and-grooved edges, use clips at unsupported edges. Clips are commercially available and should be installed in accordance with the manufacturer's instructions. For 16-inch rafter spacing, 3/8-inch plywood is the minimum thickness to be used; 1/2-inch-thick plywood is preferable.

ADDING ROOF OVERHANG

As mentioned previously the addition of a roof overhang, where there is none, will soon pay for itself in reduced maintenance on siding and exterior trim. Without the overhang, water washes down the face of the wall, creating moisture problems in the siding and trim and, consequently, more frequent painting is required. Additional roof overhang also does much to improve the appearance of the house.

Where new sheathing is being added, the sheathing can be extended beyond the edge of the existing roof to provide some overhang. This is a minimum solution and the extension should not be more than 12 inches where 1/2-inch plywood sheathing is used. Any greater extension would require some type of framing.

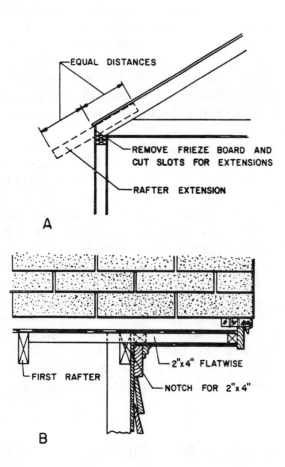

Figure 73--Extension of roof overhang; A, rafter extension at eaves; B, extension at gable end.

Framing can usually be extended at the eave by adding to each rafter. First, remove the frieze board, or, in the case of a closed cornice, remove the fascia. Nail a 2-by-4 to the side of each rafter, letting it extend beyond the wall the amount of the desired overhang. The 2-by-4 should extend inside the wall a distance equal to the overhang. Framing for an overhang at

the gable ends can be accomplished by adding a box frame. Extensions of the ridge beam and eave fascia are required to support this boxed framing. An alternate extension is possible with a plank placed flat, cut into gable framing, extending back to the first rafter.

ROOF COVERINGS

A wide variety of roof coverings is available, and most can be used in rehabilitation in the same manner as for new construction. Sometimes there are local code requirements for fire safety.

Cost usually influences your choice. In most houses the roof is a major design element and the covering material must fit the house design. Heavy materials such as tile or slate should not be used unless they replace the same material or unless the roof framing is strengthened to support the additional load. The most popular covering materials for pitched roofs are wood, asphalt and asbestos shingles. As previously discussed, these can be applied directly over old shingles or over sheathing; however, if two layers of shingles exist from previous reroofing, it may be well to remove the old roofing before proceeding. Roll roofing is sometimes used for particularly low-cost applications or over porches with relatively low-pitched roofs. The most common covering for flat or low-pitched roofs is a built-up roof with a gravel topping.

An underlay of 15- or 30-pound asphalt-saturated felt should be used in moderate and low-sloped roofs covered with asphalt, asbestos shingles, slate shingles or tile roofing. It is not commonly used under wood shingles or shakes. A 45-pound or heavier smooth-surface roll roofing should be used as a flashing along the eave line in areas where moderate to severe snowfalls occur.

The flashing should extend to a point 36 inches inside the warm wall. If two strips are required, use mastic to seal the joint. Also use mastic to seal end joints. This flashing gives protection from ice dams which are formed when melting snow runs down the roof and freezes at the colder cornice area. The ice gradually forms a dam that backs up water under the shingles. The wide flashing at the eave will minimize the chances of this water entering the ceiling or the wall. Good attic ventilation and sufficient ceiling insulation are also important in eliminating ice dams. This will be described more in detail under "Ventilation". Roll roofing 36 inches wide is also required at all valleys.

Where shingle application is over old wood or asphalt shingles, industry recommendations include certain preparations. First, remove about 6-inch-wide strips of old shingles along the eaves and gables, and apply nominal 1-inch boards at these locations. Thinner boards may be necessary where application is over old asphalt shingles. Remove the old covering from ridges or hips and replace it with bevel siding, butt edge up. Place a strip of lumber over each valley to separate old metal flashing from new. Double the first shingle course.

Wood shingles - Wood shingles used for house roofs should be No. 1 grade which are all heartwood, all edge grain and tapered. Principal species used commercially are western red cedar and redwood, which have heartwood with high decay resistance and low shrinkage. Widths of shingles vary, and the narrower shingles are most often found in the lower grades. Recommended exposures for common shingle sizes are shown below.

The general rules for applying wood shingles are:

1. Extend shingles 1-1/2 to 2 inches beyond the eave line and about 3/4-inch beyond the rake (gable) edge.

2. Nail each shingle with two rust-resistant nails spaced about 3/4-inch from the edge and 1-1/2 inches above the butt line of the next course. Use threepenny nails for 16- and 18-inch shingles and fourpenny nails for 24-inch shingles.

   Where shingles are applied over old wood shingles, use longer nails to penetrate through the old roofing and into the sheathing. A threaded ring-shank nail is recommended where the plywood roof sheathing is less than 1/2-inch thick.

3. Allow a 1/8- to 1/4-inch space between each shingle for expansion when wet. Lap vertical joints at least 1-1/2 inches by the shingles in the course above. Space the joints in succeeding courses so that the joint in one course is not in line with the joint in the second course above it.

4. Shingle away from valleys, selecting and precutting wide valley shingles. The valley should be 4 inches wide at the top and should increase in width at the rate of 1/8-inch per foot from the top. Use valley flashing with a standing seam. Do not nail through the metal.

   Valley flashing should be a minimum of 24 inches wide for roof slopes under 4-in-12; 18 inches wide for roof slopes of 4-in-12 to 7-in-12; and 12 inches wide for roof slopes of 7-in-12 and over.

5. Place a metal edging along the gable end of the roof to aid in guiding the water away from the endwalls.

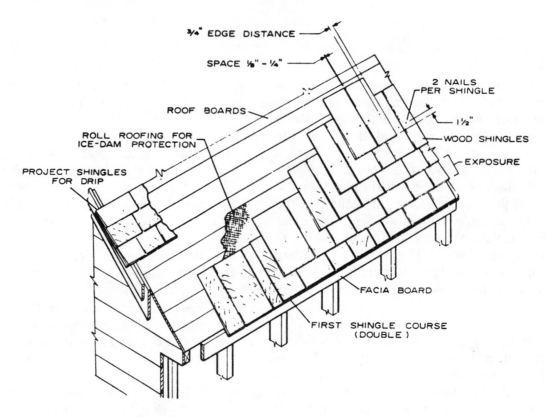

Figure 74--Application of wood-shingle roofing over boards.

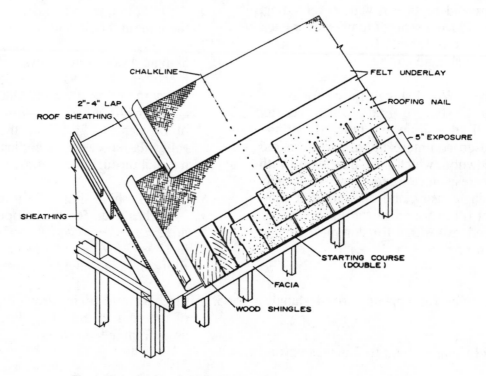

Figure 75--Application of asphalt shingle roofing over plywood with strip shingles.

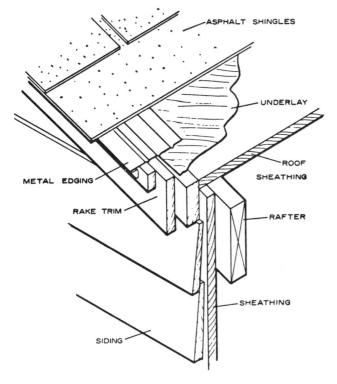

Figure 76--Application of metal edging at gable end.

weather. Bundles should be piled flat so that strips will not curl when the bundles are opened for use. An underlayment of 15-pound saturated felt is often used.

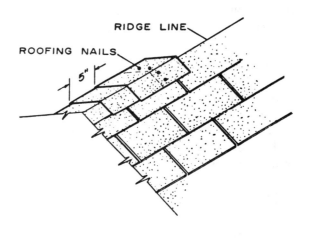

Figure 77--Boston ridge using asphalt shingles.

Wood shakes - Apply wood shakes in much the same manner as shingles, except longer nails must be used because the shakes are thicker. Shakes have a greater exposure than shingles because of their length. Exposure distances are 8 inches for 18-inch shakes, 10 inches for 24-inch shakes and 13 inches for 32-inch shakes. Butts are often laid unevenly to create a rustic appearance. An 18-inch-wide underlay of 30-pound asphalt felt should be used between each course to prevent wind-driven snow from entering between the rough faces of the shakes. Position the underlay above the butt edge of the shakes a distance equal to double the weather exposure. Where exposure distance is less than one-third the total length, underlay is not usually required.

Asphalt shingles - The most common type of asphalt shingle is the square-butt strip shingle, which is 12-by-36 inches, has three tabs and is usually laid with 5 inches exposed to the

Begin application of the roofing by first applying a wood-shingle course or a metal edging along the eave line. The first course of asphalt shingles is doubled and extended downward beyond the wood shingles (or edging) about 1/2-inch to prevent the water from backing up under the shingles. A 1/2-inch projection should also be used at the rake. Make several chalklines on the underlayment parallel to the roof slope to serve as guides in aligning the shingles so that the tabs are in a straight line. Follow the manufacturer's directions in securing the shingles. Nailing each 12-by-36-inch strip with six 1-inch galvanized roofing nails is prudent in areas of high winds. Seal-tab or lack shingles should be used in these areas. When a nail penetrates a crack or knothole, remove the nail, seal the hole, and replace the nail in sound wood. If the nail is not in sound wood, it will gradually work out and cause a bump in the shingle above it.

Built-up roof - Built-up roof coverings are limited to flat or low-pitched roofs and are installed by contractors who specialize in this work. The roof consists of three, four or five layers of roofers' felt, with each layer mopped down with tar or asphalt. The final surface is then coated with asphalt, which is usually covered with gravel embedded in asphalt or tar.

Other roof coverings - Other roof coverings, such as asbestos, slate, tile and metal, require specialized applicators. For this reason, their application is not described in detail. They are generally more expensive and are much less widely used than wood or asphalt shingles and built-up roofs.

RIDGE

The Boston ridge is the most common method of treating the roof ridge and is also applicable to hips. Where asphalt shingles are used, cut the 12-by-36-inch strips into 12-by-12-inch sections. Bend them slightly and use in a lap fashion over the ridge with a 5-inch exposure distance. Locate nails where they will be covered by the lap of the next section. A small spot of asphalt cement under each exposed edge will give a positive seal.

Wood-shingle roofs can also be finished with a Boston ridge. Flashing should first be placed over the ridge. Six-inch-wide shingles are alternately lapped, fitted and blind-nailed. Exposed shingle edges are alternately lapped.

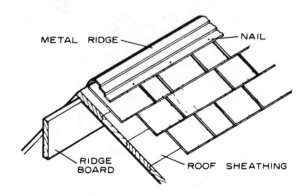

Figure 79--Metal ridge roll.

A metal ridge roll can also be used on asphalt-shingle or wood-shingle roofs. This ridge of copper, galvanized iron or aluminum is formed to the roof slope.

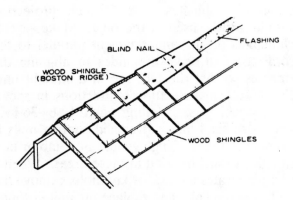

Figure 78--Boston ridge using wood shingles.

20. OPENINGS

WINDOWS

Windows may need repair, replacement or relocation. Until recent years, windows were not generally treated with a preservative; so, moisture may have gotten into some joints, resulting in decay. Also, older windows may allow more air infiltration than newer types. It will often be desirable to replace the windows. This is not difficult where the same size window can be used; however, where the window size is no longer produced, replacement of the window will also mean reframing. An alternative to explore is the addition of storm windows. Even if custom-made, the cost of storm windows may be significantly lower than that of reframing and replacing all windows.

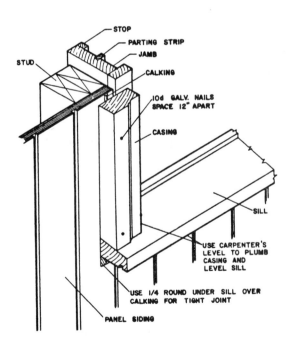

Figure 80–Installation of double-hung window frame.

If the decision is made to replace your windows, the sequence of window replacement will depend on the type of siding used. Where new panel siding is being applied, the window is installed after the siding. Where horizontal siding is used, the window must be installed before the siding.

REPAIR OF EXISTING WINDOWS

Where the wood in windows is showing some signs of deterioration, but the window is still in good operating condition, a water-repellent preservative may arrest further decay. First, remove existing paint. Then, brush on the preservative, let it dry and repaint the window. Paint cannot be used over some preservatives; so, make sure a paintable preservative is used.

A double-hung sash may bind against the stops, jambs or parting strip. Before doing any repair, try waxing the parts coming into contact. If this does not eliminate the problem, try to determine where the sash is binding. Excessive paint buildup is a common cause of sticking and can be corrected by removing paint from stops and parting strips. Nailed stops can be moved slightly away from the sash. If stops are fastened by screws, it will probably be easier to remove them and plane them lightly on the face contacting the sash. Loosening the contact between sash and stop too much will result in excessive air infiltration at the window. If the sash is binding against the jamb, remove the sash and plane the vertical edges slightly.

It may be desirable to add full-width weatherstripping and spring balance units to provide a good airtight window that will not bind. These are easily installed, requiring only removal of the parting strip and stops. Install the units in accordance with the manufacturer's instructions and replace the stops.

REPLACEMENT OF EXISTING WINDOWS

If windows require extensive repairs, it will probably be more economical to replace them. New windows are usually purchased as a complete unit, including sash, frame and exterior trim. These are easily installed where a window of the same size and type is removed. Many older houses have tall, narrow windows of sizes that are no longer commercially produced. In some cases it may be desirable to change the size or type of your windows. Most window manufacturers list rough-opening sizes for each of their windows. Some general rules for rough-opening sizes are:

A. **Double-hung window (single unit)**
Rough opening width = glass width plus 6 inches
Rough opening height = total glass height plus 10 inches

B. **Casement window (two sash)**
Rough opening width = total glass width plus 11-1/4 inches
Rough opening height = total glass height plus 6-3/8 inches

After the existing window is removed, take off the interior wall covering to the rough opening width for the new window. If a larger window must be centered in the same location as the old one, half the necessary additional width must be cut from each side; otherwise, the entire additional width may be cut from one side.

For windows 3-1/2 feet or less in width, no temporary support of ceiling and roof should be required. Where windows more than 3-1/2 feet wide are to be installed, provide some temporary support for the ceiling and roof before removing existing framing in bearing walls. Remove framing to the width of the new window and frame the window. The header must be supported at both ends by cripple studs. Headers are made up of two 2-inch-thick members, usually spaced with lath or wood strips to produce the same width as the 2-by-4 stud space.

For wider openings, independent design may be necessary. Do not oversize headers on the theory that, if a little is good, more is better. Cross-grain shrinkage causes distortion and should be kept to a minimum.

Cut the sheathing, or panel siding used without sheathing, to the size of the rough opening. If bevel siding is used, it must be cut to the size of the window trim so that it will butt against the window casing. Determine the place to cut the siding by inserting the preassembled window frame in the rough opening and marking the siding around the outside edge of the casing.

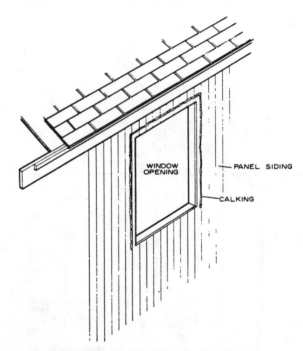

Figure 81--Caulk around window before installing frame.

Before installing the window frame in the rough opening, precautions must be taken to ensure that water and wind do not come in around the finished window. Where panel siding is used, place a ribbon of caulking sealant (rubber or similar base) over the siding at the location of the side and head casing. Where horizontal siding is used over sheathing, loosen the siding around the opening and slide strips of 15-pound asphalt felt between the sheathing and siding around the opening.

Place the frame in the rough opening, preferably with the sash in place to keep it square, and level the sill with a carpenter's level. If necessary, use shims under the sill on the inside. Make sure the side casing and jamb are level and square; then, nail the frame in place with tenpenny galvanized nails. Nail through the casing into the side studs and header, spacing the nails about 12 inches apart. When double-hung windows are used, slide the sash up and down while nailing the frame to be sure that the sash works freely. For installation over panel siding, place a ribbon of caulking sealer at the junction of the siding and the sill. Install a small molding; such as, a quarter-round over the caulking.

RELOCATION OF WINDOWS

It may be desirable to move a window to a different location or to eliminate a window and add a new one at another location. The method for installing a window was described in the preceding section. Where a window is removed, close the opening as follows. Add 2-by-4 vertical framing members spaced no more than 16 inches apart. Keep framing in line with existing studs under the window or in sequence with wall studs so that covering materials can be nailed to them easily. Toenail new framing to the old window header and to the sill using three eightpenny or tenpenny nails at each joint. Install sheathing of the same thickness as that existing, add insulation and apply a vapor barrier on the inside face of the framing. Make sure the vapor barrier covers the rough framing of the existing window and overlaps any vapor barrier in the remainder of the wall. Insulation and vapor barriers are discussed more fully in separate sections. Apply interior and exterior wall covering to match the existing coverings on the house.

STORM WINDOWS

In cold climates, storm windows are necessary for comfort, for economy of heating and to avoid damage from excessive condensation on the inside face of the window. If old windows are not of standard sizes, storm windows must be made by building a frame to fit the existing window and fitting glass to the frame. Storm windows are commercially available to fit all standard size windows. One of the most practical types is the self-storing or combination storm and screen. These have minor adjustments for width and height, and can be custom fabricated for odd-size windows at moderate cost.

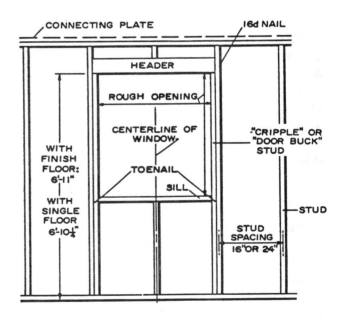

Figure 82--Framing at window opening and height of window and door headers.

21. DOORS

Doors in houses of all ages frequently cause problems by sticking and by failure to latch. To remedy the sticking door, first determine where it is sticking. If the frame is not critically out of square, some minor adjustments may remedy the situation. The top of the door could be planed without removing the door. If the side of the door is sticking near the top or bottom, the excess width can also be planed without removing the door; however, the edge will have to be refinished or repainted. If the side of the door sticks near the latch or over the entire height of the door, remove the hinges and plane the hinge edge. Then, additional routing is required before the hinges are replaced. Where the door is binding on the hinge edge, the hinges may be routed too deeply. This can be corrected by loosening the hinge leaf and adding a filler under it to bring it out slightly.

If the latch does not close, remove the strike plate and shim it out slightly. Replace the strike plate by first placing a filler, such as a match-stick, in the screw hole and reinserting the screw so that the strike plate is relocated slightly away from the stop.

EXTERIOR DOORS

If exterior doors are badly weathered, it may be desirable to replace them rather than to attempt a repair. Doors can be purchased separately or with frames, including exterior side and head casing with jamb and sill. Exterior doors should be either panel or solid-core flush. Several styles are available, most of them featuring some type of glazing. Hollow-core flush doors should be limited to interior use, except in warm climates, because they warp excessively during the heating season when used as exterior doors. The standard height for exterior doors is 6 feet 8 inches; standard thickness, 1-3/4 inches. The main door should be 3 feet wide; the service or rear door, at least 2 feet 6 inches, preferably 3 feet wide.

Where rough framing is required either for a new door location or because old framing is not square, provide header and cripple studs. Rough opening height should be the height of the door, plus 2-1/4 inches above the finished floor; the width should be the width of the door, plus 2-1/2 inches. Use doubled 2-by-6s for headers and fasten them in place with two six-teenpenny nails through the stud into each member. If the stud space on each side of the door is not accessible, toenail the header to the studs. Nail cripple (door buck) studs, supporting the header on each side of the opening, to the full stud with twelvepenny nails spaced about 16 inches apart and staggered.

After sheathing or panel siding is placed over the framing, leaving only the rough opening, the door frame can be installed. Apply a ribbon of caulking sealer on each side and above the opening where the casing will fit. Place the door frame in the opening and secure it by nailing through the side and head casing. Nail the hinge side first. In a new installation the floor joists and header must be trimmed to receive the sill before the frame can be installed. The top of the sill should be the same height as the finish floor so that the threshold can be installed over the joint. Shim the sill when necessary so that it will have full bearing on the floor framing. When joists are parallel to the sill, headers and a short support member are necessary at the edge of the sill. Use a quarter-round molding in combination with caulking under the door sill when a panel siding or other single exterior covering is used. Install the threshold over the junction with the finish floor by nailing it to the floor and sill with finishing nails.

Exterior doors are usually purchased with an entry lock set which is easily installed. Any trimming to reduce the width of the door is done on the hinge edge. Hinges are routed or mortised into the edge of the door with about 3/16- or 1/4-inch back spacing.

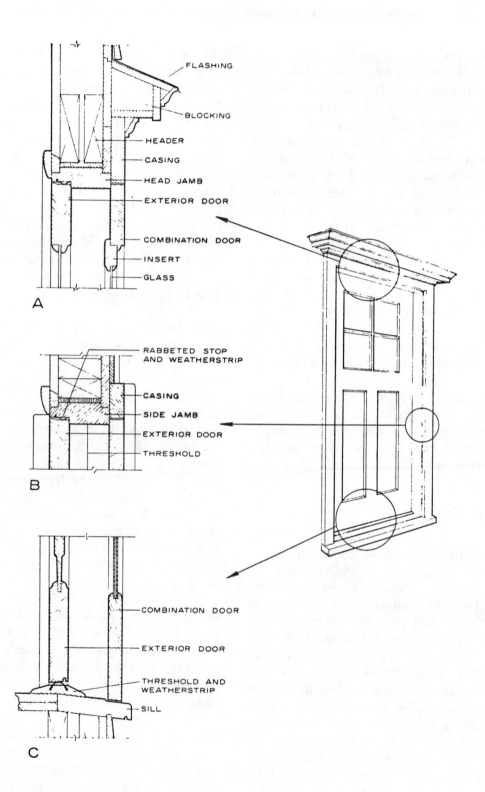

Figure 83--Exterior Door and frame. Exterior door and combination-door (screen and storm) cross sections: A, head jamb; B, side jamb; C, sill.

In-swinging exterior doors require 3-1/2-by-3-1/2-inch loose-pin hinges. Nonremovable pins are used on out-swinging doors. Use three hinges to minimize warping. Bevel edges slightly toward the side that will fit against stops. Carefully measure the opening width and plane the edge for the proper side clearances. Next, square and trim the top of the door for proper fit; then, saw off the bottom for the proper floor clearance. All edges should then be sealed to minimize entrance of moisture.

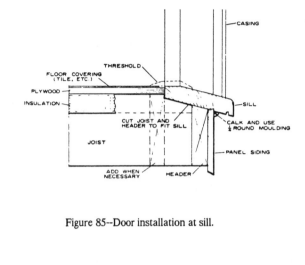

Figure 85--Door installation at sill.

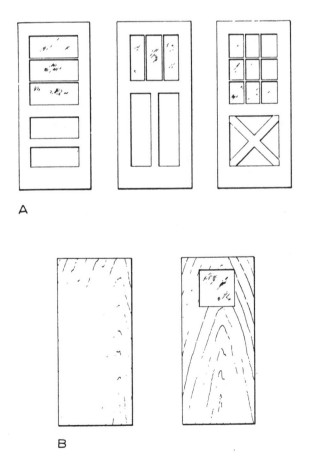

Figure 84--Exterior doors: A, panel type, B, flush type.

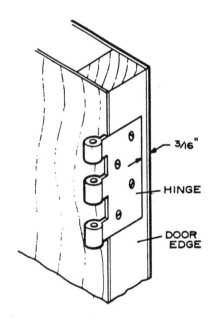

Figure 86--Installation of door hinges.

In cold climates, weatherstrip all exterior doors. Check weatherstripping on old doors, and replace it where there is indication of wear. Also consider adding storm doors. They will not only save on heat, but also protect the surface of the exterior door from weather, thereby reducing the likelihood of warping.

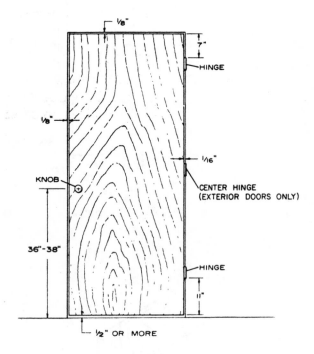

Figure 87--Door clearances

Rough framing width is 2-1/2 inches, plus the door width; height is 2 inches, plus the door height above the finished floor. The head jamb and two side jambs are the same width as the overall wall thickness when wood casing is used. When metal casing is used with drywall, the jamb width is the same as the stud depth. Jambs are often purchased in precut sets and can even be purchased complete with stops and with the door prehung in the frame. Jambs can also easily be made in a small shop with a table or radial-arm saw.

The prehung door is by far the simplest to install and is usually the most economical because of the labor savings. Even where the door and jambs are purchased separately, the installation is simplified by prehanging the door in the frame at the building site. The door then serves as a jig to set the frame in place quite easily. Before installing the door, temporarily put in place the narrow wood strips used as stops. Stops are usually 7/16-inch thick and may be 1-1/2 to 2-1/4 inches wide. Install them with a mitered joint at the junction of the head and side jambs. A 45-degree bevel cut 1 to 1-1/2 inches above the finish floor will eliminate a dirt pocket and make cleaning easier. This is called a sanitary stop.

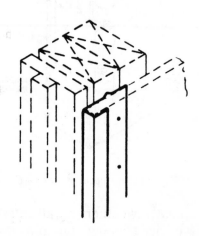

Figure 88--Metal casing used with drywall.

INTERIOR DOORS

If a new interior door is added or the framing is replaced, the opening should be rough framed in a manner similar to that for exterior doors.

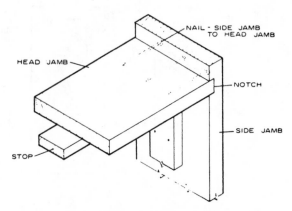

Figure 89--Door jamb assembly.

Fit the door to the frame, using the clearances shown here. Bevel edges slightly toward the side that will fit against the stops. Route or mortise the hinges into the edge of the door with about a 3/16- or 1/4-inch back spacing. Make adjustments, if necessary, to provide sufficient edge distance so that screws have good penetration in the wood. For interior doors, use two 3-by-3-inch loose-pin hinges. If a router is not available, mark the hinge outline and depth of cut; remove the wood with a wood chisel. The surface of the hinge should be flush with the wood surface. After attaching the hinge to the door with screws, place the door in the opening, block it for proper clearances and mark the location of door hinges on the jamb. Remove the door and route the jamb to the thickness of the hinge half. Install the hinge halves on the jamb, place the door in the opening and insert the pins.

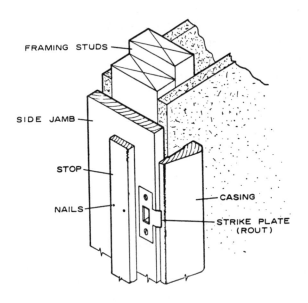

Figure 91–Installation of door strike plate.

Lock sets are classified as:

(a)   Entry lock sets (decorative, keyed locks)

(b)   Privacy lock sets (inside lock controls with a safety slot for opening from the outside)

(c)   Keyed lock sets

(d)   latch sets (without locks).

The lock set is usually purchased with, and may even be installed with, the door. If not installed, directions are provided, including paper templates which provide for the exact location of holes. After the latch is installed, mark the location of the latch on the jamb when the door is in a near-closed position. Mark the outline of the strike plate for this position and route the jamb so the strike plate will be flush with the face of the jamb.

The stops which were temporarily nailed in place can now be permanently installed. Nail the stop on the lock side first, setting it against

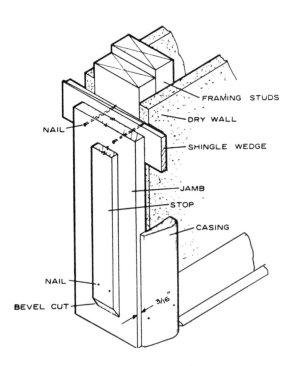

Figure 90–Installation of door trim.

the door face when the door is latched. Nail the stops with finishing nails or brads 1-1/2 inches long and spaced in pairs about 16 inches apart. The stop at the hinge side of the door should allow a clearance of 1/32-inch.

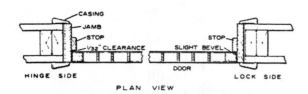

Figure 92--Door stop clearances (plan view).

To install a new door frame, place the frame in the opening and plumb and fasten the hinge side of the frame first. Use shingle wedges between the side jamb and the rough door buck to plumb the jamb. Place wedge sets at hinge and latch locations, plus intermediate locations along the height, and nail the jamb with pairs of eightpenny nails at each wedge area. Continue installation by fastening the opposite jamb in the same manner. After the door jambs are installed, cut off the shingle wedges flush with the wall.

Casing is the trim around the door opening. Shapes are available in thicknesses from 1/2- to 3/4-inch and widths varying from 2-1/4 to 3-1/2 inches. A number of styles are available. Metal casing used at the edge of drywall eliminates the need for wood casing.

Position the casing with about a 3/16-inch edge distance from the face of the jamb. Nail it with sixpenny or sevenpenny casing or finishing nails, depending on the thickness of the casing. Casing with one thin edge should be nailed with 1-1/2-inch brads along the edge. Space nails in pairs about 16 inches apart. Casings with molded forms must have a mitered joint where the head and side casings join, but rectangular casings are butt-joined.

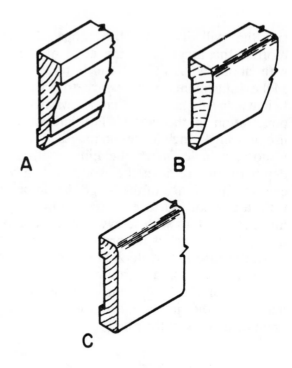

Figure 93--Styles of door casings: A, colonial; B, ranch; C, plain.

Metal casing can be installed by either of two methods. In one method, the casing is nailed to the door buck around the opening; then, the dry wall is inserted into the groove and nailed to the studs in the usual fashion.

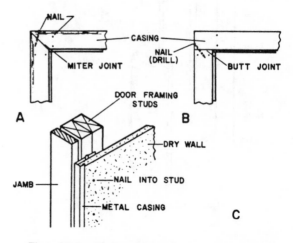

Figure 94--Installation of door trim: A, molded casing; B, rectangular casing; C, metal casing.

The other method consists of first fitting the casing over the edge of the dry wall, positioning the sheet properly and then nailing through the dry wall and casing into the stud behind. Use the same type of nails and spacing as for dry wall alone.

Interior doors are either panel or flush type. Flush doors are usually hollow core. Moldings are sometimes included on one or both faces. Such moldings can also be applied to existing doors where added decoration is desired. The panel-type doors are available in a variety of patterns. Two popular patterns are the five-cross-panel and the colonial.

Standard door height is 6 feet 8 inches; however, a height of 6 feet 6 inches is sometimes used with low ceilings, such as in the upstairs of a story-and-a-half house or in a basement. Door widths vary, depending on use and personal taste; however, minimums may be governed by building regulations. Usual widths are: (a) Bedrooms and other rooms, 2 feet 6 inches; (b) bathrooms, 2 feet 4 inches; (c) small closets and linen closets, 2 feet.

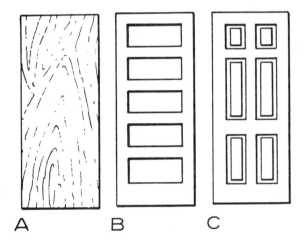

Figure 95--Interior doors: A, flush; B, five-cross panel; C, colonial panel type.

22. INSULATION AND MOISTURE CONTROL

Insulation

The importance of insulation depends upon the climate. Ceiling insulation is beneficial in most climates, although not essential in extremely mild climates where there are neither hot nor cold extremes. Wall insulation is not as essential as ceiling insulation, but it is required for comfort in cold climates and will pay for itself in heat savings. Floor insulation is also necessary for comfort in the crawl-space house located in a cold climate.

When planning to insulate, consider all major causes of heat loss. Heat loss per unit area through windows and exterior doors is much greater than through most wall materials. Another major heat loss is from air infiltration around doors and windows. Storm doors and storm windows will reduce air infiltration and will reduce heat transfers by 50 per cent or more through the exposed surface. Weather-stripping around doors and windows may result in another major heat savings.

Regardless of type and location of insulation, vapor barriers are required on the warm side of the insulation.

CEILING INSULATION

Most houses have an accessible attic with exposed ceiling framing so that any type of insulation can easily be applied. If batt or blanket type is used, get the width that will conform to joist spacing -- usually 16 or 24 inches. Loose-fill insulation could also be used by simply dumping it between joists and screeding it off to the desired thickness. In the northern states with severe winters, at least 6 inches of fill or batt insulation should be used. The same thickness is recommended in the Central States. In the South, thickness of ceiling insulation could be reduced for heating requirements, but

cooling requirements may dictate 6 inches or more.

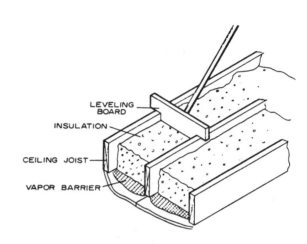

Figure 96--Installation of loose-fill ceiling insulation.

WALL INSULATION

Wood-frame walls in existing houses are usually covered both inside and out; so, application of batt or blanket insulation is impractical. It is possible, however, to blow fill-type insulation into each of the stud spaces. This is done by a contractor equipped for such work. On houses having wood siding, the top strip just below the top plates and the strips below each window are removed. Two-inch-diameter holes are cut through the sheathing into each stud space. The depth of each stud space is determined by using a plumb bob, and additional holes are made below obstructions in the spaces. Insulation under slight pressure is forced through a hose and nozzle into the stud space until it is completely filled. Special care should be taken to insulate spaces around doors and windows and at intersections of partitions and outside walls.

Stucco, brick and stone veneer walls can be insulated in a similar manner. The same method can also be used in attic and roof spaces that are not accessible for application of other types of insulation.

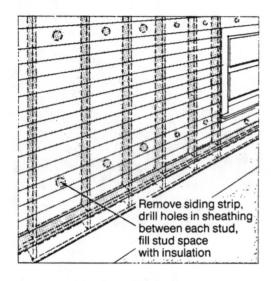

Figure 97--Reinsulating a wall.

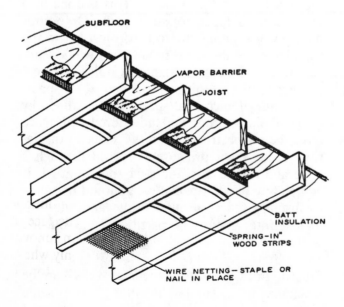

Figure 98--Installing insulating batts in floor

Solid masonry walls, such as brick, stone and concrete, can be insulated only by applying insulation to the interior surface. Remember that in doing this some space is being lost. One method of installing such insulation is to adhesively bond insulating board directly to the interior surface. The insulating board can be plastered, left exposed or covered with any desired finish material. Thicker insulating board can be used for added effectiveness.

Another method of installing insulation on the inside surface of masonry walls is through attachment of 2-by-2-inch furring strips to the walls at 16-inch centers and installation of 1-inch blanket insulation between strips. Thicker furring strips would permit use of thicker blanket insulation. The techniques used on masonry walls above grade can also be applied to basement walls.

FLOOR INSULATION

Houses with basements usually do not require insulation under floors because the heating unit warms the basement. The crawl-space house should have an insulated floor in severe climates; insulated floors will add much to comfort even in moderate climates. Batt-type insulation is often used for floors, although blanket insulation can also be used. Friction batts fit tightly between joists, and are secured to the bottom side of the subfloor with an adhesive. Batts that are not friction type require some support, in addition to the adhesive. This can be provided by wood strips cut slightly longer than the joist space so that they spring into place. They should be about 3/16-by-3/4 inch and spaced 24 to 36 inches apart. Another method of supporting floor insulation is by nailing or stapling wire netting between joists. This method can be used for blanket as well as batt type.

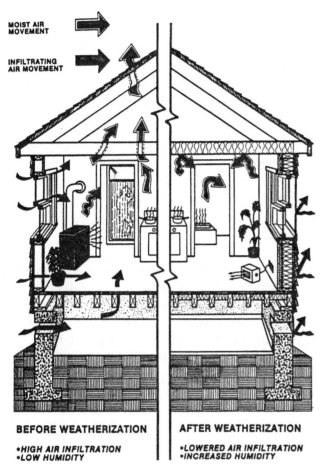

Figure 99--Effects of insulating old structures.

Vapor Barriers

Vapor barriers are essential wherever insulation is used. They are always placed on the warm side of the surface; they must be continuous over the surface to be effective. Since insulation reduces heat flow, the surface of a wall or roof is colder if insulation is used than when the wall is not insulated. This colder surface is likely to be below the dewpoint of the air inside of the house; so, condensation occurs.

The common functions of cooking, bathing, laundry and respiration contribute to moisture inside a house. Additional water vapor may be added by humidifiers operated during the winter. The high vapor pressure inside causes vapor to move out through every available

crack and even through most building materials. This water vapor condenses in the wall at the point where the temperature is below the dewpoint of the inside atmosphere. The purpose of a vapor barrier is to slow the rate of vapor flowing into the wall to a rate lower than that to the outside atmosphere.

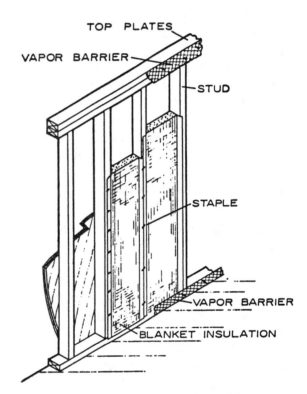

Figure 100--Installation of blanket insulation with vapor barriers on one side.

CONTINUOUS MEMBRANE

The most effective vapor barrier is a continuous membrane which is applied to the inside face of studs and joists in new construction. In renovations, such a membrane can be used only where new interior covering materials are to be applied.

The rate of vapor movement through a material is measured in perms. The lower the perm rating of a material, the more effective it is as a vapor barrier. Suitable materials for a membrane are polyethylene 2 mils or more in thickness, asphalt-impregnated and surface-coated kraft papers and duplex or laminated paper consisting of two sheets of paper cemented together with asphalt.

These vapor barriers can be stapled to furring strips before applying new ceiling or dry wall. If the old ceiling or wall finish is removed, staple the vapor barrier directly to the studs or joists. This type of barrier can also be laid on a subfloor directly under any finish floor or floor covering material. When installing the membrane, be sure to lap all joints at least 2 inches, being careful not to puncture it. Naturally, nail anchorages of finished floor will puncture the barrier; however, this will not greatly reduce its effectiveness.

BLANKET INSULATION WITH VAPOR BARRIER

Most blanket insulation has a vapor barrier on one side. Place the insulation with the vapor barrier toward the warm surface. Tabs on the blanket must be stapled to the inside face of the stud or joist, and adjacent tabs should lap each other. Tabs stapled to the side of studs or joists in the cavity will be ineffective because vapor will move out between the tabs and framing members. In rehabilitation, this type of vapor barrier can be used only where the old interior covering materials are completely removed or where furring strips are added on the inside. Insulation is installed between furring strips in the same manner as between studs.

VAPOR-RESISTANT COATING

Where loose-fill insulation has been used in walls and ceilings and no new interior covering is planned, a vapor-resistant coating should be applied to the inside surface. One method for applying such a coating is to paint the interior surface of all outside walls with two coats of aluminum primer, which are subsequently covered with decorative paint. This does not offer as much resistance to vapor movement as a membrane; so, it should be used only where other types cannot be used. If the exterior wall covering is permeable enough to allow moisture to escape from the wall, a vapor-resistant coating on the inside should be adequate.

SOIL COVER

Crawl spaces can be ventilated to effectively remove most moisture, but a soil cover will keep a lot of moisture from ever entering the crawl space. Any of the continuous membranes just mentioned can be used. Lay the membrane so that it contacts the outside walls and has a lap of at least 2 inches at all joints. Use bricks or stones on top of the membrane to hold it down and to prevent curling. Ventilation requirements are greatly reduced where a soil cover is used.

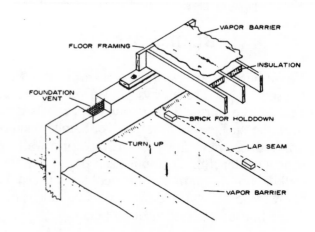

Figure 101—Vapor barrier for crawl space (ground cover).

Ventilation

Ventilation of attics and crawl spaces is essential in all houses located where the average

January temperature is 35 degrees Fahrenheit or lower. Vapor barriers help to control moisture problems, but there are always places, such as around utility pipes, where some moisture escapes. In the older house that does not have proper vapor barriers, ventilation is especially important.

ATTIC AND ROOF

Moisture escaping from the house into the attic tends to collect in the coldest part of the attic. Relatively impermeable roofing, such as asphalt shingles or a built-up roof, complicates the problem by preventing the moisture from escaping to the outside. The only way to get the moisture out is to ventilate the attic. Attic ventilation also helps keep a house cool during hot weather.

Where possible, inlet vents should be provided in the soffit area and outlet vents should be provided near the ridge. This results in natural circulation regardless of wind direction. The warm air in the attic rises to the peak, goes out the vents and fresh air enters through the inlet vents to replace the exhausted air. In some attics only gable vents can be used. Air movement is then somewhat dependent upon wind. The open area of the vent must be larger than where both inlet and outlet vents are provided.

Hip roofs cannot have gable vents near the peak; so, some other type of outlet ventilator must be provided. This can be either a ventilator near the ridge or a special flue provided in the chimney with openings into the attic space. Both types require inlet vents in the soffit area. The hip roof can also be modified to provide a small gable for a conventional louvered vent.

Flat roofs with no attic require some type of ventilation above the ceiling insulation. If this space is divided by joists, each joist space must be ventilated. This is often accomplished by a continuous vent strip in the soffit. Drill through all headers that impede passage of air to the opposite eave.

Cathedral ceilings require the same type of ventilation as flat roofs. A continuous ridge vent is also desirable because, even with holes in the ridge rafter, air movement through the rafter space is very sluggish without a ridge vent. Houses with intersecting roofs or hip roofs create special problems.

Methods of ventilating gable roofs and the amount of ventilation for the many types vary. The size of the requisite vent opening varies with total ceiling area. The open area required should be completely unobstructed. Where 16-mesh screen is used to cover the opening, the vent area should be doubled.

CRAWL SPACE

An enclosed crawl space under the house floor receives moisture from the soil below. This moisture produces both a decay and termite hazard. To keep the crawl space dry, vents are required with a total free area of not less than 1/150 of the ground area. This vent area must be divided into four or more openings distributed around the foundation. If yours is a partial basement, the crawl space can be vented to the basement instead of to the outside. Where a soil cover or a vapor barrier is laid over the entire area of the crawl space, the required ventilation area is greatly reduced. A total free area of only 1/1500 of the ground area is sufficient. These minimum areas are free areas and must be enlarged when screens or other obstructions are included with the vent.

Several types of foundation vents can be purchased commercially for easy installation in the appropriate size opening. Screen sizes vary, depending on whether they are insect-proof or rodent-proof.

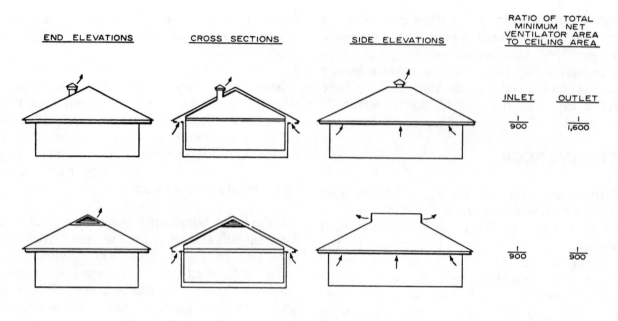

Figure 102 --Attic ventilation with hip roof.

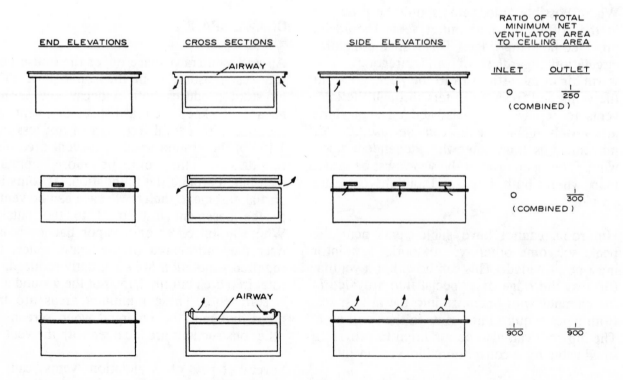

Figure 103--Ventilation of ceiling space in flat roof.

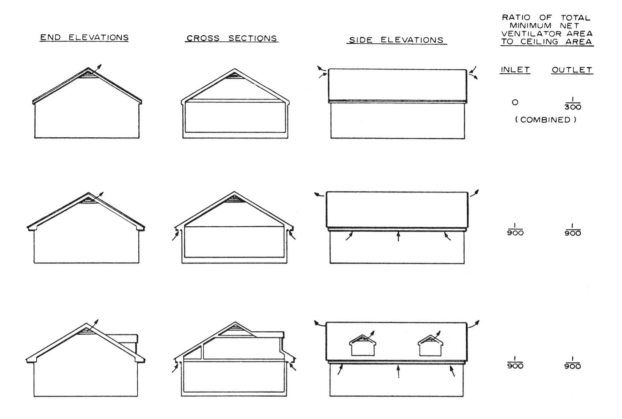

Figure 104--Attic ventilation with gable roof.

23. INTERIOR ITEMS

Relocating Partitions

One of the most common occurrences in remodeling is the moving of partitions for a more convenient room layout. It may mean eliminating a partition or adding a partition in another location.

REMOVING A PARTITION

The nonbearing partition is easily removed because none of the structure depends upon it. If the covering material is plaster or gypsum board, it cannot be salvaged; so, remove it from the framing any way you find easiest. The framing can probably be reused if it is removed carefully.

The main problem presented by removing a nonbearing partition is the unfinished strip left in the ceiling, wall and floor. This unfinished strip in the ceiling and wall is easily finished by plastering to the same thickness as the existing plaster or by cutting strips of gypsum board to fit snugly into the unfinished strip and finishing the joints with joint compound and tape. Flooring can also be patched by inserting a wood strip of the same thickness and species as the existing floor. If existing flooring runs parallel to the wall, patching is fairly effective; however, where the flooring runs perpendicular to the wall, the patch will always be obvious unless a new floor covering is added. In making the patch, cut the flooring to fit as snugly as possible. Even where the flooring is well fitted and of the same species, it may not be exactly the same color as the existing flooring.

Removing a loadbearing partition involves the same patching of walls, ceiling and floor as the nonbearing partition. In addition, however, some other means of supporting the ceiling joists must be provided. If attic space above the partition is available, a supporting beam can be placed above the ceiling joists in the attic so that the joists can hang from the beam. The ends of the beam must be supported on an exterior wall, a bearing partition or a post that will transfer the load to the foundation. Wood hanger brackets are installed at the intersection of the beam with each joist. One method is illustrated below. This type of support can be installed before the wall is removed, eliminating the need for temporary support.

Where an exposed beam is not objectionable, it can be installed after the partition is removed. A series of jacks with adequate blocking or some other type of support is required on each side of the partition while the transition between the partition and a beam is being made. The bottom of the beam should be at least 6 feet 8 inches above the floor.

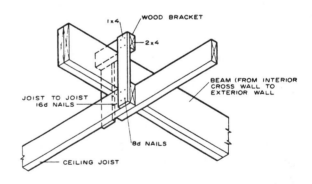

Figure 105--Framing for flush ceiling with wood brackets.

There may be situations where an exposed beam is undesirable and no attic space is available, as in the ground floor of a two-story house. A beam can be provided in the ceiling with joists framing into the sides of it. Temporary support for the joists is required similar to that used for installing the exposed beam. The joists must be cut to make room for the beam. Install joist hangers on the beam where each joist will frame into it. Put the beam in place and repair the damaged ceiling.

The size of the required beam will vary greatly, depending on beam span, span of joists framing into it and material used for the beam. Determination of beam size should be made by an engineer or someone experienced in construction.

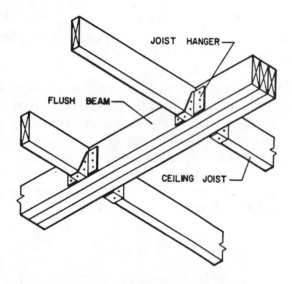

Figure 106--Flush beam with joist hangers.

ADDING A PARTITION

A partition is added by simply framing it in, much as in new construction. Framing is usually done with 2-by-4s, although 2- by-3-inch framing is also considered adequate for partitions. The first step in framing should be to install the top plate. If ceiling joists are perpendicular to the partition, nail the top plate to each joist using sixteenpenny nails. If ceiling joists are parallel to the partition and the partition is not directly under a joist, install solid blocking between joists at no more than 2-foot spacing; nail the top plate to the blocking. To assure a plumb partition hold a plumb bob along the side of the top plate at several points and mark these points on the floor. Nail the sole plate to the floor joists or to solid blocking between joists in the same manner as the top plate was nailed to the ceiling joists.

The next step is to install studs to fit firmly between the plates at a spacing of 16 inches. Check the required stud length at several points. There may be some variation. Toenail the studs to the plates, using eightpenny nails. If conditions permit, it may be easier to partially assemble the wall on the floor and tilt it into place. First, the top plate is nailed to the studs and the frame tilted into place, after which studs are toenailed to the bottom plate as above. Frame in doors, where desired, in the manner described under the section on doors. The partition is then ready for wall finish and trim, both of which are herein discussed.

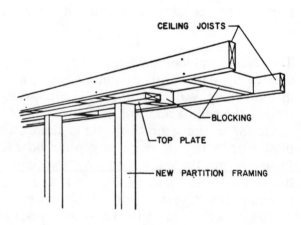

Figure 107--Blocking between joists to which the top plate of a new partition is nailed.

Interior Wall Finish

Minor cracks in plaster or dry wall can be easily patched by filling the crack with a plaster-patching mix and sanding after the plaster dries. A fiberglass fabric applied over the crack helps prevent recurrence. This works well when the cracks are limited in number; however, if plaster is generally cracked or pulled loose from its backing, a new covering material should be used.

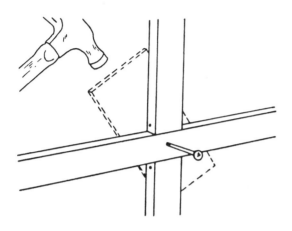

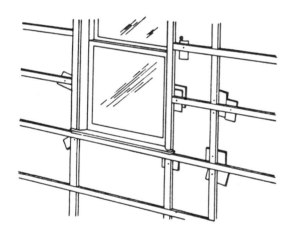

Figure 108--Shingle shims behind furring to produce a smooth surface.

In houses that require a new wall finish, some type of dry wall sheet material is usually the most practical. The application of most drywall requires no special tools or skills, and it can be applied in a manner to smooth out unevenness and to cover imperfections. The most common forms of dry wall are gypsum board, plywood, hardboard, fiberboard and wood paneling. Dry wall is usually applied to framing or to furring strips over the framing or existing wall finish. If the existing wall finish is smooth, new wall finish can sometimes be glued or nailed directly to the existing wall. In this direct application there is no thickness requirement for the new

covering because it is continuously supported. For dry wall applied over framing or furring, the recommended thicknesses for 16- and 24-inch spacing of fastening members are listed in the following tabulation:

Finish	Minimum thickness when framing is spaced	
	16 in.	24 in.
Gypsum board	3/8	1/2
Plywood	1/4	3/8
Hardboard	1/4	
Fiberboard	1/2	3/4
Wood paneling	3/8	1/2

The 1/4-inch plywood or hardboard may be slightly wavy unless applied over 3/8-inch gypsum board.

In order to prepare a room for a new wall finish, first locate each stud. They are usually spaced 16 inches apart and at doors and windows. The easiest way to find them is to look for nailheads in the dry wall or baseboard. These nails have been driven into studs. Where there is no evidence of nailheads, tap the wall finish with a hammer. At the stud, the sound will be solid; whereas, the space between studs will sound hollow. Commercial stud finders are also available at hardware and building supply stores. These operate by the use of a magnet that points to nail heads. Mark the stud locations in order to attach horizontal furring strips or to nail on paneling applied without furring strips.

Check walls for flatness by holding a straight 2-by-4 against the surface. Mark locations that are quite uneven. Also check for true vertical alignment by holding a large carpenter's level on the straight 2-by-4 against the wall. As furring is applied, use shingles as shims behind the furring where needed to produce a smooth vertical surface.

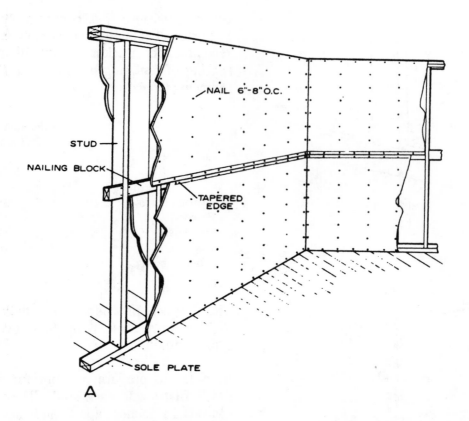

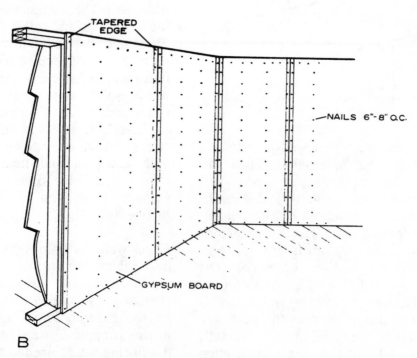

Figure 109--Installing gypsum board on walls: A, horizontal application; B, vertical application.

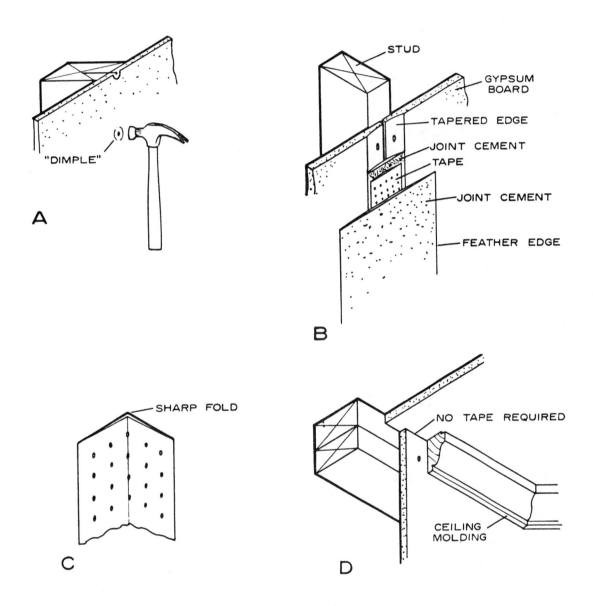

Figure 110--Preparing gypsum dry-wall sheets for painting: A, drive nails in "dimple" fashion; B, detail of joint treatment; C, corner tape; D, ceiling molding.

Apply standard 1-by-2-inch furring horizontally at 16- or 24-inch spacing, depending on the covering material to be used. Nail the furring at each stud. Remove existing base trim, window and door casings and apply furring around all openings. Also use vertical furring strips where vertical joints will occur in the dry wall.

After this preparation, any of the usual dry wall materials can be applied.

GYPSUM BOARD

Gypsum board is one of the lowest cost materials for interior finish; however, the labor required to finish joints may offset the low material cost. This sheet material is composed of a gypsum filler faced with paper. Recessed edges accommodate tape for joints. Sheets are 4 feet wide and 8 feet long or longer; they can be applied vertically or horizontally. Sheets the entire length of a room can be applied horizontally, leaving only one joint at the midheight of the wall.

For both horizontal and vertical applications, nail completely around the perimeter of the sheet and at each furring strip; for direct application to framing, nail at each stud. Use fourpenny cooler-type nails for 3/8-inch-thick gypsum board and fivepenny cooler-type nails for 1/2-inch-thick gypsum board. Space the nails 6 to 8 inches apart. Lightly dimple the nail location with the hammerhead, being careful not to break the surface of the paper. The minimum edge nailing distance is 3/8-inch. Screws are sometimes used instead of nails.

The conventional method of preparing gypsum sheets for painting includes the use of a joint cement and perforated joint tape. Some gypsum board is supplied with a strip of joint paper along one edge, which is used in place of the tape. After the gypsum board has been installed and each nail driven in a "dimple" fashion, the walls are ready for treatment.

Joint cement ("spackle" compound), which comes in powder or ready-mixed form, should have a soft putty consistency so that it can be easily spread with a trowel or wide putty knife. The gypsum board edges are usually tapered so that, where two sheets are joined, there is a recessed strip to receive joint cement and tape. If a sheet has been cut, the edge will not be tapered. A square edge is taped in much the same manner as the beveled edge, except the joint cement will raise the surface slightly at the seam and edges have to be feathered out further for a smooth finish. Complete instructions are included with the taping material. A brief description of the procedure for taping is as follows:

1. Use a wide spackling knife (5 inches) and spread the cement over the tapered and other butt edges, starting at the top of the wall.

2. Press the tape into the recess with the knife until the joint cement is forced through the small perforations.

3. Cover the tape with additional cement to a level surface, feathering the outer edges -- allow to dry.

4. Sand lightly and apply a thin second coat, feathering the edges again. A third coat may be required after the second coat has dried.

5. After cement is dry, sand smooth.

6. For hiding nail indentations at members between edges, fill with joint cement. A second coat is usually required. Again, sand when dry.

Interior and exterior corners may be treated with perforated tape. Fold the tape down the center to a right angle. Now, (a) apply cement on each side of the corner, (b) press tape in place with the spackle or putty knife, and (c) finish with joint cement and sand when dry. Wallboard corner beads of metal or plastic also can be added to provide strength. Such metal corners are recommended. They are nailed to outside corners and are treated with joint cement. The junction of the wall and ceiling can also be finished with a wood molding in any desired shape, which will eliminate the need for joint treatment. Use eightpenny finishing nails spaced 12 to 16 inches apart and nail into the top wallplate.

Treatment around window and door openings depends on the type of casing used. When a casing head and trim are used instead of a wood casing, the jambs and the beads may be installed before or during application of the gypsum wall finish. These details are covered in the section on "Doors".

PLYWOOD AND HARDBOARD

Plywood and hardboard are usually in 4-by-8-foot sheets for vertical application. However, 7-foot-long panels can sometimes be purchased for use in basements or other low-ceiling areas. Plywood can be purchased in a number of species and finishes, with wide variations in cost. Hardboard imprinted with a wood grain pattern is generally less expensive. The better hardboard paneling uses a photograph of wood to provide the woodgrain effect, which produces a very realistic pattern. Both plywood and hardboard can be purchased with a hard, plastic finish that is easily wiped clean. Hardboard is also available with vinyl coatings in many patterns and colors.

The plywood or hardboard interior finish material should be delivered to the site well before application to allow the panels to assume conditions of moisture and temperature in the room. Stack the panels, separated by full length furring strips, to allow air to get to all panel faces and backs. Panels should remain in the room at least a couple of days before application.

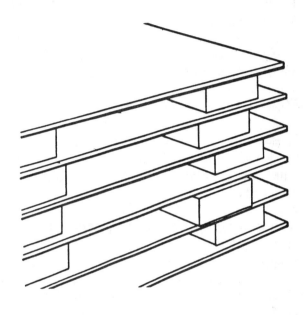

Figure 111–Stacking panels for conditioning to room environment prior to use.

In applying the panels to the walls, the start depends partly on whether or not the wall corners are truly vertical. If the starting corner is straight, the first panel is merely butted to the corner and subsequent panels located so they lap on studs. If the panel corner or other surface is not truly vertical, place the panel edge on a vertical line 50 inches from the surface, plumb that edge with a carpenter's level and use an art compass to scribe the outline of the cut to be made on the other edge. Cut the panel and move it against the corner. After the first panel is placed, install successive panels by butting edges against the previous panel, being careful to maintain a true vertical line. Any misalignment is less noticeable, of course, if all walls are paneled. A similar procedure can be used for fitting panels against the ceiling.

Panels can be fastened with nails or adhesive. Adhesive is sometimes preferable because there are no nailheads to mar the finish. Most adhesives include instructions for application; follow these instructions carefully. Use an adhesive that allows enough open assembly time to adjust the panel for a good fit. Where panels are nailed, use small finishing nails (brads). Use 1-1/2-inch-long nails for 1/4- or 3/8-inch-thick materials and space 8 to 10 inches apart on edges and at intermediate supports. Most panels are grooved and nails can be driven in these grooves. Set nails slightly with a nail set. Many prefinished materials are furnished with small nails having heads that match the color of the finish; thus, no setting is required.

WOOD AND FIBERBOARD PANELING

Wood and fiberboard paneling elements are tongued-and-grooved and are available in various widths. Wood is usually limited to no more than 8 inches in nominal width. Fiberboard paneling is often 12 or 16 inches wide. Paneling should also be stacked in the room to be paneled, as recommended for plywood and hardboard, to stabilize at the temperature and moisture conditions of the room. Paneling is usually applied vertically, but at times is applied horizontally for special effects.

Vertically applied paneling is nailed to horizontal furring strips or to nailing blocks between studs. Nail with 1-1/2- to 2-inch finishing or casing nails. Blind nail through the tongue; for 8-inch boards, face nail near the opposite edge. Where 12- or 16-inch-wide fiberboard is used, two face nails may be required. Color-matched nails are sometimes supplied with the fiberboard. Staples may also be used in the tongue of fiberboard instead of nails. Where adhesive is used, the only nailing is the blind nail in the tongue.

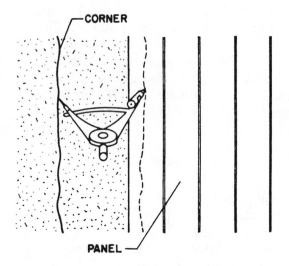

Figure 112–Scribing of cut at panel edge to provide exact fit in a corner or at ceiling.

Ceilings

Ceilings can be finished with gypsum board or other sheet materials in much the same manner as interior walls. Or, a variety of ceiling tiles can be used, including the type for use with suspended metal or wood hangers. The suspended ceiling is particularly useful in renovations having high ceilings. It covers many imperfections and lowers the ceiling to a more practical height. The space above the new ceiling may be used for electrical wiring, plumbing or heating ducts added during remodeling. In so doing, this mechanical equipment remains easily accessible.

Cracks in plaster ceilings can be repaired with plaster patching in the same manner as walls are patched; however, where cracks are extensive, a new ceiling is the only cure.

GYPSUM BOARD

Gypsum board can be applied directly to ceiling joists by first removing existing ceiling material. It may also be applied directly over plaster or to furring strips nailed over the existing ceiling where plaster is uneven. Use 2-by-2-inch or 2-by-3-inch furring strips oriented perpendicular to the joists and spaced 16 inches on centers for 3/8-inch gypsum board or 24 inches on centers for 1/2-inch gypsum board. Nail the furring strips with two tenpenny nails at each joist.

Apply the gypsum boards with end joints staggered and centered on a joist or furring strip. Place the sheets so there is only light contact at joints. One or two braces slightly longer than the ceiling height are quite useful in installing the gypsum sheets. Nail the gypsum board to all supporting members with nails spaced 7 to 8 inches apart. Use fivepenny cooler-type nails for 1/2-inch gypsum board and fourpenny nails for 3/8-inch gypsum board. Nailheads should not penetrate the surface. Each nailhead location should be slightly dimpled with the hammerhead, being careful not to break the surface of the paper. Finish the joints and nailheads in the same manner described under "Interior Wall Finish". Where gypsum board is used, it should be applied to the ceiling before wall finish is applied.

CEILING TILE

Ceiling tile is available in a variety of materials and patterns, with a wide range in cost. It can be applied directly to a smooth backing, but the usual application is to furring strips.

If the existing ceiling has a flat surface, tile can be fastened with adhesive. Use an adhesive recommended by the tile manufacturer and follow directions carefully. A small spot of adhesive at each corner and center is usually sufficient. Edged-matched tile can also be stapled if the backing is wood.

A more common method of installing ceiling tile is fastening them to furring strips. Nominal 1-by-3- or 1-by-4-inch furring strips are used where ceiling joists are spaced no more than 24 inches apart. Nail strips with two sevenpenny or eightpenny nails to each joist. Where trusses or ceiling joists are spaced up to 48 inches apart, use nominal 2-by-2- or 2-by-3-inch furring nailed with two tenpenny nails to each joist. The furring should be a low-density wood, such as the softer pines, if tile is to be stapled to the furring.

Locate the strips by first measuring the width of the room (parallel to joists). Place the first furring strip at the center of the room, establish the number of complete courses and adjust edge spacing so that edge courses are equal in width. Plan spacing perpendicular to joists in the same manner so that the end courses will be equal.

Start at one side and continue across the room. For a close fit, do not cut the tile until the last row is being installed. Ceiling tile usually has a tongue on two adjacent edges and grooves on the other edges. In installing, keep the tongue edges on the open side so that they can be stapled to nailing strips. Use a small finishing nail or adhesive at the edge of the tile next to the wall. Use one staple at each furring strip on the leading edge and two staples along the side. A small finishing nail or adhesive is again required in the edge of the tile against the wall where each row is completed.

In applying the tile, be careful not to soil the surface; it is usually factory-finished and requires no painting.

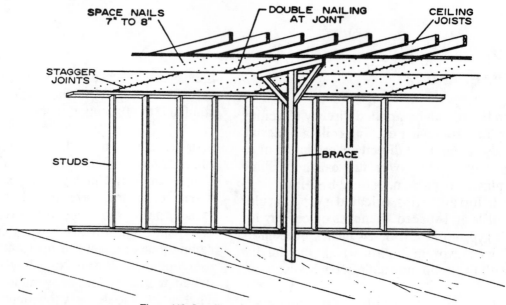

Figure 113--Installing gypsum board on ceiling.

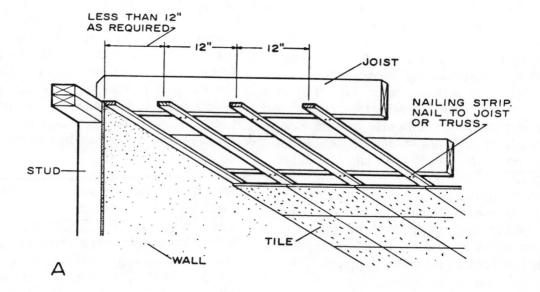

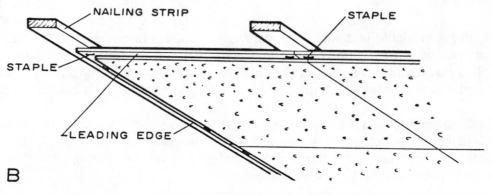

Figure 114--Ceiling tile installation: A, nailing strip location; B, stapling.

SUSPENDED CEILING

Suspended ceilings consist of a grid of small metal or wood hangers, supported by hanging them from the ceiling framing with wire or strap, and drop-in panels sized to fit the grid system. This type of ceiling can be adjusted to any desired height. Where the existing ceiling is normal height, the hangers can be supported only 2 or 3 inches below the ceiling and still cover any bulging plaster or other unevenness. Where existing ceilings are high, adjust the hangers to the desired ceiling height.

Suspended ceilings are purchased as a system, assuring the   panels are compatible with the supporting grid.   Detailed instructions for installation are usually supplied by the manufacturer.

Interior Trim

Interior trim consists of window and door casings and various moldings. Such trim in existing houses varies considerably, depending on age, style and quality of the house. The trim found in many older houses is probably no longer on the market; so, matching it requires expensive custom fabrication. If the plan is to use existing trim, remove pieces carefully where windows, doors or partitions are changed. In so doing, be sure to mark each piece so that it can be reused where needed.

Where new trim is planned, the type of finish desired is the basis for selecting the species of wood to be used. For a paint finish, the material should be smooth, close-grained and free from pitch streaks. Some species that meet these requirements are ponderosa pine, northern white pine, redwood, mahogany and spruce. The additional qualities of hardness and resistance to hard usage are provided by such species as birch, gum and yellow-poplar. For a natural finish, the wood should have a pleasing

texture, hardness and uniform color. These requirements are satisfied by species such as ash, birch, cherry, maple, oak and walnut.

CASING

Casing is the interior edge trim for door and window openings. New casing patterns vary in width from 2-1/4 to 3-1/2 inches; in thickness from 1/2 to 3/4 inch. Place the casing with about a 3/16-inch edge distance from door and window jambs. Nail with sixpenny or sevenpenny casing or finishing nails, depending on thickness of the casing. Space nails in pairs about 16 inches apart, nailing to both jambs and framing. Rectangular casings can be butt-joined at corners, but molded forms must have a mitered joint.

BASEBOARD

Baseboard, the finish between the finished wall and floor, is also available in several sizes and forms. It may be either one or two piece. The two-piece base consists of a baseboard topped with a small base cap which conforms to any irregularities in the wall finish. Except where carpet is installed, most baseboards are finished with a base shoe. The base shoe is nailed into the subfloor, conforming to irregularities in the finished floor.

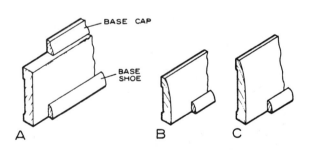

Figure 115--Baseboard: A, two piece; B, narrow; C, medium width.

Install square-edged baseboard with a butt joint at inside corners and a mitered joint at outside corners. Nail at each stud with two eightpenny finishing nails. Molded base, base cap and base shoe require a coped joint at inside corners and a mitered joint at outside corners.

CEILING MOLDINGS

Ceiling moldings are used at the junction of wall and ceiling. They may be strictly decorative where there is a finished joint or they may be specifically for the purpose of hiding a poorly fitted joint. They are particularly useful with wood paneling or other dry wall which is difficult to fit and where plaster patching cannot be used to finish the joint., Attach the molding with finishing nails driven into the upper wallplates. Large moldings should also be nailed to the ceiling joists.

MISCELLANEOUS DECORATIVE MOLDINGS

Many decorative moldings can be used in a variety of ways. They can be applied to walls or doors to give the effect of relief paneling or carved doors. They can also be used to add interest to existing cabinetwork. Check with a local building supplier for available types and ideas on how to use them.

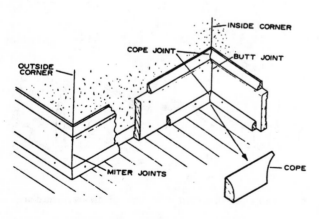

Figure 116--Installation of base molding.

Closets

Many older homes are lacking in closet space and often the closets provided are not well arranged for good usage. Remodeling may involve altering existing closets or adding new ones.

ALTERING EXISTING CLOSETS

One thing that can do much to improve closets is to provide full front openings to replace small doors. Doors are available in a great variety of widths, particularly accordion doors. Remove wall finish and studs to the width required for a standard accordion-fold or double-hinged door set. Standard double doors may also be suitable. Where the closet wall is loadbearing, use header sizes listed for window openings.

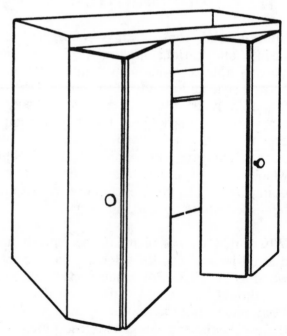

Figure 117--Double hinged door set for full-width opening closet.

The header can be eliminated for a nonload-bearing wall, and a full ceiling-height accordion-fold door can be used. Frame the opening in the same manner as other door openings, with the rough framed opening 2-1/2 inches wider than the door or set of doors. Install closet doors in a manner similar to other interior doors. Special types of doors, such as double-hinged doors, are usually supplied with installation instructions.

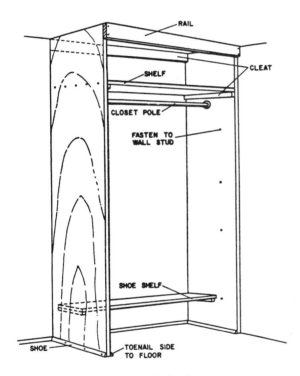

Figure 118--Wardrobe closet.

Closets can sometimes be made more useful by additions or alterations in shelves and clothes rods. The usual closet has one rod with a single shelf over it. Where hanging space is quite limited, install a second clothes rod about half way between the existing rod and the floor. This type of space can be used for children's clothing or for shorter adult clothing. Shelves can also be added in any manner to fit a particular need.

To add either a shelf or a pole, support them by 1-by-4-inch cleats nailed to the end walls of the closet. Nail these cleats with three sixpenny nails at each end of the cleat and at the intermediate stud. Shelf ends can rest directly on these cleats. Attach clothes rods to the cleats that support the shelf.

NEW CLOSETS

New closets can be built in a conventional manner or wardrobe closets of plywood or particleboard can be built at a lower cost.

Conventional closets are constructed by adding a partition around the closet area, using 2-by-3-inch or 2-by-4-inch framing and gypsum board or other cover material. The method of installing partitions is described under "Adding Partitions". Provide a cased opening for the closet door.

Wardrobe closets require less space because the wall is a single material without framing. Use 5/8- or 3/4-inch plywood or particleboard supported on cleats.

Use a 1-by-4-inch top rail and back cleat. Fasten the cleat to the wall, and in a corner fasten the sidewall to a wall stud. Toenail base shoe moldings to the floor to hold the bottom of the sidewalls in place. Add shelves and closet poles where desired. Similar units can be built with shelves for linens or other items. Any size or combination of these units can be built. Add plywood doors or folding doors as desired.

24. SPECIAL ITEMS

Framing for Utilities

Updating the heating, plumbing and electrical systems in an older house usually requires a skilled, licensed craftsman; so, the details for accomplishing this are not within the scope of this manual. Certain construction practices, however, are required to accommodate the utilities. Because heating ducts, plumbing stacks and drains, heater piping and electrical conduit must be run throughout the house, it is usually difficult to avoid cutting into the structure to accommodate them.

Mechanical trades should be cautioned against cutting; instruct them in the exact manner of cutting, when unavoidable. At critical points the structure can be altered, but only by or at the direction of someone qualified. Cut members can often be reinforced, and any new walls or other framing can be built to accommodate mechanical items.

CUTTING FLOOR JOISTS

Floor joists must often be cut to accommodate pipe for water supply lines or electrical conduit. This may be in the form of notches at top or bottom of the joist or as holes drilled through the joist. Notching of joists should be done only in the end quarter of the span and to not more than one-sixth of the depth. If more severe alteration is required, floor framing should be altered.

Holes can also be drilled through joists if the size of hole is limited to 2 inches in diameter and the edges of the hole are not less than 2-1/2 inches from the top or bottom of the joist.

Where a joist must be cut and the above conditions cannot be met, add an additional joist next to the cut joist or reinforce the cut joist by nailing scabs to each side.

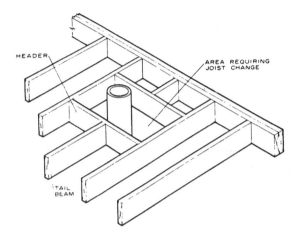

Figure 119--Headers for joists to eliminate cutting.

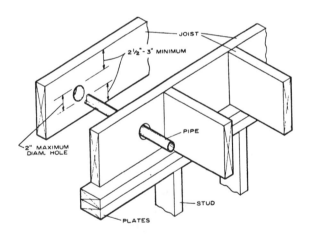

Figure 120--Boring holes in joists.

BATHTUB FRAMING

Where a bathtub is to be added, additional framing may be necessary to support the heavy weight of the tub filled with water. Where joists are parallel to the length of the tub, double the joists under the outer edge of the tub. The other edge is usually supported on the wall framing which also has a double joist under it. Hangers or wood blocks support the bathtub at the enclosing walls.

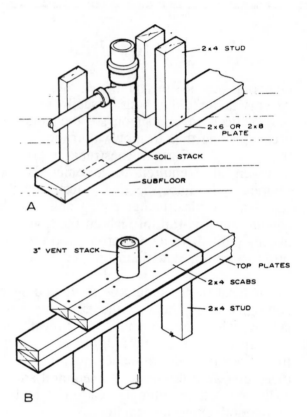

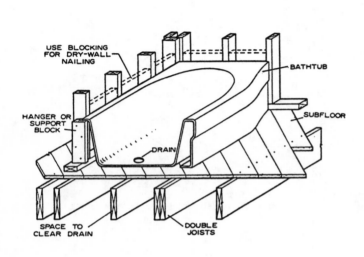

Figure 121--Framing for bathtub.

Figure 122--Framing for vent stack: A,, 4 inch soil pipe; B, 3 inch stack vent.

UTILITY WALLS

Walls containing plumbing stack or vents may require special framing. Four-inch soil stacks will not fit in a standard 2-by- 4-inch stud wall. Where a thicker wall is needed, it is usually constructed with 2-by-6-inch top and bottom plates and 2-by-4-inch studs placed flatwise at the edge of the plate. This leaves the center of the wall open for running both supply and drain pipes through the wall.

Three-inch vent stacks do fit into 2-by-4-inch stud walls; however, the hole for the vent requires cutting away most of the top plate, and may cause problems if the plumbing is not centered properly. Scabs cut from 2-by-4s are then nailed to the plate on each side of the vent to reinforce the top plate.

CHIMNEYS AND FIREPLACES

Defective chimneys and fireplaces are difficult to repair; so, it may be best to replace a poor

chimney. When gas or oil heaters are used, only small metal vents may be required. Check with local code authorities for the type and allowable length of run. These can sometimes be placed in the stud space of an interior partition for low-capacity heaters; then, the defective chimney can be eliminated. If fuels requiring chimneys are used, fabricated metal chimneys can usually be installed at a much lower cost than the conventional masonry chimney. Check local codes for requirements for prefabricated chimneys.

Well-built chimneys have flue linings which keep the flue tight even though there are cracks in the masonry. Where flues are not lined, stainless steel flue lining can be installed. This lining can be purchased in 2- or 2-1/2 foot-lengths and in cross sections to fit most standard size chimneys. Sections are connected together and inserted from the top, with additional sections being added until the required length is achieved. Note that this type of lining can only be used with a reasonably straight flue. The flue lining will ensure safe operation, but cracks in mortar should also be repaired by regrouting.

Fireplaces have several requirements for good draft and smoke-free operation. If they were not built with proper proportions, a metal extension across the top of the fireplace opening will sometimes improve the draft. This improvement can be tested by holding a board against the fireplace just above the opening and by observing the change in draft. Draft can sometimes be improved by extending the height of the flue or by adding a chimney cap for venturi action. Another possible solution where draft is inadequate is to install a fan in the chimney for forced exhaust.

In cold climates, a damper that can be closed when the fireplace is not in use is quite important. Where there is no damper, an asbestos card can be cut to fit the flue opening at the top of the fireplace, supporting it on some type of bracket. This card would have to be completely removed when the fireplace is in use. Although inconvenient, this method eliminates heat loss or cold drafts from the flue.

If a new fireplace is desired, professional help is usually required; however, prefabricated metal fireplaces are available which require no special skills for installation. They can be placed on the conventional floor without a separate foundation, and no masonry work is required. Fireplace liners are also available which only require masonry added around them. Though requiring a complete foundation and separate chimney the same as a conventional fireplace, these liners are a convenient guide for ensuring proper proportions.

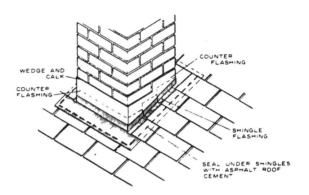

Figure 123--Chimney flashing.

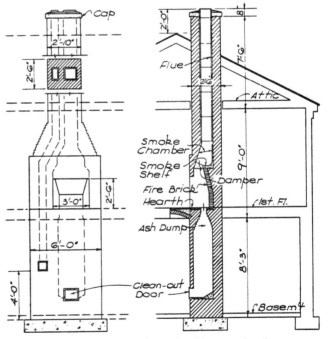

Figure 124--Diagram of an entire chimney such as is commonly built to serve the house heating unit and one fireplace.

25. PORCH

If examination of the porch showed all parts to be in a generally deteriorated condition, complete removal and replacement is recommended. However, it may be feasible to replace components, such as steps, floor, posts or roof, when all other components are in good condition.

STEPS

When wood steps are used, the bottom step and carriage should not be in contact with soil. A concrete step can be cast on the ground to support the carriage or it can be supported on a treated wood post. Apply a water-repellent preservative to all wood used in the steps.

If only one step is required and treated posts are used for support, the step can be supported on the same post that supports the edge of the porch. Use treated posts of 5- to 7-inch diameter embedded in the soil at least 5 feet. Nail and bolt the crossmember to the post, and block the inner end to the floor framing with a short 2-by-4.

Where more steps are required, use a 2-by-12 stringer at each end of the steps with the lower end of each stringer bolted to a treated post. The upper end can be attached to the porch framing. Concrete or masonry piers can be used in place of treated posts. The important thing is that the stringer be kept from contact with the soil.

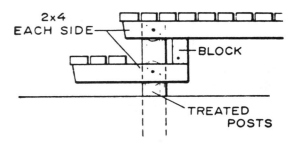

Figure 126--Single porch step supported on a treated post.

FLOOR

If floor framing is decayed, it should be completely replaced, and all replacement members should be treated with a water-repellent preservative. Framing members should be at least 18 inches above the ground, and good ventilation should be provided under the porch. Framing should be installed to give the finished floor an outward slope of at least 1/8-inch per foot.

Porch flooring is 1-by-4-inch lumber, dressed and matched. It is blind-nailed at each joist in the same manner as regular flooring. Apply a good stain or deck paint as soon as possible after installation.

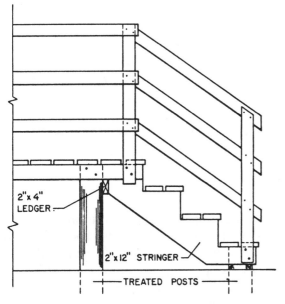

Figure 125--Step stringer supported by porch framing and posts.

POSTS

Where a post rests directly on the porch floor, the base of the post may be decayed. The best solution may be to replace the post. When this is done, provide some way to support the post slightly above the porch floor. Standard post anchors can be purchased for this purpose.

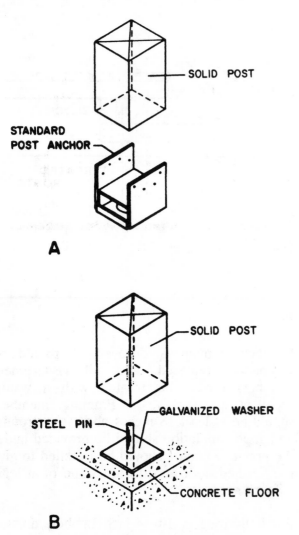

A

B

Figure 127–Base for post: A, standard post anchor for resistance to uplift; B, galvanized washer and pin where resistance to uplift is not critical.

Another way to accomplish this is by using a small 3/8- or 1/2-inch-diameter pin and a large galvanized washer. Drill a hole for the pin in the end of the post and a matching hole in the floor. Apply a mastic caulk to the area and position with the pin inserted and the washer between the post and the floor. This will allow moisture to evaporate from the end of the post and prevent decay. This pinned method should be used only on small porches that will not have a major wind uplift load.

If the existing porch posts are ornamental, it may be desirable to cut off the decayed portion near the base and save the good portion. Perhaps a base slightly larger than the post can be added to replace the decayed portion. Some method of ventilating the base of the post should be provided to avoid further decay. One solution is to use a pin and large washer, as described above for a new post.

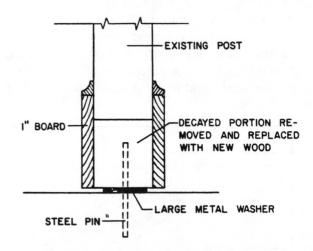

Figure 128–Replacement of decayed end of porch post.

ROOF

A porch roof can be repaired in much the same manner as repairing the house roof. The difference may be that porch roofs frequently have a very low slope and are often covered with roll roofing. Simply apply an underlayment of asphalt-saturated felt and follow with mineral surfaced half-lap roll roofing applied in accordance with manufacturer's instructions. Use a ribbon of asphalt roof cement or lap seal material under the lapped edge, and avoid using any exposed nails. Extend the roofing beyond the fascia enough to form a natural drip edge.

If wood or asphalt shingles are used on the porch roof, apply them as described in the section on "Roofs".

26. PAINTING AND FINISHING

Painting and finishing of your house during remodeling will usually include repainting or refinishing the existing surfaces, as well as providing a finish over new siding, interior wall surfaces, floors and trim. Exterior finishes are required for appearance and protection from weathering; interior finishes are primarily for appearance, wear resistance and ease in maintaining the surface.

Wood Properties and Finish Durability

The durability of an existing finish is materially affected by the wood's characteristics. Woods that are high in density (heavy), such as dense hardwoods, will be more difficult to finish effectively than lightweight woods. Western red cedar and redwood are two species that have the a high degree of the desired qualities.

The amount and distribution of summerwood (darker grained portions) on the surface of softwood lumber also influence the success of the finishing procedure. Finishes, particularly paints, will last longer on surfaces with a low proportion of summerwood.

The manner in which lumber is sawn from the log influences its finishing characteristics. Paint-type and film-forming finishes always perform best on vertical-grain lumber because the summerwood is better distributed on the surface and because vertical-grain lumber is low in swelling across the width of the board.

All woods shrink or swell as they lose or absorb water. Species which shrink and swell the least are best for painting. Checking and warping of wood and paint peeling are more likely to be critical on woods which are hard, dense and high in swelling.

Wood that is free of knots, pitch pockets and other defects is the preferred base for paints, but these defects have little adverse effect on penetrating-type finishes. Smoothly planed surfaces are best for paint finishes, while rougher or sawn surfaces are preferred for penetrating (nonfilm-forming) finishes.

Exterior Finishes

UNFINISHED WOOD

Permitting the wood to weather naturally without protection of any kind is, of course, very simple and economical. Wood fully exposed to all the elements -- rain and sun having the most severe effect -- will wear away at the approximate rate of only 1/4-inch in a century. The time required for wood to weather to a final gray color will depend on the degree of exposure. Wood in protected areas will be much slower to gray than wood fully exposed to the sun on the south side of a building. Early in the graying process, the wood may take on a blotchy appearance because of the growth of microorganisms on the surface. Migration of wood extractives to the surface also will produce an uneven and unsightly discoloration, particularly in areas that are not washed by rain.

Unfinished lumber will warp more than lumber protected by paint. Warping varies with the wood density, width, thickness, basic wood structure and species. Because warp increases with the density and width of the board, board width should not exceed eight times the thickness. Flat-grain boards warp more than vertical-grain lumber. Bald cypress, the cedars and redwood are species which have only a slight tendency to warp.

WATER-REPELLENT-PRESERVATIVE FINISHES

A simple treatment of an exterior wood surface with a water-repellent preservative markedly alters the natural weathering process. Most pronounced is the retention of a uniform natural tan color in the early stages of weathering and a retardation of the uneven graying process which is produced by the growth of mildew on the surface.

Water-repellent finishes generally contain a preservative (usually pentachlorophenol), a small amount of resin and a very small amount of a water repellent that is frequently wax-like in nature. The water-repellency imparted by the treatment greatly reduces the tendency toward warping, excessive shrinking and swelling which lead to splitting. It also retards the leaching of extractives from the wood and the staining from water at ends of boards.

This type of finish is quite inexpensive, easily applied and very easily refinished. Water-repellent preservatives can be applied by brushing, dipping and spraying. Rough surfaces will absorb more solution than smoothly planed surfaces; the treatment will also be more durable. It is important to thoroughly treat all lap and butt joints and the ends of all boards. Many brands of effective water-repellent preservatives are on the market.

Initial applications may be short lived (1 year), especially in humid climates and on species that are susceptible to mildew, such as sapwood and certain hardwoods. Under more favorable conditions, such as on rough cedar surfaces which will absorb large quantities of the solution, the finish will last more than 2 years.

When blotchy discolorations of mildew start to appear on the wood, remove blotches and rain spatters and lighten dark areas by steel brushing with the grain. Retreat the surface with water repellent-preservative solution. If extractives have accumulated on the surface in protected areas, clean these areas by mild scrubbing with a detergent of trisodium-phosphate solution.

The continued use of these water-repellent-preservative solutions will effectively prevent serious decay in wood in above-ground installation. This finishing method, therefore, is recommended for all wood species and surfaces exposed to the weather.

Only aluminum or stainless steel nails will prevent discoloration on the siding. Galvanized nails will show light stains after several years. Steel nails without rust-resistant treatment should not be used.

PENETRATING PIGMENTED STAIN FINISHES

Penetrating stains are also effective and economical finishes for all kinds of lumber and plywood surfaces. They are especially well suited for rough-sawn, weathered and textured wood and plywood. Knotty wood boards and other lower quality grades of wood which would be difficult to paint can be finished successfully with penetrating stains.

These stains penetrate into the wood without forming a continuous film on the surface. Because there is no film or coating, there can be no failure by cracking, peeling and blistering. Stain finishes are easily prepared for refinishing and are easily maintained.

Penetrating pigmented stains form a flat and semi-transparent finish, which allow to show through only part of the wood-grain pattern. A variety of colors is available, including shades of brown, green, red and gray. The only color which is not available is white; it can be provided only through the use of white paint.

Stains are quite inexpensive and easy to apply. To avoid the formation of lap marks, the entire length of a course of siding should be finished without stopping. Only one coat is recommended on smoothly planed surfaces; it will last 2 to 3 years. After refinishing, however, the second coat will last 6 to 7 years because the weathered surface has absorbed more of the stain than the smoothly planed surface.

Two-coat staining is possible on rough-sawn or weathered surfaces, but both coats should be applied within a few hours of each other. When using a two-coat system, the first coat should never be allowed to dry before the second is applied. If it does, the surface will be sealed, preventing the second coat from penetrating. A finish life of up to 10 years can be achieved when two coats are applied to a rough or weathered surface.

A stained surface should be refinished only when the colors fade and the bare wood is beginning to show. A light steel-wooling or steel brushing with the grain, followed by a hosing with water to remove surface dirt and mildew, is all that is needed to prepare the surface. Restain after the surfaces have thoroughly dried.

A number of penetrating pigmented stain finishes are on the market; a satisfactory home version can also be prepared by mixing the Forest -Products Laboratory natural finish. Its composition, preparation and application is described in "Forest Products Laboratory Natural Finish" from the USDA Forest Service, U.S. Department of Agriculture. This finish has a linseed oil vehicle; a preservative, pentachlorophenol, to protect the oil from mildew; and a water repellent, paraffin wax, to protect the wood from excessive penetration of water.

CLEAR FILM FINISHES

Clear finishes based on varnish, which form a coating or film on the surface, should not be used on wood exposed fully to the weather. These finishes are quite expensive and often begin to deteriorate within one year. Refinishing is a frequent, difficult and time-consuming process.

EXTERIOR PAINTS

Of all finishes, paints provide the widest selection of color. When properly selected and applied, paint will provide wood the greatest protection against weathering. The durability of paint coatings on exterior wood, however, is affected by many variables; much care is needed in the selection of the wood surface material, type of paint and method of application. The original and maintenance costs are higher for a paint finish than for either the water-repellent preservative treatment or penetrating-stain finish.

Paint performance is affected by such wood variables as species, density, structure, extractives and defects such as knots and pitch pockets.

Maximum paint durability will be achieved on select high grades of vertical-grain western red cedar, redwood and low-density pines. Exterior-grade plywood which has been overlaid with medium-density resin-treated paper is another wood-base material on which paint will perform very well.

Follow these three simple steps when painting wood:

(1) Apply water-repellent preservatives to all joints by brushing or spraying. Treat all lap and butt joints, ends and edges of lumber and window sash and trim. Allow 2 warm days of drying before painting.

(2) Prime the treated wood surface with an oil-base paint free of zinc-oxide pigment. Do not use a porous low-luster oil paint as primer on wood surfaces. Apply sufficient primer so that the grain of the wood cannot be seen. Open joints should be caulked after priming.

(3) Apply two topcoats of high-quality oil, alkyd or latex paint over the primer. The south side has the most severe exposure; so, two topcoats are particularly important on that side of the house.

EFFECT OF IMPREGNATED PRESERVATIVES ON PAINTING

Wood treated with water-soluble preservatives in common use can be painted satisfactorily after it is redried. The coating may not last quite as long as it would have on untreated wood, but there is no vast difference. Certainly, a slight loss in durability is not enough to offer any practical objection to using treated wood where preservation against decay is necessary, protection against weathering desired and appearance of painted wood important. Coal-tar creosote or other dark oily preservatives tend to stain through paint unless the treated wood has been exposed to the weather for many months before it is painted.

Repainting

Repaint only when the old paint has worn thin and no longer protects the wood. Faded or dirty paint can often be freshened by washing. Where wood surfaces are exposed, spot prime with a zinc-free linseed oil primer before applying the finish coat. Too-frequent repainting produces an excessively thick film that is more sensitive to the weather and also that is likely to crack abnormally across the grain of the paint, which is the direction of the last brush strokes. Complete paint removal is the only cure for cross-grain cracking.

For the topcoat, use the same brand and type of paint originally applied. A change in paints is advisable only if one has given you trouble. When repainting with latex paint, apply a non-porous, oil-base primer overall before applying the latex paint.

When inter-coat peeling -- which indicates a weak bond between coats of paint -- occurs, complete paint removal is the only satisfactory procedure. To avoid inter-coat peeling, clean the old painted surface well before repainting. Allow no more than 2 weeks between coats in two-coat repainting. Do not repaint sheltered areas, such as eaves and porch ceilings, every time the weathered body of the house is painted. When sheltered areas require repainting, wash the old painted surface with trisodium phosphate or detergent solution to remove surface contaminants that will interfere with adhesion of the new coat of paint. Following washing, rinse all sheltered areas with copious amounts of water; then, let them dry thoroughly before repainting.

BLISTERING AND PEELING

When too much water gets into wood, the paint may blister and peel. Moisture blisters normally appear first; peeling follows. Sometimes, however, paint peels without blistering. At other times, the blisters go unnoticed. Moisture blisters usually contain water when they form, or soon afterward, and eventually dry out. Small blisters may disappear completely upon drying; however, fairly large ones may leave a rough spot on the surface. If the blistering is severe, the paint may peel.

New, thin coatings -- as compared to old, thick coatings -- are more likely to blister because of too much moisture under them. Older and thicker coatings are too rigid to stretch and form blisters; they do, however, tend to crack and peel. When this occurs, the old paint must be completely burned off; residing may be more economical.

House construction features that will minimize water damage of outside paint are: (a) wide roof overhang, (b) wide flashing under shingles at roof edges, (c) effective vapor barriers, (d) adequate eave troughs and properly hung downspouts and (e) adequate ventilation of the house. If these features are lacking in a house, persistent blistering and peeling may occur.

DISCOLORATION BY COLOR EXTRACTIVES

Water-soluble color extractives occur naturally in western red cedar and redwood. It is to these substances that the heartwood of these two species owes its attractive color, good stability and natural decay resistance. Discoloration occurs when the extractives are dissolved and leached from the wood by water. When the solution of extractives reaches the painted surface, the water evaporates, leaving the extractives as a reddish-brown stain. The water that gets behind the paint and causes moisture blisters also causes migration of extractives. The discoloration produced by water wetting the siding from the back side frequently forms a rundown or streaked pattern.

Emulsion paints and so-called "breather" or low-luster oil paints are more porous than conventional oil paints. If these are used on new wood without a good oil primer, or if any paint is applied too thinly on new wood (a skimpy two-coat paint job, for example), rain or even heavy dew can penetrate the coating and reach the wood. When the water dries from the wood, the extractives are brought to the surface of the paint. Discoloration of paint by this process forms a diffused pattern.

On rough surfaces, such as shingles, machine-grooved shakes and rough-sawn lumber siding, it is difficult to obtain an adequately thick coating on the high points. Extractive staining, therefore, is more likely to occur on such surfaces by water penetrating through the coating. But the reddish-brown exctractives will

be less conspicuous if dark-colored paints are used.

INTERIOR FINISHES

Interior finishes for wood, dry-wall or plaster surfaces are usually intended to serve one or more of the following purposes:

(1) Make the surface easy to clean

(2) Enhance the natural beauty of wood

(3) Achieve a desired color decor

(4) Impart wear resistance

The type of finish depends largely upon the type and use of the area in question. Wood surfaces can be finished with either a clear finish or a paint. Plaster-base materials are painted.

PREPARING OLD SURFACES

Repainting of old surfaces depends upon the materials used and their condition:

(1) In the following cases, complete removal of old paint is required; a new covering material may be more practical.

- Kalsomine over sand-textured plaster
- Kalsomine applied alternately with oil-base paint
- Incompatible paints that have resulted in inter-coat peeling
- Paints applied in kitchens or other areas over a grease film.

(2) All plaster cracks should be repaired with fiberglass tape and plaster patching.

(3) Old varnish should be cleaned with strong trisodium. Paint the surface soon

after it has dried. Heavily alligatored varnish must be completely removed before cleaning.

4. Old radiators painted gold or aluminum should be coated with bronzing liquid before painting.

5. Plastered chimneys may have creosote soaking through the plaster resulting from an accumulation in the chimney. This will continue to soak through; so, the wall should be framed out around the chimney before adding a new covering material.

WOOD FLOORS

Hardwood floors of oak, birch, beech and maple are usually finished by applying two coats of wood seal, also called floor seal, with light sanding or steel wooling between coats. A final coat of paste wax is then applied and buffed. This finish is easily maintained by rewaxing. The final coat can instead be a varnish, which provides a high gloss.

When floors are to be painted, an undercoat is used. Then, at least one topcoat of floor and deck enamel is applied.

WOOD PANELING AND TRIM

Wood trim and paneling are most commonly finished with a clear wood sealer or a stain-sealer combination. Then, the surface is top-coated, after sanding, with at least one additional coat of sealer or varnish. The final coat of sealer or varnish can also be covered with a heavy coat of paste wax to produce a surface which is easily maintained by rewaxing. Good depth in a clear finish can be achieved by finishing first with one coat of high-gloss varnish followed with a final coat of semigloss varnish.

Wood trim of nonporous species such as pine can also be painted by first applying a coat of primer or undercoat, followed by a coat of latex, flat or semigloss oil-base paint. Semigloss and gloss paints are more resistant to soiling and are more easily cleaned by washing than the flat oil and latex paints. Trim of porous wood species, such as oak and mahogany, requires filling before painting.

KITCHEN AND BATHROOM WALLS

Kitchen and bathroom walls -- normally of plaster or dry-wall construction -- are finished best with a coat of undercoat and two coats of semigloss enamel. This type of finish wears well, is easy to clean and is quite resistant to moisture.

DRYWALL AND PLASTER

Plaster and drywall surfaces which account for the major portion of the interior area are finished with two coats of either flat oil or latex paint. An initial treatment with size or sealer will improve holdout (reduced penetration of succeeding coats), thereby reducing the quantity of paint required for good coverage.

GLOSSARY

Attic ventilators - In houses, screened openings provided to ventilate an attic space. They are located in the soffit area as inlet ventilators and in the gable ends or along the ridge as outlet ventilators. They can also consist of power-driven fans used as an exhaust system. See also "Louver".

Backfill - The replacement of excavated earth into a trench around and against a basement foundation.

Base or baseboard - A board placed against the wall around a room next to the floor to finish properly the area between the floor and wall.

Base molding - Molding used to trim the upper edge of interior baseboards.

Base shoe - Molding used next to the floor on interior baseboards. Sometimes called a carpet strip.

Batten - Narrow strips of wood used to cover joints or as decorative vertical members over plywood or wide boards.

Beam - A structural member transversely supporting a load.

Bearing partition - A partition that supports any vertical load in addition to its own weight.

Bearing wall - A wall that supports any vertical load in addition to its own weight.

Blind-nailing - Nailing in such a way that the nail heads are not visible on the face of the work -- usually at the tongue or matched boards.

Boston ridge - A method of applying asphalt or wood shingles at the ridge or at the hips of a roof as a finish.

Brace - An inclined piece of framing lumber applied to wall or floor to stiffen the structure. Often used on walls as temporary bracing until framing has been completed.

Brick veneer - A facing of brick laid against and fastened to sheathing of a frame wall or tile wall construction.

Built-up roof - A roofing composed of three to five layers of asphalt felt laminated with coat tar, pitch or asphalt. The top is finished with crushed slag or gravel. Generally used on flat or low-pitched roofs.

Butt joint - The junction where the ends of two timbers or other members meet in a square-cut joint.

Casement frames and sash - Frames of wood or metal enclosing part or all of the sash, which may be opened by means of hinges affixed to the vertical edges.

Casing - Molding of various widths and thicknesses used to trim door and window openings at the jambs.

Checking - Fissures that appear with age in many exterior paint coats. They are at first superficial, but in time they may penetrate entirely through the coating.

Collar beam - Nominal 1- or 2-inch-thick members connecting opposite roof rafters. They serve to stiffen the roof structure.

Column - In architecture, a perpendicular supporting member, circular or rectangular in section, usually consisting of a base, shaft and capital. In engineering, a vertical structural compression member which supports loads acting in the direction of its longitudinal axis.

Combination doors or windows - Combination doors or windows used over regular openings. They provide winter insulation and summer protection and often have self-storing or removable glass and screen inserts. This eliminates the need for handling a different unit each season.

Condensation - In a building, beads or drops of water (and frequently frost in extremely cold weather) that accumulate on the inside of the exterior covering of a building when warm, moisture-laden air from the interior reaches a point where the temperature no longer permits the air to sustain the moisture it holds. Use of louvers or attic ventilators will reduce moisture condensation in attics. A vapor barrier under the gypsum lath or dry wall on exposed walls will reduce condensation in them.

Construction dry wall - A type of construction in which the interior wall finish is applied in a dry condition, generally in the form of sheet materials or wood paneling, as contrasted to plaster.

Construction, frame - A type of construction in which the structural parts are wood or depend upon a wood frame for support. In codes, if masonry veneer is applied to the exterior walls, the classification of this type of construction is usually unchanged.

Coped joint - See "Scribing".

Corner bead - A strip of formed sheet metal, sometimes combined with a strip of metal lath, placed on corners before plastering to reinforce them. Also, a strip of wood finish three-quarters-round or angular placed over a plastered corner for protection.

Corner boards - Used as trim for the external corners of a house or other frame structure against which the ends of the siding are finished.

Corner braces - Diagonal braces at the corners of frame structure to stiffen and strengthen the wall.

Cornice - Overhang of a pitched roof at the eave line, usually consisting of a fascia board, a soffit for a closed cornice and appropriate moldings.

Cornice return - That portion of the cornice that returns on the gable end of a house.

Counterflashing - A flashing usually used on chimneys at the roof line to cover shingle flashing and to prevent moisture entry.

Cove molding - A molding with a concave face used as trim or to finish interior corners.

Crawl space - A shallow space below the living quarters of a basement-less house, normally enclosed by the foundation wall.

Cripple stud - A stud that does not extend full height.

d. - See "Penny".

Dado - A rectangular groove across the width of a board or plank. In interior decoration, a special type of wall treatment.

Decay - Disintegration of wood or other substance through the action of fungi.

Deck paint - An enamel with a high degree of resistance to mechanical wear, designed for use on such surfaces as porch floors.

Density - The mass of a substance in unit volume. When expressed in the metric system, it is numerically equal to the specific gravity of the same substance.

Dewpoint - Temperature at which a vapor begins to deposit as a liquid. Applies especially to water in the atmosphere.

Dimension - See "Lumber dimension".

Direct nailing - To nail perpendicular to the initial surface or to the junction of the pieces joined. Also termed "face nailing".

Door jamb, interior - The surrounding case into which and out of which a door closes and opens. It consists of two upright pieces, called side jambs, and a horizontal head jamb.

Dormer - An opening in a sloping roof, the framing of which projects out to form a vertical wall suitable for windows or other opening.

Downspout - A pipe, usually of metal, for carrying rainwater from roof gutters.

Dressed and matched (tongued and grooved) - Boards or planks machined in such a manner that there is a groove on one edge and a corresponding tongue on the other.

Drip - (a) A member of a cornice or other horizontal exterior-finish course that has a projection beyond the other parts for throwing off water. (b) A groove in the underside of a sill or drip cap to cause water to drop off on the outer edge instead of drawing back and running down the face of the building.

Drip cap - A molding placed on the exterior top side of a door or window frame to cause water to drip beyond the outside of the frame.

Dry wall - Interior covering material, such as gypsum board or plywood, which is applied in large sheets or panels.

Ducts - In a house, usually round or rectangular metal pipes for distributing warm air from the heating plant to rooms, or air from a conditioning device or as cold air returns. Ducts are also made of asbestos and composition materials.

Eaves - The margin or lower part of a roof projecting over the wall.

Fascia or facia - A flat board, band or face, used sometimes by itself but usually in combination with moldings, often located at the outer face of the cornice.

Filler (wood) - A heavily pigmented preparation used for filling and leveling off the pores in open-pored woods.

Fire stop - A solid, tight closure of a concealed space, placed to prevent the spread of fire and smoke through such a space. In a frame wall, this will usually consist of 2-by-4 cross blocking between studs.

Fishplate - A wood or plywood piece used to fasten the ends of two members together at a butt joint with nails or bolts. Sometimes used at the junction of opposite rafters near the ridge line.

Flashing - Sheet metal or other material used in roof and wall construction to protect a building from water seepage.

Flat paint - An interior paint that contains a high proportion of pigment and dries to a flat or luster-less finish.

Flue - The space or passage in a chimney through which smoke, gas or fumes ascend. Each passage is called a flue, which together with any others and the surrounding masonry make up the chimney.

Flue lining - Fire clay or terra-cotta pipe, round or square, usually made in all ordinary flue sizes and in 2-foot lengths, used for the inner lining of chimneys with the brick or masonry work around the outside. Flue lining in chimney runs from about a foot below the flue connection to the top of the chimney.

Fly rafters - End rafters of the gable overhang supported by roof sheathing and lookouts.

Footing - A masonry section, usually concrete, in a rectangular form wider than the bottom of the foundation wall or pier it supports.

Foundation - The supporting portion of a structure below the first-floor construction, or below grade, including the footings.

Framing, balloon - A system of framing a building in which all vertical structural elements of the bearing walls and partitions consist of single pieces extending from the top of the foundation sill plate to the roof-plate to which all floor joists are fastened.

Framing, platform - A system of framing a building in which floor joists of each story rest on top plates of the story below or on the foundation sill for the first story, and the bearing walls and partitions rest on the subfloor of each story.

Frieze - In house construction , a horizontal member connecting the top of the siding with the soffit of the cornice

Frostline - The depth of frost penetration in soil. This depth varies in different parts of the country. Footings should be placed below this depth to prevent movement.

Fungi, wood - Microscopic plants that live in damp wood and cause mold, stain and decay.

Fungicide - A chemical that is poisonous to fungi.

Furring - Strips of wood or metal applied to a wall or other surface to even it and normally to serve as a fastening base for finish material.

Gable - In house construction, the portion of the roof above the eave line of a double-sloped roof.

Gable end - An end wall having a gable.

Gloss enamel - A finishing material made of varnish and sufficient pigments to provide opacity and color, but little or no pigment of low opacity. Such an enamel forms a hard coating with maximum smoothness of surface and a high degree of gloss.

Gloss (paint or enamel) - A paint or enamel that contains a relatively low proportion of pigment and dries to a sheen or luster.

Girder - A large or principal beam of wood or steel used to support concentrated loads at isolated points along its length.

Grain - The direction, size arrangement, appearance or quality of the fibers in wood.

Grain, edge (vertical) - Edge-grain lumber has been sawed parallel to the pitch of the log and approximately at right angles to the growth rings; i.e., the rings form an angle of 45 degrees or more with the surface of the piece.

Grain, flat - Flat-grain lumber has been sawed parallel to the pitch of the log and approximately tangent to the growth rings; i.e., the rings form an angle of less than 45 degrees with the surface of the piece.

Grain, quartersawn - Another term for edge grain.

Grounds - Guides used around openings and at the floorline to strike off plaster. They can consist of narrow strips of wood or of wide subjambs at interior doorways. They provide a level plaster line for installation of casing and other trim.

Grout - Mortar made of such consistency (by adding water) that it will just flow into the joints and cavities of the masonry work and fill them solid.

Gusset - A flatwood, plywood or similar type member used to provide a connection at intersection of wood members. Most commonly used at joints of wood trusses. They are fastened by nails, screws, bolts or adhesives.

Gutter or eave trough - A shallow channel or conduit of metal of wood set below and along the eaves of a house to catch and carry off rainwater from the roof.

Gypsum plaster - Gypsum formulated to be used with the addition of sand and water for base-coat plaster.

Header - (a) A beam placed perpendicular to joists and to which joists are nailed in framing for chimney, stairway or other openings. (b) A wood lintel.

Heartwood - The wood extending from the pitch to the sapwood, the cells of which no longer participate in the life processes of the tree.

Hip - The external angle formed by the meeting of two sloping sides of a roof.

Hip roof - A roof that rises by inclined planes from all four sides of a building.

Humidifier - A device designed to increase the humidity within a room or a house by means of the discharge of water vapor It may consist of individual room-size units or larger units attached to the heating plant to condition the entire house.

Insulation board, rigid - A structural building board made of coarse wood or cane fiber in 1/2- or 25/32-inch thicknesses. It can be obtained in various size sheets, in various densities and with several treatments.

Insulation, thermal - Any material high in resistance to heat transmission that, when placed in the walls, ceiling or floors of a structure, will reduce the rate of heat flow.

Interior finish - Material used to cover the interior framed areas or materials of walls and ceilings.

Jack post - A hollow metal post with a jack screw in one end so that it can be adjusted to the desired height.

Jack rafter - A rafter that spans the distance from the wallplate to a hip, or from a valley to a ridge.

Jamb - The side and head lining of a doorway, window or other opening.

Joint - The space between the adjacent surfaces of two members of components joined and held together by nails, glue, cement, mortar or other means.

Joint cement - A powder that is usually mixed with water and used for joint treatment in gypsum-wallboard finish. Often called "spackle".

Joist - One of a series of parallel beams, usually 2 inches in thickness, used to support floor and ceiling loads and supported in turn by larger beams, girders or bearing walls.

Knot - In lumber, the portion of a branch or limb of a tree that appears on the edge or face of the piece.

Landing - A platform between flights of stairs or at the termination of a flight of stairs.

Lath - A building material of wood, metal, gypsum or insulating board that is fastened to the frame of a building to act as a plaster base.

Ledger strip - A strip of lumber nailed along the bottom of the side of a girder on which joists rest.

Let-in brace - Nominal 1-inch-thick boards applied into notched studs diagonally.

Lintel - A horizontal structural member that supports the load over an opening; such as, a door or window.

Lookout - A short wood bracket or cantilever to support an overhang portion of a roof or the like, usually concealed from view.

Louver - An opening with a series of horizontal slats so arranged as to permit ventilation, but to exclude rain, sunlight or vision. See also "Attic ventilators".

Lumber - Lumber is the product of the sawmill and planing mill not further manufactured other than by sawing, resawing and passing lengthwise through a standard planing machine, crosscutting to length and marching.

Lumber, board - Yard lumber less than 2 inches thick and 2 or more inches wide.

Lumber, dimension - Yard lumber from 2 inches to, but not including, 5 inches thick and 2 or more inches wide. Includes joists, rafter, studs, plank and small timbers.

Lumber, dressed size - The dimension of lumber after shrinking from green dimension and after machining to size or pattern.

Lumber, matched - Lumber that is dressed and shaped on one edge in a grooved pattern and on the other in a tongued pattern.

Lumber, shiplap - Lumber that is edge-dressed to make a close rabbeted or lapped joint.

Lumber timbers - Yard lumber 5 or more inches in least dimension. Includes beams, stringer, posts, caps, sills, girders and purlins.

Lumber, yard - Lumber of those grades, sizes and patterns which are generally intended for ordinary construction; such as, framework and rough coverage of houses.

Mantel - The shelf above a fireplace. Also used in referring to the decorative trim around a fireplace opening.

Masonry - Stone, brick, concrete, hollow-tile, concrete block, gypsum block or other similar building units or materials or a combination of the same, bonded together with mortar to form a wall, pier, buttress or similar mass.

Mastic - A pasty material used as a cement (as for setting tile) or a protective coating (as for thermal insulation or waterproofing).

Metal lath - Sheets of metal that are slit and drawn out to form openings. Used as a plaster base for walls and ceilings and as reinforcing over other forms of plaster base.

Millwork - Generally all building materials made of finished wood and manufactured in millwork plants and planing mills are included under the term "millwork". It includes such items as inside and outside doors, window and door frames, blinds, porchwork, mantels, panelwork, stairways, moldings and interior trim. It normally does not include flooring, ceiling or siding.

Miter joint - The joint of two pieces at an angle that bisects the joining angle. For example, the miter joint at the side and head casing as a door opening is made at a 45-degree angle.

Moisture content of wood - Weight of the water contained in the wood, usually expressed as a percentage of the weight of oven dry wood.

Molding - A wood strip having a curved or projecting surface used for decorative purposes.

Mullion - A vertical bar or divider in the frame between windows, doors or other openings.

Muntin - A small member which divides the glass or openings of sash or doors.

Natural finish - A transparent finish which does not seriously alter the original color or grain of the natural wood. Natural finishes are usually provided by sealers, oils, varnishes, water-repellent preservatives and other similar materials.

Nonbearing wall - A wall supporting no load other than its own weight.

Nosing - The projecting edge of a molding or drip. Usually applied to the projecting molding on the edge of a stair tread.

O.C., on center - The measurement of spacing for studs, rafters, joists and the like in a building from the center of one member to the center of the next.

Outrigger - An extension of a rafter beyond the wall line. Usually a smaller member nailed to a larger rafter to form a cornice or roof overhang.

Paint - A combination of pigments with suitable thinners or oils to provide decorative and protective coatings.

Panel - In house construction, a thin flat piece of wood, plywood or similar material, framed by stiles and rails as in a door, or fitted into grooves of thicker material with molded edges for decorative wall treatment.

Paper, building - A general term, without reference to properties or uses, for papers, felts and similar sheet materials used in buildings.

Paper, sheathing - A building material, generally paper or felt, used in wall and roof construction as a protection against the passage of air and sometimes moisture.

Parting stop or strip - A small wood piece used in the side and head jambs of double-hung windows to separate upper and lower sashes.

Partition - A wall that subdivides spaces within any story of a building.

Penny - As applied to nails, it originally indicated the price per hundred. The term now serves as a measure of nail length and is abbreviated by the letter "d".

Perm - A measure of water vapor movement through a material (grains per square foot per hour per inch of mercury difference in vapor pressure).

Pier - A column of masonry, usually rectangular in horizontal cross section, used to support other structural members.

Pigment - A powdered solid in suitable degree of subdivision for use in paint or enamel.

Pitch - The incline slope of a roof or the ratio of the total rise to the total width of a house; i.e., an 8-foot rise and 24-foot width is a one-third pitch roof. Roof slope is expressed in the inches of rise per foot of run.

Pith - The small, soft core at the original center of a tree around which wood formation takes place.

Plaster grounds - Strips of wood used as guides or strike-off edges around window and door openings and at base of walls.

Plate - Sill plate: A horizontal member anchored to a masonry wall. Sole plate: Bottom horizontal member of a frame wall. Top plate: Top horizontal member of a frame wall supporting ceiling joists, rafters or other members.

Plough - To cut a lengthwise groove in a board or plank.

Plumb - Exactly perpendicular; vertical.

Ply - A term to denote the number of thicknesses or layers of roofing felt, veneer in plywood, or layers in built-up materials, in any finished piece of such material.

Plywood - A piece of wood made of three or more layers of veneer joined with glue, and usually laid with the grain of adjoining plies at right angles. Almost always an odd number of plies are used to provide balanced construction.

Preservative - Any substance that, for a reasonable length of time, will prevent the action of wood-destroying fungi, borers of various kinds and similar destructive agents when the wood has been properly coated or impregnated with it.

Primer - The first coat of paint in a paint job that consists of two or more coats; also, the paint used for such a first coat.

Putty - A type of cement usually made of whiting and boiled linseed oil, beaten or kneaded to the consistency of dough, and used in sealing glass in sash, filling small holes and crevices in wood and for similar purposes.

Quarter round - A small molding that has the cross section of a quarter circle.

Rabbet - A rectangular longitudinal groove cut in the corner edge of a board or plank.

Radiant heating - A method of heating, usually consisting of a forced hot water system with pipes placed in the floor, wall or ceiling; or with electrically heated panels.

Rafter - One of a series of structural members of a roof designed to support roof loads. The rafters of a flat roof are sometimes called roof joists.

Rafter, hip - A rafter that forms the intersection of an external roof angle.

Rafter, valley - A rafter that forms the intersection of an internal roof angle. The valley rafter is normally made of double 2-inch-thick members.

Rail - Cross members of panel doors or of a sash. Also the upper and lower members of a balustrade or staircase extending from one vertical support, such as a post, to another.

Rake - Trim members that run parallel to the roof slope and form the finish between the wall and a gable roof extension.

Reflective insulation - Sheet material with one or both surfaces of comparatively low heat emissivity, such as aluminum foil. When used in building construction the surfaces face air spaces, reducing the radiation across the air space.

Reinforcing - Steel rods or metal fabric placed in concrete slabs, beams or columns to increase their strength.

Relative humidity - The amount of water vapor in the atmosphere, expressed as a percentage of the maximum quantity that could be present at a given temperature. The actual amount of water vapor that can be held in space increases with the temperature.

Ribbon (Girt) - Normally a 1-by-4-inch board let into the studs horizontally to support ceiling or second-floor joists.

Ridge - The horizontal line at the junction of the top edges of two sloping roof surfaces.

Ridge board - The board placed on edge at the ridge of the roof into which the upper ends of the rafters are fastened.

Rise - In stairs, the vertical height of a step or flight of stairs.

Riser - Each of the vertical boards closing the spaces between the treads of stairways.

Roll roofing - Roofing material, composed of fiber and saturated with asphalt, that is supplied in 36-inch wide rolls with 108 square feet of material. Weights are generally 45 to 90 pounds per roll.

Roof sheathing - The boards or sheet material fastened to the roof rafters on which the shingle or other roof covering is laid.

Rout - The removal of material, by cutting, milling or gouging, to form a groove.

Run - In stairs, the net width of a step or the horizontal distance covered by a flight of stairs.

Saddle - Two sloping surfaces meeting in a horizontal ridge, used between the back side of a chimney, or other vertical surface, and a sloping roof.

Sapwood - The outer zone of wood, next to the bark. In the living tree it contains some living cells (the heartwood contains none), as well as dead and dying cells. In most species it is lighter colored than the heartwood. In all species, it is lacking in decay resistance.

Sash - A single light frame containing one or more lights of glass.

Saturated felt - A felt which is impregnated with tar or asphalt.

Scratch coat - The first coat of plaster, which is scratched to form a bond for the second coat.

Screed - A small strip of wood, usually the thickness of the plaster coat, used as a guide for plastering.

Scribing - Fitting woodwork to an irregular surface. In moldings, cutting the end of one piece to fit the molded face of the other at an interior angle to replace a miter joint.

Sealer - A finishing material, either clear or pigmented, that is usually applied directly over uncoated wood for the purpose of sealing the surface.

Semigloss paint or enamel - A paint or enamel made with a slight insufficiency of nonvolatile vehicle so that its coating, when dry, has some luster but is not very glossy

Shake - A thick hand split shingle, resawed to form two shakes, usually edge-grained.

Sheathing - The structural covering, usually wood boards or plywood, used over studs or rafters of a structure. Structural building board is normally used only as wall sheathing.

Sheathing paper - See "Paper, sheathing".

Sheet metal work - All components of a house employing sheet metal, such as flashing, gutters and downspouts.

Shellac - A transparent coating made by dissolving in alcohol "lac", a resinous secretion of the lac bug (a scale insect that thrives in tropical countries, especially India).

Shingles - Roof covering of asphalt, asbestos, wood, tile, slate or other material cut to stock lengths, widths and thicknesses.

Shingles, siding - Various kinds of shingles, such as wood shingles or shakes and non-wood shingles, that are used over sheathing for exterior sidewall covering of a structure.

Shiplap - See "Lumber, shiplap".

Shutter - Usually lightweight louvered or flush wood or non-wood frames in the form of doors located at each side of a window. Some are made to close over the window for protection; others are fastened to the wall as a decorative device.

Siding - The finish covering of the outside wall of a frame building, whether made of horizontal weatherboards, vertical boards with battens, shingles or other material.

Siding, bevel (lap siding) - Wedge-shaped boards used as horizontal siding in a lapped pattern,. This siding varies in butt thickness from 1/2- to 3/4-inch and in widths up to 12 inches. It is normally used over some type of sheathing.

Siding, Dolly Varden - Beveled wood siding which is rabbeted on the bottom edge.

Siding, drop - Usually 3/4-inch thick and 6 to 8 inches wide with tongued-and-grooved or shiplap edges. Often used as siding without sheathing in secondary buildings.

Sill - The lowest member of the frame of a structure, resting on the foundation and supporting the floor joists or the uprights of the wall. The member framing the lower side of an opening, as a door sill, window sill, etc.

Sleeper - Usually, a wood member embedded in concrete, as in a floor, that serves to support and to fasten subfloor or flooring.

Soffit - Usually the underside of an overhanging cornice.

Soil cover (ground cover) - A light covering of plastic film, roll roofing or similar material used over the soil in crawl spaces of buildings to minimize moisture permeation of the area.

Soil stack - A general term for the vertical main of a system of soil, waste or vent piping.

Sole or sole plate - See "Plate".

Solid bridging - A solid member placed between adjacent floor joists near the center of the span to prevent joists from twisting.

Span - The distance between structural supports such as walls, columns, piers, beams, girders and trusses.

Splash block - A small masonry block laid with the top close to the ground surface to receive roof drainage from downspouts and to carry it away from the building

Square - A unit of measure - 100 square feet -- usually applied to roofing material. Sidewall coverings are sometimes packed to cover 100 square feet and are sold on that basis.

Stain, shingle - A form of oil paint, very thin in consistency, intended for coloring wood with rough surfaces, such as shingles, without forming a coating of significant thickness or gloss.

Stair carriage - Supporting member for stair treads. Usually a 2-inch plank notched to receive the treads; sometimes called a "rough horse".

Stair landing - See "Landing".

Stair rise - See "Rise".

Stile - An upright framing member in a panel door.

Stool - A flat molding fitted over the window sill between jambs and contacting the bottom rail of the lower sash.

Storm sash or storm window - An extra window usually placed on the outside of an existing one as additional protection against cold weather.

Story - That part of a building between any floor and the floor or roof next above.

Strike plate - A metal plate mortised into or fastened to the face of a door-frame side jamb to receive the latch or bolt when the door is closed.

Strip flooring - Wood flooring consisting of narrow, matched strips.

String, stringer - A timber or other support for cross members in floors or ceilings. In stairs, the support on which the stair treads rest; also stringboard.

Stucco - Most commonly refers to an outside plaster made with Portland cement as its base.

Stud - One of a series of slender wood or metal vertical structural members placed as supporting elements in walls and partitions (Plural: Studs or studding).

Subfloor - Boards or plywood laid on joists over which a finish floor is to be laid.

Suspended ceiling - A ceiling system supported by hanging it from the overhead structural framing.

Termites - Insects that superficially resemble ants in size, general appearance and habit of living in colonies; hence, they are frequently called "white ants". Subterranean termites establish themselves in buildings not by being carried in with lumber, but by entering from ground nests after the building has been constructed. If unmolested, they eat out the woodwork, leaving a shell of sound wood to conceal their activities; damage may proceed so far as to cause collapse of parts of a structure before discovery. There are about 56 species of termites known in the United States; but the two major ones, classified by the manner in which they attack wood, are ground-inhabiting or subterranean termites (the most common) and drywood termites, which are found almost exclusively along the extreme southern border and the Gulf of Mexico in the United States.

Threshold - A strip of wood or metal with beveled edges used over the finish floor and the sill or exterior doors.

Toenailing - To drive a nail at a slant with the initial surface in order to permit it to penetrate into a second member.

Tongued and grooved - See "Dressed and matched".

Tread - The horizontal board in a stairway on which the foot is placed.

Trim - The finish materials in a building, such as moldings, applied around openings (window trim, door trim) or at the floor and ceiling of rooms (baseboard, cornice and other moldings).

Trimmer - A beam or joist to which a header is nailed in framing for a chimney, stairway or other opening.

Truss - A frame or jointed structure designed to act as a beam of long span, while each member is usually subjected to longitudinal stress only, either tension or compression.

Turpentine - A volatile oil used as a thinner in paints and as a solvent in varnishes. Chemically, it is a mixture of terpenes.

Undercoat - A coating applied prior to the finishing or top coats of a paint job. It may be the first of two or the second of three coats. In some uses of the word it may become synonymous with priming coat.

Underlayment - A material placed under finish coverings, such as flooring or shingles, to provide a smooth, even surface for applying the finish.

Valley - The internal angle formed by the junction of two sloping sides of a roof.

Vapor barrier - Material used to retard the movement of water vapor into walls and prevent condensation in them. Usually considered as having a perm value of less than 1.0. Applied separately over the warm side of exposed walls or as a part of batt or blanket insulation.

Varnish - A thickened preparation of drying oil or drying oil and resin suitable for spreading on surfaces to form continuous, transparent coatings, or for mixing with pigments to make enamels.

Vehicle - The liquid portion of a finishing material; it consist of the binder (nonvolatile) and volatile thinners.

Veneer - Thin sheets of wood made by rotary cutting or slicing of a log.

Vent - A pipe or duct which allows flow of air as an inlet or outlet.

Water-repellent preservative - A liquid designed to penetrate into wood and impart water repellency and a moderate preservative protection. It is used for millwork, such as sash and frames, and is usually applied by dipping.

Weatherstrip - Narrow or jamb-width sections of thin metal or other material to prevent infiltration of air and moisture around windows and doors. Compression weather stripping prevents air infiltration, provides tension and acts as counterbalance.

APPENDIX

Renovation Estimate Checklist 237
Cost Estimate Summary 243
Item Estimate Work Sheet 245
Purchase Order 247
Purchase Order Control Log 249
Plan Analysis Checklist 253
Suppliers/Subcontractors Reference Sheet 255
Subcontractor's Agreement 259
Subcontractor's Affidavit 261
Lighting and Appliance Order 263
Draw Schedule Sheet 265

RENOVATION ESTIMATE CHECKLIST

ADDRESS_____ DATE_____

OWNER_____ PHONE_____ YEARS OWNED_____

Instructions:Grade the condition of each problem--1=Minor Repair, 5=Total Replacement
Fill in the estimated cost-to-repair from your estimate or bid.

PROBLEM	PRESENT CONDITION	EST. COST
FOUNDATION		
[ ] Cracks in piers	_____	_____
[ ] Crack between foundation & frame	_____	_____
[ ] Sagging floor joists	_____	_____
[ ] Cracks in basement wall	_____	_____
[ ] Cracks in brick veneer	_____	_____
[ ] Crumbling mortar	_____	_____
[ ] Dry or no caulking at joints	_____	_____
[ ] Damp or leaky basement wall	_____	_____
[ ] White mineral deposits on wall	_____	_____
[ ] Finish grade sloped to foundation	_____	_____
DECAY AND INSECTS		
[ ] Presence of fungus growth	_____	_____
[ ] Wood spongy and flakey	_____	_____
[ ] Termite tubes visible on foundation	_____	_____
[ ] Termite pellets visible	_____	_____
[ ] Bore holes visible in framing	_____	_____
CHIMNEY & FIREPLACES		
[ ] Cracks or crumbling mortar	_____	_____
[ ] Clogged or impaired flue	_____	_____
[ ] Fails to draw properly	_____	_____
INSULATION AND MOISTURE CONTROL		
[ ] No vapor barrier in walls	_____	_____
[ ] No vapor barrier in ceiling	_____	_____
[ ] No vapor barrier under floor	_____	_____
[ ] High energy usage for home	_____	_____
[ ] Poor or no wall insulation	_____	_____
[ ] Poor or no ceiling insulation	_____	_____
[ ] No air vents in soffit or attic	_____	_____

Page Total _____

<u>Problem</u>	<u>Present Condition</u>	<u>Est. cost</u>

FLOOR FRAMING
[ ] Wood posts imbedded in concrete
[ ] Decay present
[ ] Sagging girders
[ ] Termite tracks present
[ ] Springy or noisy floor
[ ] Warped or disconnected subfloor
[ ] Floor not level

WALL FRAMING
[ ] Doors out of line
[ ] Windows bind or do not open
[ ] Decay at foundation
[ ] Decay around steps
[ ] Splits or nail pops in drywall

ROOF
[ ] Sagging ridge line
[ ] Buckled or warped roof decking
[ ] Signs of leakage around perimeter
[ ] Signs of leakage around chimney
[ ] Water stains on rafters
[ ] Cracked or split shingles
[ ] Wood shingles cracked or split
[ ] Shingles covered with tar & fungus
[ ] Flashing corroded or absent
[ ] Gutters & downspouts corroded

SIDING AND TRIM
[ ] Decayed fascia or trim
[ ] Water stains & decay on soffit
[ ] Excessive gaps between lap siding
[ ] Splits & warpage in siding and trim
[ ] Shingle siding worn & broken

MECHANICAL AND PLUMBING
[ ] Heating system is deteriorated
[ ] No air conditioning system
[ ] Water pressure is low
[ ] Inadequate hot water supply
[ ] Drainage pipes clogged or broken
[ ] Fixtures worn or out of style
[ ] Electrical amp service inadequate
[ ] Wiring frayed or rotten
[ ] Inadequate outlets

Page Total _____

Problem	**Present Condition**	**Est. cost**

WINDOWS AND DOORS

[ ] Windows loose fitting and warped

[ ] Window caulking dried and broken

[ ] Drafts around window

[ ] Window counterweights broken

[ ] Window size insufficient

[ ] Decay around sash and sill

[ ] Doors warped or binding

[ ] Door bottom decayed

[ ] Door trim warped or decayed

PAINT AND WALL COVERING

[ ] Exterior paint chipped or blistered

[ ] Exterior paint covered with fungus

[ ] Layers of chipped paint present

[ ] Interior paint blistered

[ ] Interior trim paint chipped

[ ] Wallpaper blistered or peeling

[ ] Drywall buckled or unsound

INTERIOR FLOOR COVERING

[ ] Wood floor buckled or warped

[ ] Wood floor has gaps between pieces

[ ] Resilient tile cracked or broken

[ ] Underlayment under tile uneven

[ ] Flooring spongy, dark and decayed

[ ] Carpet faded or mildewed

[ ] Carpet pad flat or crumbly

TRIM AND CABINETS

[ ] Trim damaged or warped

[ ] Cabinet doors split or uneven

[ ] Cabinet finish chipped or scaled

[ ] Counter tops decayed or delaminated

KITCHEN AND BATH

[ ] Kitchen appliances need replacing

[ ]   Refrigerator

[ ]   Stove

[ ]   Sink

[ ] Bath appliances need replacing

[ ]   Sink

[ ]   Toilet

[ ]   Shower

Page Total _____

Report Total _____

COST ESTIMATE SUMMARY

	EST. COST	ACTUAL COST	OVER/UNDER
LICENSES AND FEES			
PREPARATION OF LOT			
FOOTINGS			
FOUNDATION			
ADDITIONAL SLABS			
MATERIALS (PACKAGE)			
FRAMING LABOR			
TRIM LABOR			
ROOFING			
HVAC			
ELECTRIC			
INTERIOR FINISH (SHEETROCK)			
PAINTING			
FLOOR COVERING			
WALKS, DRIVES, STEPS			
LANDSCAPING			
CABINETS AND VANITIES			
APPLIANCES AND LIGHTS			
INSULATION			
CLEANING			
DEVELOPED LOT COST			
CONSTRUC. CLOSING AND INTEREST			
SUPERVISORY FEE			
REAL ESTATE COMMISSION			
POINTS AND CLOSING			
CONTINGENCY (MISC. EXPENSES)			
SEPTIC			
FIREPLACE			
GUTTERS			
TOTAL			

ITEM ESTIMATE WORK SHEET

VENDOR NAME	ITEM NO.	DESCRIPTION	MEASURING QTY. UNIT	CONVERSION FACTOR	ORDERING QTY. UNIT	PRICE EACH	COST	TAX	TOTAL COST	COST TYPE

EXPENSE CATEGORY	MATERIAL COST	LABOR COST	SUBCONT. COST	TOTAL COST

PURCHASE ORDER

INV. NO. _____

VENDOR CODE _____

JOB NO. _____

CAT. NO. _____

_____

_____

_____

_____

TO:

_____

_____

_____

_____

DELIVER TO:

_____

_____

_____

_____

TERMS: PAGE ____ OF ____   DATE:

TRANSACTION	INVOICE NO.	ACCOUNT NO.	SALESMAN	CUST P.O. NO.	REFERENCE		
B/O	QTY.	ITEM CODE	DESCRIPTION	UNITS	PRICE/UNIT	TOTAL	CAT.
							NET SALE
							SALES TAX
							TOTAL

PURCHASE ORDER CONTROL LOG

P.O. NO.	DATE ORDERED	DESCRIPTION	VENDOR NAME	DATE DEL	DISCOUNT RATE	DUE	CK.#	AMT.	PAYMENTS CK.#	AMT	CK.#	AMT	TOTAL PAID

PURCHASE ORDER CONTROL LOG

P.O. NO.	DATE ORDERED	DESCRIPTION	VENDOR NAME	DATE DEL.	DISCOUNT RATE	DISCOUNT DUE	CK.#	AMT.	PAYMENTS CK.#	AMT	CK.#	AMT	TOTAL PAID

PLAN ANALYSIS CHECKLIST

PROPERTY:_____ PLAN NUMBER: _____

CIRCULATION:

Is there access between the following without going through another room?

Living Room to Bathroom .... YES____ NO____
Living Room to Bathroom .... YES____ NO____
Family Room to Bathroom .... YES____ NO____
Each Bedroom to Bathroom.. YES____ NO____
Kitchen to Dining Room .... YES____ NO____
Living Room to Dining Room...................................... YES____ NO____
Kitchen to Outside Door .... YES____ NO____

ROOM SIZE AND SHAPE:

Are all rooms adequate size and
    reasonable shape based on planned use? .... YES____ NO____
Can Living Room wall accommodate sofa
    and end tables (minimum 10 ft.)? .... YES____ NO____
Can wall of Den take sofa and end tables
    (minimum 10 ft.)? .... YES____ NO____
Can wall of master Bedrooms(s) take
    double bed and end tables?... YES____ NO____

STORAGE AND CLOSETS:

Guest closet near front entry.. YES____ NO____
Linen closet near baths .... YES____ NO____
Broom closet near kitchen.. YES____ NO____
Tool and lawnmower storage.. YES____ NO____
Space for washer and dryer .... YES____ NO____

EXTERIOR:

Is the house style "normal" architecture?...................... YES____ NO____
Is the house style compatible with
    surrounding architecture?.. YES____ NO____

SITE ANALYSIS:

Does the house conform to the neighborhood? .... YES____ NO____
Is the house suited to the lot? .... YES____ NO____
Is the topography good?... YES____ NO____
Will water drain away from the house?........................ YES____ NO____
Will grade of driveway be reasonable?......................... YES____ NO____
Is the lot wooded?... YES____ NO____
Is the subject lot as good as others
    in the neighborhood? .... YES____ NO____

SUPPLIERS/SUBCONTRACTORS REFERENCE SHEET

Date _____ How contacted? _____

Name _____ Phone _____

Address_____ Call when? _____

Type of product _____

REFERENCES	PHONE	COMMENTS
_____	_____	_____
_____	_____	_____
_____	_____	_____

PRICES/COMMENTS _____
_____
_____
_____
_____

Date _____ How contacted? _____

Name _____ Phone _____

Address_____ Call when? _____

Type of product _____

REFERENCES	PHONE	COMMENTS
_____	_____	_____
_____	_____	_____
_____	_____	_____

PRICES/COMMENTS _____
_____
_____
_____
_____

Date _____ How contacted? _____

Name _____ Phone _____

Address_____ Call when? _____

Type of product _____

REFERENCES	PHONE	COMMENTS
_____	_____	_____
_____	_____	_____
_____	_____	_____

PRICES/COMMENTS _____
_____
_____
_____

SUPPLIERS/SUBCONTRACTORS REFERENCE SHEET

Date _____ How contacted? _____

Name _____ Phone _____

Address_____ Call when? _____

Type of product _____

REFERENCES	PHONE	COMMENTS
_____	_____	_____
_____	_____	_____
_____	_____	_____

PRICES/COMMENTS _____
_____
_____
_____

Date _____ How contacted? _____

Name _____ Phone _____

Address_____ Call when? _____

Type of product _____

REFERENCES	PHONE	COMMENTS
_____	_____	_____
_____	_____	_____
_____	_____	_____

PRICES/COMMENTS _____
_____
_____
_____

Date _____ How contacted? _____

Name _____ Phone _____

Address_____ Call when? _____

Type of product _____

REFERENCES	PHONE	COMMENTS
_____	_____	_____
_____	_____	_____
_____	_____	_____

PRICES/COMMENTS _____
_____
_____

SUBCONTRACTOR'S AGREEMENT

JOB NO. _____   DESCRIPTION_____

ORDER DATE _____   PLAN NUMBER _____

NAME_____   HAVE WORKMANS COMP. YES___ NO ___

_____   WORKMANS COMP. NO. _____

_____   EXPIRATION DATE _____

PHONE _____   TAX ID NO. _____

PAYMENT TO BE MADE AS FOLLOWS:

_____   _____

_____   _____

_____   _____

DEDUCT _____ % FOR RETAINAGE.

All material is guaranteed to be as specified. All work to be completed in a timely manner acccccording to standard practices. Any alteration or deviation from specifications below involving extra costs will be executed only upon written order (refer to Change Authorization Form).

SPECIFICATIONS: (Attach extra sheets if necessary.)

AGREEMENT_____   BID AMOUNT _____

_____   BID GOOD UNTIL _____
Subcontractor   Date

DATE	CHECK NO.	AMOUNT PAID	AMOUNT DUE
_____	_____	_____	_____
_____	_____	_____	_____
_____	_____	_____	_____

SUBCONTRACTOR'S AFFIDAVIT

STATE OF: _____

COUNTY OF: _____

Personally appeared before the undersigned attesting officer, _____
_____, who being duly sworn, on oath says that he was the contractor
in charge of improving the property owned by
_____,
located at _____.

Contractor says that all work, labor, services and materials used in such improvements were
furnished and performed at the contractor's instance; that said contractor has been paid or partially
paid the full contract price for such improvements; that all work done or material furnished in
making the improvements have been paid for at the agreed price, or reasonable value, and there are
no unpaid bills for labor and services performed or materials furnished; and that no person has any
claim or lien by reason of said improvements.

_____
(Seal)

Sworn to and subscribed before me,
this _____ day of _____, 19_____.

_____
Notary Public

LIGHTING AND APPLIANCE ORDER

DATE_____

JOB _____   LIGHTING BUDGET_____

DESCRIPTION	QTY.	STYLE NO.	UNIT PRICE	TOTAL PRICE
Front Entrance				
Rear Entrance				
Dining Room				
Living Room				
Den				
Family Room				
Kitchen				
Kitchen sink				
Breakfast Area				
Dinette				
Utility Room				
Basement				
Master Bath				
Hall Bath 1				
Guest Bath				
Hall				
Hall				
Stairway				
Master Bedroom				
Bedroom 2				
Bedroom 3				
Bedroom 4				
Closets				
OUTDOOR:				
Front Porch				
Rear Porch				
Porch/Patio				
Carport/Garage				
Post/Lantern				
Floodlights				
Chimes				
Pushbuttons				
APPLIANCES				
Oven				
Hood				
Dishwasher				
Disposal				
Refrigerator				
SIGNATURE			TOTAL:	

DRAW SCHEDULE SHEET

JOB DESCRIPTION _____ JOB NO. _____ BLDG. PERMIT NO. _____

NAME OF BANK _____ ADDRESS _____

LOAN PAYOFF .... _____

CONSTRUCTION LOAN CLOSING AMOUNT .... _____

DRAW	DESCRIPTION	DATE	AMOUNT
One	_____	_____	_____
Two	_____	_____	_____
Three	_____	_____	_____
Four	_____	_____	_____
Five	_____	_____	_____
Six	_____	_____	_____
Seven	_____	_____	_____
Eight	_____	_____	_____

TOTAL DRAW AMOUNT .... _____

TOTALS OF CLOSINGS AND DRAWS .... _____

TOTAL INTEREST PAID ON CONSTRUCTION LOAN .... _____

INDEX

Adding partition, 194
Additions
    bathroom, 129-131
    floor (storey), 145-6
    sunroom, 146
    to existing house, 146-7
Advertising, 31-2
Affidavits, 100-1
    subcontractor's, 261
Agents, real estate, 31
Agreement, subcontractor's, 259
Amenities checklist, 63
American Institute of Real Estate
    Appraisers, 41
Ants, Carpenter, 53
Appearance of house, preserving,
    114
Appliances, kitchen, 119
Appraisals
    cost method, 39
    income method, 39
    market comparison method, 39-
        41
    methods of, 38-9
    professional, 41
Asphalt shingles, 171
Attic conversion, 64
Attic finishing, 136-7
Attic space addition, 135-8
Attic ventilators, defined, 221
Auctions, 32

Backfill, defined, 221
Base molding, defined, 221
Base or baseboard, defined, 221
Base shoe, defined, 221
Basements
    ceilings, 144
    conversion, 63-4
    dampness, overcoming, 139
    finishing, 138-144
    finishing, natural light, 139
    floors, 141-2
    footings, 152
    inspection of, 44
    posts, 152
    walls, 143-4
    windows, 139-140

Bathrooms
    compartmented, 131-2
    floor plan, 129
    layout sheet, 133
    options to consider, 129-131
    remodeling, 64-5, 127-133
        major, 127-8
        minor, 127
        planning the work, 127-8
    space utilization, 129
Bathtub framing, 207-8
Batten, defined, 221
Beam, defined, 221
Bearing partition, defined, 221
Bearing wall, defined, 221
Beetles, Powder Post, 52-3
Benefits of remodeling over new
    construction, 11-2
Bidding process
    with material suppliers, 103-4
    with subcontractors, 101-2
Bids, importance of, 76
Blanket insulation with vapor bar-
    rier, 188
Blind-nailing, defined, 221
Blistering and peeling, paint, 218-9
Block, concrete, subcontractor, 74
Blueprints, 26
Boston ridge, 172
    defined, 221
Brace, defined, 221
Brick, estimating cost, 69
Brick veneer, defined, 221
Builder's Risk Insurance, 28, 30
Building permits, 28, 30
Built-up roof, 172
    defined, 221
    inspection of, 49
Business license, subcontractor, 101
Butt joint, defined, 221

Cabinetry subcontractor, 75
Cabinets
    estimating cost, 74
    existing, modifying, 123
    inspection of, 50-1

Cabinets (cont.)
    kitchen, 122
        examples, 124
        new, 123
Capital gains tax, 23
Carpenter ants, 53
Carpeting, 157
Casement frames and sash, defined,
    221
Cash flow, 18
    negative, 18
Cash payments, to subcontractors,
    100
Casing, defined, 221
Caution, words of, 12-3
Cautionary comments, 59
Ceilings
    basement, 144
    garage, 145
    moldings, 204
    repair, 200
    suspended, 203
    tile, installation, 201-2
Checking, defined, 221
Checklists
    amenities, 63
    cost estimate, 79-95
    floor plan, 63
    location evaluation, 42
    plan analysis, 253
    renovation estimate, 237-241
Chimney
    inspection of, 46
    repair/replacement, 208-9
Clear film finishes, 217
Closets, 113
    existing, renovating, 204-5
    new, 205
    remodeling/adding, 204-5
    wardrobe, 205
Collar beam, defined, 221
Colors, kitchen, 121
Column, defined, 221
Combination doors or windows, de-
    fined, 222
Compartmented bathroom, 131-2
Concrete, estimating costs, 68

Concrete block foundations, cost estimating, 69

Concrete finishing subcontractor, 74

Concrete walls, poured, estimating costs, 69

Condensation, defined, 222

Construction, frame, defined, 222

Construction costs, new, estimating, 67-74

Construction dry wall, defined, 222

Continuous membrane vapor barrier, 187-8

Contractor, remodeling, 97

Contractor accounts, with suppliers, 103

Conversions
attic, 64
basement, 63-4
rental homes, 24

Coped joint - see "Scribing", 222

Corner bead, defined, 222

Corner boards, defined, 222

Corner braces, defined, 222

Cornice
defined, 222
material, estimating cost, 72
return, defined, 222
subcontractor, 74

Cosmetic improvements, importance of, 61

Cost estimate, as part of loan application package, 26

Cost estimate checklist, 79-95

Cost estimate summary, 77, 243

Cost estimating, 18

Costs, hidden, 67

Counterflashing, defined, 222

Counters, kitchen, 119-120

Countertops, kitchen, 125

Courthouse, county, as source of information, 32

Cove molding, defined, 222

Covenants, as legal considerations, 28-9

Coverings
miscellaneous, estimating cost, 73-4
roof, 168-171

Cracks, concrete foundation, 151

Crawl space, defined, 222

Creative financing techniques, 26-8

Credit cards, as source of financing, 26-7

Cripple stud, defined, 222

d. - see "Penny", 222

Dado, defined, 222

Damage by termites, U.S. map, 150

Decay damage, wood, 51-2

Decay, defined, 222

Deck paint, defined, 222

Decks, addition of, 64

Decorative moldings, 204

Density, defined, 222

Depreciation rates, affected by tax law changes, 23

Description of materials, as part of loan application package, 26

Design, kitchen, 120-3

Dewpoint, defined, 223

Dimension, see "Lumber Dimension", 223

Direct nailing, defined, 223

Doing it yourself
jobs better left to pros, 98
jobs to consider, 98
potential savings,97

"Don't wanters", 17-8, 31

Door hinges, installation, 179

Door jamb, interior, defined, 223

Doors, 48, 177-183
exterior, 177-180
installation, 177-183
interior, 180-3
inspection of, 50
types of, 183
prehung, 180

Dormer
defined, 223
gable, attic, 136
shed, attic, 138

Downspout, defined, 223

Drainage, good, importance of, 35

Drainage system, inspection of, 56

Draw schedule sheet (form), 265

Dressed and matched (tongued and grooved), defined, 223

Drip, defined, 223

Drip cap, defined, 223

Drive by's, 32

Drywall
application, 195-8
defined, 223
estimating cost, 72
preparing for painting, 197

Drywall/plaster surfaces, painting, 220

Ducts, defined, 223

Easements, as legal considerations, 28

Eaves, defined, 223

Electrical subcontractor, 75

Electrical system, inspection of, 57-8

Elevations, kitchen, 120

Energy efficiency improvements, 65

Equipment, provided by subcontractor, 101

Equity
building by remodeling, 17
buildup, 23

Equity loans, 27

Estimating costs
brick, 69
cabinets, 74
concrete block foundations, 69
concrete, 68
cornice material, 72
coverings, miscellaneous, 73-4
drywall, 72
excavation, 67-8
flooring, 73
framing, 69-70
insulation, 72
mortar, 69
new construction costs, 67-74
remodeling costs, 67-95
roofing shingles, 71
siding, 71
trimwork, 72-3

Evaluating remodeling potential, 35-42

Evaluating the structure, 43-59

Excavation costs, estimating, 67-8

Exterior doors, 177-180

Exterior paints, 217

Exterior wood painting, recommended steps, 217

Fascia (or facia), defined, 223

Filler (wood) defined, 223

Financial statement, personal, 25

Financing, 25-8
by owner, 27
options, 17-8
techniques, creative, 26-8

Finding properties with remodeling potential, 31-3

Finishes
clear film, 217
exterior, inspection of, 48-9

Finishing
kitchen and bathroom walls, 220
wood floors, 220
wood paneling and trim, 220

Fire stop, defined, 223

Fireplace
inspection of, 46
prefabricated, 209
addition of, 65
renovation/replacement, 208-9
subcontractor, 75

Fishplate, defined, 223
Fixtures, plumbing, inspection of, 57
Flashing
    defined, 223
    inspection of, 49
Flat paint, defined, 223
Floor (storey) addition, 145-6
Floor covering, new, 154-5
Floor framing
    estimating cost, 70
replacement, 153
Floor leveling, 153
Floor plan
    bathroom, 129
    checklist, 63
    layout, importance of, 63
Floor squeaks, elimination, 153-4
Floor
    garage, 144
    hardwood, subcontractor, 76
Floor system, 153-8
Flooring
    estimating cost, 73
    hardwood, 155
    installation, 155
        miscellaneous, 154-7
        subcontractor, 76
    seamless, 157
    softwood, 155
    strip, 155
    wood or wood-base tile, 156
Flooring and trim improvements,
    importance of, 62
Floorplan, kitchen, developing, 117
Floors
    basement, 141-2
    inspection of, 46-7
    wood, inspection of, 50
Flue, defined, 223
Flue lining, defined, 224
Fly rafters, defined, 224
Footings
    basement, 152
    defined, 224
    subcontractor, 74
For Sale by Owner, 31, 32
Foreclosures, as remodeling
    prospects, 32
Forest Products Laboratory, 43
Foundation
    concrete
        cracks, 151
        uneven settlement, 152
    defined, 224
    inspection of, 43
    renovation, 149-152
    termite control, 149

Foundation (poured), subcontractor,
    75
Framing
    balloon, 224
    bathtub, 207-8
    estimating cost, 69-70
    floor, estimating cost, 70
    floor, replacement, 153
    for utilities, 207
    platform, defined, 224
        roof, 167
        estimating cost, 70-1
    walls, estimating cost, 70
    subcontractor, 74
Frieze, defined, 224
Frostline, defined, 224
FSBO's, 31
Functional obsolescence, 62-3
Fungi, wood, defined, 224
Fungicide, defined, 224
Furring defined, 224

Gable, defined, 224
Gable dormer, attic, 136
Gable end, defined, 224
Garage
    addition of, 65
    ceiling, 145
    door subcontractor, 75
    finishing, 144-5
    floor, 144
    walls, 145
Girder, defined, 224
Gloss (paint or enamel), defined, 224
Glossary of terms, 221-233
Grading subcontractor, 75
Grain
    defined, 224
    edge (vertical), defined, 224
    flat, defined, 224
    quartersawn, defined 225
Grounds, defined, 225
Grout, defined, 225
Gusset, defined, 225
Gutter or eave trough, defined 225
Gutters subcontractor, 75
Gypsum board
    application, 198-9
    ceiling application, 201
Gypsum plaster, defined, 225

Hardboard, installation, 199-200
Hardboard siding, 161
Header, defined, 225
Heartwood, defined, 225
Heater, water, inspection of, 56-7
Heating system, inspection of, 57-8

Hidden costs, 67
Hip, defined, 225
Hip roof, defined, 225
Home equity loan, 21, 25
Home improvement loan, 25
    unsecured, 26
Horizontal wood siding, 161
Humidifier, defined, 225
HVAC equipment, inspection of, 55-
    8
HVAC subcontractor, 75

Insect damage, wood, 51-2
Inspection of materials, 104
Installation
    door hinges, 179
    doors, 177-183
    flooring, 155
    windows, 174-5
Insulation, 53-5, 185-8
    ceiling, 185
    estimating cost, 72
    floor, 186
    thermal, defined, 225
    wall, 185-6
Insulation and moisture control,
    185-191
Insulation board, rigid, defined, 225
Insulation subcontractor, 75
Interest deductions
    mortgage loans, 21-2
    personal mortgage loans, 21-2
Interior doors, 180-3
    types of, 183
Interior finish, defined, 225
Interior layout of house, importance
    of, 37-8
Interior renovations, 193-205
Interior surfaces, preparing for
    painting, 219-220
Interior trim, 203-4
Interior wall coverings, inspection of,
    50
Interior wall finish, repair, 194-5
Inventory control, materials, 104-5
Investment, remodeling as, 17-9
Investment property remodeling,
    owner financing, 17-8
Item estimate work sheet, 245

Jack post, defined, 225
Jack rafter, defined, 225
Jamb, defined, 225
Joint, defined, 225
Joint cement, defined, 225
Joist, defined, 226

Kitchen
appliances, 119
cabinets, 122
examples, 124
new, 123
colors, 121
corridor type, 118
counter tops, 125
counters, 119-120
design, 120-3
elevations, 120
floorplan, developing, 117
importance of location/size, 37
"L" shape, 118
layout sheet, 126
lighting, 122
remodeling, 64, 117-126
planning the work, 117
sidewall type, 118
traffic pattern, planning for, 118
"U" shape, 118
work triangle, 118
Kitchen/bathroom walls, finishing, 220
Knee walls, attic, 138
Knot, defined, 226

Landing, defined, 226
Landscaping improvements, importance of, 62
Landscaping subcontractor, 75
Lath, defined, 226
Layout
traffic circulation, 110
upgrading, 109
Layout sheet
bathroom, 133
kitchen, 126
Lease with option to buy, 27-8
Ledger strip, defined, 226
Legal considerations
builder's risk insurance, 28
building permits, 28
covenants, 28
easements, 28
liens, 28
subcontractor contracts, 28
variances, 28
workmen's compensation, 28
zoning, 28
Legal issues, 28-30
Let-in brace, defined, 226
Leveling, floor, 153
Leverage, 26
License, business, subcontractor, 101
Liens, as legal considerations, 28, 29
Light, adequate, how to provide, 112
Lighting, kitchen, 122

Lighting and appliance order, (form), 263
Line of credit, unsecured, 27
Linoleum, 157
Lintel, defined, 226
Loadbearing partition, 193
Loadbearing walls, location of, 38
Loan application package, 25
Location, importance of, 35-6
Location Evaluation Checklist, 42
Lock sets, 181
Lookout, defined, 226
Lot, importance of, 35
Louver, defined, 226
Lumber
board, defined, 226
defined, 226
dressed sized, defined, 226
matched, defined, 226
shiplap, defined, 226
yard, defined, 226
Lumber dimension, defined, 226
Lumber timbers, defined, 226

MAI (Member of the Appraisal Institute), 41
Maintenance costs, reducing, 18-9
Mantel, defined, 226
Map, U.S.
damage by termites, 150
recommended average moisture content for woodwork, 150
Market comparison method of appraisal, 39-41
Masonry, defined, 226
Masonry veneer siding, 165
Masonry veneers, inspection of, 45-6
Masonry walls and piers, inspection of, 43
Mastic, defined, 226
Material arrangements, with subcontractor, 101
Material suppliers, working with, 103-5
Materials
inspection and handling, 104
inventory control, 104-5
Mechanical systems, inspection of, 55-8
Metal lath, defined, 226
Millwork, defined, 227
Miter joint, defined, 227
Moisture content of wood, defined, 227
Moisture content recommended for interior finish woodwork, U.S. map, 150

Moisture control, 53-5
Moisture control and insulation, 185-191
Molding, defined, 227
Moldings
ceiling, 204
decorative, 204
Monolithic slabs, cost estimating, 68
Mortar
crumbling, 151-2
estimating cost, 69
Mortgage
purchase money, 27
second, 25
Mortgage loan interest deductions, 21-2
Mullion, defined, 227
Multiple listing services, 31
Muntin, defined, 227
Natural finish, defined, 227
Negative cash flow, 18
Neighborhood
evaluation
danger signals, 36-7
things to look for, 36
importance of quality of, 36
New construction costs, estimating, 67-74
"No money down" financing options, 17-8
Non-wood siding, 165
Nonbearing wall, defined, 227
Nosing, defined, 227

O.C., on center, defined, 227
Obsolescence, functional, 62-3
Occupied home, remodeling, 98
Openings, 173-5
Outrigger, defined, 227
Overhang, 50
roof, 114-5
Owner financing, 27
investment property remodeling, 17-8

Paint, defined, 227
Paint blistering and peeling, 218-9
Paint removal before repainting, 218
Painted walls, inspection of, 50
Painting
drywall/plaster surfaces, 220
importance of, 61
interior finishes, 219-220
Painting and finishing, 215-220
exterior surfaces, 215-8
Painting and stain subcontractor, 76

Painting preparation, interior surfaces, 219-220
Paints, exterior, 217
Panel, defined, 227
Panel siding, 159-161
Paneling, wood and fiberboard, 200
Paper
    building, defined, 227
    sheathing, defined, 227
Parting stop or strip, defined, 227
Partitions
    adding, 194
    changing, 111
    defined, 227
    loadbearing, 111, 193
    relocating, 193-4
Payments to subcontractors, 100
Penetrating pigmented stains, 216-7
Penny, defined, 227
Perm, defined, 228
Personal financial statement, 25
Pest control subcontractor, 75
Pier, defined, 228
Pigment, defined, 228
Pitch, defined, 228
Pith, defined, 228
Plan analysis checklist, 253
Planning, 17-103, 117
Plaster grounds, defined, 228
Plate - Sill Plate, defined, 228
Plough, defined, 228
Plumb, defined, 228
Plumbing
    inspection of, 55-6
    subcontractor, 75
Plumbing fixtures, inspection of, 57
Ply, defined, 228
Plywood
    conditioning, 199
    defined, 228
    installation, 199-200
    siding, 160-1
Poisoning, soil, 149
Pool, swimming, 66
Porches, 114
    inspection of, 48
    renovation, 211-3
Prehung door, 180
Preservative, defined, 228
Preservatives
    impregnated, effect on painting, 218
    water-repellent, 215-6
Primer, defined, 228
Priority list, remodeling projects, 61
Professional appraisal, 41
Properties to buy, advertising, 31-2

Properties with remodeling potential, how to find, 31-3
Purchase money mortgage, 27
Purchase order (form), 247
Purchase order control log (form), 249-251
Purchase orders, 104
Putty, defined, 228

Quarter round, defined, 228

Rabbet, defined, 228
Radiant heating, defined, 228
Rafters
    defined, 228
    hip, defined, 228
    sagging, 167
    valley, defined, 229
Rail, defined, 229
Rake, defined, 229
Real estate agents, 31
Real estate losses, 22
    carry forward benefit, 22-3
Real estate write-offs, 22
Reducing maintenance costs, 18-9
References, subcontractors, 99
Reflective insulation, defined, 229
Reinforcing, defined, 229
Rejection of remodeling prospect, reasons for, 58
Relative humidity, defined, 229
Relocating partitions, 193-4
Remodeling
    adding space, 135-147
    as investment, 17-9
    bathroom, 127-133
    beginning the work, 109
    kitchen, 117-126
Remodeling contractor, 97
Remodeling costs, estimating, 67-95
Remodeling decision reasons for, 58-9
Remodeling investment properties, 17-8
Remodeling occupied home, 98
Remodeling potential
    factors to evaluate, 35
    how to find, 11
Remodeling projects, priority list, 61
Remodeling prospect, rejection of, 58
Remodeling vs. new construction, benefits of, 11-2
Remodeling wood-frame construction, 115

Renovation estimate checklist, 237-241
Rent increases, after remodeling, 19
Rental home conversions, 24
Rental property remodeling, 18
Repainting, 218
Restrictions, zoning, 29
Resume, as part of loan application package, 25-6
Ribbon (girt), defined, 229
Ridge
    Boston, 172
    defined, 229
    roof, 172
Ridge board, defined, 229
Ridge poles, roof, sagging, 167
Rise, defined, 229
Riser, defined, 229
Roll roofing, defined, 229
Roof
    built-up, 172
    inspection of, 49
    new, 66
Roof coverings, 168-171
    miscellaneous, 172
Roof framing
    estimating cost, 70-1
    inspection of, 47
Roof overhang, 114-5
    added, 167-8
Roof sheathing, 167
    defined, 229
Roof system, renovation of, 167-172
Roofing subcontractor, 75
Roofing, built-up, inspection of, 49
Room addition, 65
Rout, defined, 229
Run, defined, 229

Saddle, defined, 229
Sapwood, defined, 229
Sash, defined, 229
Saturated felt, defined, 229
Savings, potential
    by acting as contractor, 97
    by providing labor yourself, 97-8
    doing it yourself, 97
Scratch coat, defined, 229
Screed, defined, 230
Scribing, defined, 230
Sealer, defined, 230
Second mortgage, 25
Selling remodeled property, importance of timing, 24
Semigloss paint or enamel, defined, 230
Septic system subcontractor, 75

Shakes
  defined, 230
  wood, 171
Sheathing
  defined, 230
  roof, 167
Sheathing paper - see "Paper, sheathing"
Shed dormer, attic, 138
Sheet metal work, defined, 230
Sheetrock
  application, 195-8
  subcontractor, 75
Shellac, defined, 230
Shelters, 21-3
Shingle siding, 162
Shingles
  asphalt, 171
    inspection of, 49
  defined, 230
  roofing, estimating cost, 71
  siding, defined, 230
  wood, 169
    application of, 169-172
    inspection of, 49
Shiplap - see "Lumber, shiplap"
Shutter, defined, 230
Siding
  bevel (lap siding), defined, 230
  defined, 230
  Dolly Varden, defined, 230
  drop, defined, 230
  estimating cost, 71
  hardboard, 161
  horizontal wood, 161-3
  installation, 159-165
  masonry veneer, 165
  new, 66
  non-wood, 165
  panel, 159-161
  plywood, 160-1
  shingle, 162
  vertical wood, 163
  wood, 159
  wood shingle and shake, 164-5
Siding and trim, inspection of, 47
Siding subcontractor, 74
Sill, defined, 230
Slabs, monolithic, cost estimating, 68
Sleeper, defined, 230
Society of Real Estate Appraisers, 41
Soffit, defined, 230
Soil cover (ground cover)
  as moisture control, 188
  defined, 231
Soil poisoning, 149
Soil stack, defined, 231
Sole or sole plate - see "Plate"

Solid bridging, defined, 231
Space additions, 135-147
  within house, 135-146
Space utilization, bathroom, 129
Span, defined, 231
Specifications, written, importance of, 100-1
Splash block, defined, 231
Square - a unit of measure, defined, 231
Squeaks, floor, elimination, 153-4
Stain, shingle, defined, 231
Stains, penetrating, 216-7
Stair carriage, defined, 231
Stair landing - see "Landing"
Stair rise - see "Rise"
Stile, defined, 233
Stonework subcontractor, 74
Stool, defined, 231
Storm sash or storm window, defined, 231
Story. defined, 231
Strategies for increasing equity through remodeling, 23-4
Stretching the remodeling dollar, 61-6
Strike plate, defined, 231
String, stringer, defined, 231
Strip flooring, defined, 231
Structural improvements, importance of, 62
Structural problems, 43
Stucco, defined, 231
Stud, defined, 231
Subcontractor
  cabinetry, 75
  ceramic tile, 76
  concrete block, 74
  concrete finishing, 74
  contracts, 28, 29
  cornice, 74
  electrical, 75
  equipment provided by, 101
  fireplace, 75
  flooring, miscellaneous, 76
  footing, 74
  foundation (poured), 75
  framing, 74
  garage door, 75
  grading, 75
  gutters, 75
  hardwood floors, 76
  HVAC, 75
  insulation, 75
  landscaping, 75
  material arrangements with, 101
  need for time flexibility, 101
  painting & stain, 76

Subcontractor (cont.)
  pest control, 75
  plumbing, 75
  roofing, 75
  septic system, 75
  sheetrock, 75
  siding, 74
  stonework, 74
  trim, 74
  wallpaper, 75
Subcontractor's affidavit, 261
Subcontractor's agreement, 259
Subcontractors
  bidding process, 101-2
  making payment to, 100
  types of, 74-6
  where/how to find, 99
  working with, 99-102
Subfloor, defined, 231
Summary, cost estimate, 77, 243
Sunroom addition, 146
Sunspaces, 65
Suppliers, material
  accounts with, 103
  bidding process, 103-4
  working with, 103-5
Suppliers/subcontractors reference sheet, 255-7
Surface water, 45
Suspended ceiling, 203
  defined, 231
Sweat equity, as source of financing, 17
Swimming pool, 66

Tax credits for remodeling, requirements for, 23
Tax laws and remodeling, 21-4
Tax Reform Act of 1986, 21-2
  effect on capital gains, 23
  effect on depreciation rates, 23
Tax shelters, 21-3
Termite control, foundation, 149
Termites, 52, 53
  defined, 231
Threshold, defined, 232
Tile
  asphalt, 157-8
  ceiling, installation, 201-2
  ceramic, subcontractor, 76
  inspection of, 50
Time flexibility, with subcontractors, 101
Toenailing, defined, 232
Tongued and grooved, defined, 232
Traffic pattern, planning for kitchen, 118

Tread, defined, 232
Trim subcontractor, 74
Trim
    cabinets, and doors, inspection of, 50
    defined, 232
    interior, 203-4
Trimmer, defined, 232
Trimwork, estimating cost, 72-3
Truss, defined, 232
Turpentine, defined, 232

Undercoat, defined, 232
Underlayment, defined, 232
Unsecured home improvement loan, 26
Unsecured line of credit, 27
Utilities, framing for, 207

Vacating property, reasons to avoid, 19
Valley, defined, 232
Vapor barriers, 54-5, 187
    continuous membrane, 187-8
    defined, 232
Vapor-resistant coating, as insulation, 188
Variances, as legal considerations, 28, 29
Varnish, defined, 2332
Vehicle, defined, 232
Veneer, defined, 232
Vent, defined, 232

Ventilation, 55, 188-191
    attic and roof, 189
    crawl space, 189
    good, how to provide, 112-3
    in attic with gable roof, 191
    in attic with hip roof, 190
    of ceiling space in flat roof, 190
Vertical wood siding, 163
Wall coverings, interior, inspection of, 50
Wall finish, interior, repair, 194-5
Wall framing, estimating cost, 70
Wallpaper subcontractor, 75
    Walls
    basement, 143-4
    garage, 145
    painted, inspection of, 50
Want ads, importance of checking, 31
Wardrobe closet, 205
Wardrobes, plywood, 113
Water, surface, 45
Water-repellent preservatives, 215-6
    defined, 233
Water heater, inspection of, 56-7
Water supply system, inspection of, 55-6
Water table, high, 45
Weatherstrip, defined, 233
Window installation, 174-5
Window placement, 112-3
Windows
    basement, 139-140
    casement, 174

Windows (cont.)
    double-hung, 174
    inspection of, 48
    relocation, 175
    repair/replacement, 173-5
    storm, 175
Windows and doors, new, 66
Wood and fiberboard paneling, 200
Wood floors
    finishing, 220
    inspection of, 50
Wood frame construction
    remodeling, 115
    inspection of, 46-54
Wood painting, exterior, recommended steps, 217
Wood paneling and trim, finishing, 220
Wood shakes, 171
Wood shingle and shake siding, 164-5
Wood siding, 159
Woods, characteristics of, 215
Work sheet, item estimate, 245
Work triangle, kitchen, 118
Working with subcontractors, 99-102
Workmen's compensation, 28, 30, 101

Zoned living, 109-110
Zoning, as a legal consideration, 28
Zoning restrictions, 29